NEW WOMEN IN
THE OLD WEST

Also by Winifred Gallagher

NEW WOMEN IN THE OLD WEST

FROM SETTLERS TO SUFFRAGISTS, AN UNTOLD AMERICAN STORY

Winifred Gallagher

PENGUIN PRESS
NEW YORK
2021

PENGUIN PRESS
An imprint of Penguin Random House LLC
penguinrandomhouse.com

Illustration credits appear on page 265.

LIBRARY OF CONGRESS CATALOGING-IN-PUBLICATION DATA
Names: Gallagher, Winifred, author.
Title: New women in the old west : from settlers to suffragists,
an untold American story /
Winifred Gallagher.
Other titles: From settlers to suffragists, an untold American story
Description: New York : Penguin Press, 2021. | Includes bibliographical
references and index.
Identifiers: LCCN 2020055750 (print) | LCCN 2020055751 (ebook) |
ISBN 9780735223257 (hardcover) | ISBN 9780735223264 (ebook)
Subjects: LCSH: Women—West (U.S.)—History. |
Frontier and pioneer life—West (U.S.)—History.
Classification: LCC HQ1438.W.W45 G35 2021 (print) |
LCC HQ1438.W.W45 (ebook) | DDC 305.40978—dc23
LC record available at https://lccn.loc.gov/2020055750
LC ebook record available at https://lccn.loc.gov/2020055751

Printed in the United States of America
1st Printing

Designed by Amanda Dewey

For women who persist

CONTENTS

—⟫•⟪—

Introduction

UNSETTLING WOMEN

THE ONGOING REFORMATION of American women's history has rightfully restored many individuals previously omitted because of race or class, but one group, distinguished by region, remains overlooked. Between the 1840s and the early twentieth century, the women's rights movement and the colonization of the West were overlapping epochs, and three generations of women were critical to both. Just as during the Revolution and wars since, the vast region's settlement disrupted society's rules of the game enough to give determined women opportunities to become more equal by acting more as equals. This book explores the lives of such courageous individuals, who emerged among the White, Black, and Asian women new to the West, and the Native American and Hispanic peoples they displaced, not just to join but also at certain crucial moments to lead the human rights revolution that, with the Nineteenth Amendment in 1920, would enfranchise half of the nation.

Told that their only place was in the home, women across Victorian America nevertheless proceeded to make stunning social, economic, and political advances toward equality. In the West, however, they often did so while also struggling to build homes, communities, and ways of life from scratch. By the watershed year of 1914, the homesteaders and town mothers, coeds and cooks, teachers and doctors in most of the region could vote—a right still denied to women in every eastern state. Yet much like the larger history of the West, which is often dismissed as flyover country short on figures such as the founding fathers and events to match the Revolution, its women's record of double-barreled achievement has been neglected.

When the West's women have not been slighted, they have often been misrepresented, whether as the anonymous aproned helpmeets portrayed in the numerous generic "Pioneer Wife" memorial statues or as feminists in boots and buckskins, allegedly liberated by frontier life. Even the western suffragist has been stereotyped, like her eastern counterpart, as a traditional White wife and mother, yet a striking number of these activists, like the West's outstanding women in general, were single, divorced, gay, or bisexual. Still others were women of color. For many Native American, Hispanic, Black, and Asian women, political activism first and foremost meant ensuring their families' survival amid the systemic racism that menaced them, yet from their ranks stalwart suffragists later fought to amplify their peoples' voices as well as their sex's. Whatever their differences, the West's trailblazing women were neither the martyrs nor Amazons of song and story but hardworking, persistent individuals who, during the heyday of Victorian domesticity and cross-continental expansion, helped extend women's place from the private home to the national homeland and made America a more just union.

The names of a few remarkable western women—perhaps Montana's Jeannette Rankin, the first woman elected to the US Congress, or Annie Oakley, the nonresident apotheosis of the new cowgirl—may be familiar, but most are not. They include Oregon's Abigail Scott Duniway, the mother of western suffrage; Nebraska's Susan La Flesche Picotte, the nation's first Native American physician; New Mexico's Adelina "Nina" Otero-Warren, a chic Hispanic educator and politician; Elizabeth Ensley, a Black teacher, clubwoman, and cofounder of Colorado's Non-Partisan Equal Suffrage Association; and Lalu Nathoy, a Chinese woman who escaped slavery in the sex trade to become Polly Bemis, a pioneer homesteader in Idaho.

American women's struggle for equality did not begin, nor has it ended, with suffrage—the right to vote in national and local elections, sit on juries, and run for elected office—but remains an incremental social, economic, and political process. Before it was so vividly illustrated in the nineteenth-century West, the connection between women's socioeconomic status and their rights was highlighted in a handful of states during and just after the Revolution. While men waged the war, many wives capably ran their families' enterprises. Abigail Adams operated the farm she shared with the future president and sold her butter and eggs for extra money; Mary Katherine Goddard assumed her brother's duties as publisher of the *Maryland Journal and the Baltimore Advertiser* and soon after became Baltimore's postmaster. In recognition of such enterprise and patriotism, the governments of New York, New Jersey, Massachusetts, and New Hampshire allowed women to vote. The Jerseyites held on till 1807, but after the men returned from war, most had been disenfranchised by the time of the Constitution's ratification in 1788.

Indeed, American women were citizens in name only. In principle, citizenship is a constellation of civic rights, such as voting, and responsibilities, such as paying taxes. In reality, it is also a status that involves complex entitlements, which in America was first limited to White men—initially landowners—whose ability to maintain and protect a household qualified them to participate in public affairs. By age-old law and custom, women, much like the enslaved, were not allowed to meet those criteria. They had no official place in civic life and very few legal rights. According to the country's version of English common law, a feme sole, or single woman, could at least own property and make contracts in her own name. Almost all women married then, however, and a wife became a feme covert, who was "covered by," or officially absorbed into, her husband's person. In exchange for his support and protection, she was legally obliged to serve and obey him; her public persona consisted of being his spouse and the mother of his offspring. She could not own, inherit, or control property, including her earnings, sue in court, run a business, divorce, or even claim custody of her own children.

As the Industrial Revolution gathered steam in a rapidly urbanizing America, women's status—at least those of adequate to ample means in towns and cities—initially declined still further. In the old agrarian economy, home and work were intermeshed on farms, where the labor of both sexes sustained the family. Now they became very different places, especially in the booming metropolises, where men's jobs in the new factories and offices supported their wives and children. Eager to codify this huge shift, an anxious Victorian establishment consigned the sexes to what were routinely called "separate spheres." Men were given the public world of industry and commerce, law and politics. Women were confined to the private world of the home, where their increasingly elaborate housework and childcare were no longer deemed economic contributions but acts of unselfish love. Agrarian women remained coproviders for their families, and enslaved and poor women had to toil, but for the well- and well-enough-off who observed the rules of the "cult of true womanhood," the only acceptable career was marriage. Indeed, they could compromise their respectable reputations if they ventured far from their domestic circles and churches, much less to a workplace.

Just as westward migration began, however, influential social architects such as Catharine Beecher, a pious, prominent teacher, reformer, and champion of female education, remodeled the cloistered Victorian home into the seat of women's new social potency. They built upon a theory, evolving since the eighteenth century, that women were not so much inferior to men, as had always been thought, as different from them: weaker and dimmer, of course, but also more elevated, nurturing, and virtuous. In *A Treatise on Domestic Economy*, published in 1841 and venerated for decades as a secular bible on how best to live, Beecher put the home and homemaker at the center of America's rapidly changing society—and its westward expansion. Women were no mere domestic drudges, she asserted, but the rightful arbiters of all questions regarding mores, manners, childrearing, religion, and charity—matters previously adjudicated by men. Indeed, she went so far as to proclaim that what was later termed their "moral authority," even superiority, created a balance of power: "It is in America, alone, that women are raised to an equality with the other sex."

The glorification of their domestic role and its gradual expansion from home to community to nation throughout the century endowed women with a potent religious and social gravitas that elevated their standing and provided a platform from which activists launched their campaign for legal and political empowerment. Poor and enslaved women could not emulate it, and others, whether agrarian wives, rights reformers, or the first female teachers and other professionals, did so qualifiedly if at all, but the aspirational model of the domestic yet righteous American Madonna suffused sentimental, religious Victorian society and migrated to the West.

Most nineteenth-century Americans, including Beecher, considered politics too base a pursuit for women, but not all. In July 1848, as migration increased, Elizabeth Cady Stanton and Lucretia Mott, both abolitionists, famously convened a meeting in Seneca

Falls, New York, to discuss what were first called "woman rights." Their later propaganda presented the event as the birthplace of the suffrage movement, but the gathering only helped formalize and publicize a cause born earlier amid the ferocious battle to abolish slavery. By the 1830s, Black abolitionists, soon personified by Sojourner Truth, upheld universal suffrage, or the right to vote regardless of race, sex, or creed. Their conviction in turn inspired White women abolitionists to rebel against their own second-class status—albeit based on gender rather than race—which prevailed even within the male-dominated anti-slavery movement, to say nothing of marriage. Moreover, Stanton and Mott were well aware of a much older precedent for women's rights in their own upstate community. Women in the democratic, egalitarian societies of the local Seneca and Oneida peoples of the Haudenosaunee or Iroquois Confederation had long owned property, divorced, and elected leaders.

After two days, the conveners of the Seneca Falls conference drew up a Declaration of Rights and Sentiments, based on the founders' democratic ideals and the inclusive "social gospel" upheld by like-minded evangelical Christians and Quakers. Elegantly rephrasing Thomas Jefferson, Stanton wrote: "All men and women are created equal." Lofty language notwithstanding, their immediate goals were distinctly down to earth and based on domesticity. These included the rights to control property, divorce, and maintain custody of their children, which would enable wives to protect themselves and their families from improvident or abusive husbands. (Anticipating change, just two months before, New York State had set an important precedent with its landmark Married Women's Property Act—the first in a series of slow, often grudging, piecemeal reforms in other states.) Of the three hundred conferees, just a hundred signed the document, and even zealots considered suffrage such a far-fetched goal that they included it in their declaration only after Black abolitionist Frederick Douglass's last-minute, passionate insistence that the vote was a universal human right. As he later put it, woman's equality "was hers before she comprehended it. It is inscribed upon all the powers and faculties of her soul, and no custom, law nor usage can ever destroy it." In mainstream society, however, the women's rights proclaimed at Seneca Falls were considered so ludicrous that some newspapers lampooned the very idea simply by printing a list of them.

From the beginning, the suffrage movement was a messy, fragmented, gradational phenomenon that waxed and waned over decades of internecine as well as public debate. Where ideology was concerned, some leaders focused first on women's right to vote in school board elections—a surprisingly contentious issue seen as the thin end of the wedge. Others stoutly claimed that women deserved full enfranchisement, whether because they were equal to men or morally superior to them. Many of the same activists who challenged their own subordination to men's authority and monopoly on political power did not consider people of color, including other suffragists, as equals; indeed, some even used the maintenance of White supremacy as a rationale for the vote. What the movement lacked in consistency, however, it made up for in sheer grit. In Oregon alone, activists began lobbying for their rights in 1870, barely a decade after statehood, then mounted five grueling campaigns to pass a suffrage referendum—a general vote by the electorate on a single issue—before winning on their sixth attempt in 1912.

The vast territory called "the West" clearly ended at the Pacific Ocean, but throughout the nineteenth century, Americans kept redefining the frontier's eastern boundary. By the 1840s, when the first settlers began to cross the country, the divide was the Mississippi River, then the Missouri, before stabilizing at the hundredth meridian: the invisible line that separates the greener East from the largely arid and semi arid terrain reaching to the opposite coast.

The West differed from the rest of America in significant ways that affected women's position, starting with demography. Until the turn of the century, White men significantly outnumbered White women there, particularly in mining towns and cities, which boosted the latter's status. Though far less populous than the East, the region was home to the great majority of the country's Native Americans, Hispanics, Mormons, and Asians, which positioned the White Anglo-Saxon Protestant women who predominated in early migration to be cast as gentle, maternal "civilizers" among "savages" in an alleged "wilderness." Indeed, the West quickly became a showcase for the ideal home—the keystone of Victorian society and now also the building block of America's transcontinental expansion—and the virtuous wife who presided over it. The idea of the high-minded "citizen-mother" of her fledgling community—and even the Greater Home that was the nation, most of which now lay in the region—became such a familiar trope that the Italian composer Giacomo Puccini later celebrated her in Minnie, the Bible-spouting heroine of his opera *La Fanciulla del West*, or "The Damsel of the West."

Women's status also benefited from conditions in the West's so-called settler society, which by definition was simpler, more forward-looking, and less encumbered by tradition, precedent, and an entrenched, oppositional establishment. During the hardscrabble settlement era, as in most of America today, it took two industrious partners to support a family, which increased women's work and its value. In agrarian areas, unmarried women had their pick of suitors among men loath to homestead without a wife to handle the house and garden and earn much-needed cash from her "home production," whether selling eggs and bread or taking in sewing or boarders. In mining towns, women used those same domestic skills to make what seemed like small fortunes by marketing hot meals and clean laundry to the overwhelmingly male population. Some settlers also increased women's civic profile by moving from the private into the public sphere as the "town mothers" who organized many of the West's first schools, churches, and charities. These homemakers and community builders could not achieve economic much less political parity with men in the patriarchal system, but their record of hard work and dedication won respect and made them a force, albeit nonelectoral, to be reckoned with.

During the Civil War, two small but influential groups of western women began to capitalize on unique opportunities to gain status and also be treated as equals by the federal government—an important political precedent. In 1862, as the conflict raged, President Abraham Lincoln and his more gender-egalitarian Republicans passed two groundbreaking laws that recognized women's importance to the Greater Reconstruction; lasting from 1845 to 1877, this sweeping scheme to create a unified, coast-to-coast nation included colonizing the West as well as eventually reclaiming the rebellious South.

In May, Congress passed the Homestead Act, which enabled female as well as male heads of households to claim free land in the West. At a time when most women had few economic opportunities at all, the chance to own real estate that could support an independent life or produce capital to fund their next ventures was a stunning advance. Importantly, these homesteaders also attained the prized landowner status that since the days of the agrarian founders had been tied to citizenship and social standing. Their names on tax rolls beside their male neighbors' later became an important argument for full citizenship.

Very few nineteenth-century Americans, especially women, had access to higher education and the professional life it enabled, but in

July, Congress passed the Morrill Land-Grant Act. The law created nearly a hundred tuition-free, coeducational public colleges and universities, two thirds of which were in the rapidly developing West. Given access to decent careers that enabled them to support themselves, women graduates had an alternative to marriage. Many who joined the ranks of the region's first, urgently needed homegrown professionals became teachers, but almost 15 percent of educated women entered traditionally male professions such as medicine, journalism, and the law, compared to the national rate of 8 percent. At the same time, other young women fled agrarian backwaters for new opportunities as clerks, seamstresses, factory workers, and waitresses in the nation's fastest-growing cities, where they often significantly outnumbered men well into the twentieth century.

Later in the Victorian era, many ambitious westerners matched the profile of the "New Woman." This appealing hybrid was suspended between the nineteenth century's domestic model of womanhood and the early twentieth century's more liberated version, based on the kind of independent, self-fulfilling way of life traditionally limited to men. Women such as Clara Shortridge Foltz, a divorced single mother who became the Pacific Coast's first female lawyer, Zitkala-Sa, a Dakota writer, rights activist, and musician, and Caroline Lockhart, a journalist, a rancher, and an author of popular Westerns, helped Americans come to terms with women's evolving role in a rapidly modernizing society.

Just as the West presented certain ambitious women with unique opportunities to own land and attend college, it gave them special advantages in their pursuit of more rights. Indeed, in 1854, just six years after Seneca Falls and a year after the Washington Territory was founded, a suffrage bill failed to pass in its legislature by a single vote. The national movement was based in the East, but when the cause reemerged after the hiatus imposed by the Civil War, suffrage took off in the West like no place else.

Even before the West's gifted suffragists developed a strong movement, their environment afforded their cause certain social and political advantages. From a purely practical standpoint, legislators in the sparsely populated region were eager to grow their electorates and thus amplify their clout in Washington, DC; attracting White women would also help balance the gender ratio and for racists counter the ballots of men of color who were enfranchised by the Fourteenth and Fifteenth Amendments. Passing such controversial laws was also easier in loosely governed, socially fluid territories than in states encumbered by a century's worth of tradition and legal precedent. Moreover, territories transitioning into states had to write constitutions, which mandated debate over issues including women's legal rights and political status. Finally, compared to their brothers in the South and East, men who witnessed women's service during ongoing settlement were notably more receptive to their empowerment—particularly if it was also to their own political advantage.

In 1869, the Wyoming Territory's women became the first in Euro-American history to be fully enfranchised, followed a year later by those of the largely Mormon Utah Territory—both a half century before the passage of the Nineteenth Amendment. It is often said that western men "gave women the vote," but after those first two gifts, other territorial and state governments responded only after women persistently lobbied for bills, saw them defeated, then tried, tried again.

In the 1870s and 1880s, while suffragists fought for full citizenship in legislatures and courtrooms, western women continued to build political power by moving from community building into large-scale social reform. Many enlisted in the powerful nationwide Woman's Christian Temperance Union, which began as a campaign against vices that jeopardized the family, particularly drunkenness. Before long, however, the WCTU embraced suffrage and a broad "Do Everything" agenda that fought against poverty, ignorance, and other evils—a shift especially popular in the pragmatic West. Native American reformers such as Susette La Flesche, an Omaha teacher and author, and Sarah Winnemucca, a Paiute writer and orator, inspired White women, including Alice Cunningham Fletcher, America's first female anthropologist, and Helen Hunt Jackson, author of the bestselling novel *Ramona*, to join their fight to achieve equality for the West's original peoples; by influencing public policy before they could vote themselves, they strengthened women's claim to the rights of full citizenship.

By the 1890s, an extraordinary number of women helped make the West the national capital of the new progressive politics, which championed women's rights as well as greater democracy and economic justice for average people and opposed corrupt government and Big Business. Many followed the Kansan homesteader-turned-lawyer Mary Elizabeth Lease into the new People's Party, which upheld women's equality while defending farmers and workers against the Industrial Age's rapacious 1 percent. Like Ella Knowles, Montana's first female lawyer, some courageous progressive women ran for public office before they were enfranchised themselves. Many others helped to shape the laws of new states, right down to the more gender-neutral wording of their constitutions. When the progressive states of Colorado and Idaho enfranchised women in 1893 and 1896 respectively, the West, along with the settler societies of Australia and New Zealand, became a global as well as national epicenter of suffrage. As immigration surged in the early twentieth century and the public debated over the question of "Who is a real American?" western women increasingly pointed to their long record of community building and local civic involvement and demanded full citizenship.

In the early twentieth century, western suffragists came up with a successful formula for winning the vote. Sophisticated young suffragists such as Cora Smith Eaton, a physician, mountaineer, and coauthor of the *Washington Women's Cook Book: Votes for Women, Good Things to Eat*, mounted splashy, creative campaigns that changed American politicking. Like Oregon's Dr. Esther Pohl Lovejoy, founder of the multiracial Everybody's Equal Suffrage League, and Harriet "Hattie" Redmond, a janitor at the US District Court in Portland and the president of its Colored Women's Equal Suffrage Association, they rallied diverse women as workers for their homes and homeland who deserved to vote. Most important, they fostered successful coalitions with other forward-looking, nonpartisan good-government groups, such as progressive political organizations, labor and farmers' unions, and liberal-minded Republicans, who needed women's votes to promote their own agendas. By 1914, suffragists had made the winning argument in Washington, California, Oregon, Arizona, Kansas, Nevada, and Montana: an unofficial union of hardworking "municipal housekeepers"—whether unpaid mothers or employees on the job—were entitled to vote to improve the homeland as well as their homes.

I ronically, by the time of the suffragists' triumph that year, the West's demography had synchronized with that of the rest of the country, and women no longer benefited from the settlement era's unprecedented opportunities. As World War I loomed, society's conservative turn, exacerbated by women's economic and political gains, created the predictable backlash. Even the rugged rodeo cowgirls who had recently competed with men were replaced by spangled rodeo queens who waved sedately from their palominos.

Like the history of the nineteenth- and early twentieth-century

West in general, the record of its women is not a seamless march of progress but a jagged trajectory of advances on one front and retreats on another, progress for some and declines for others. There is no way to balance colonization's benefits for White settlers and their descendants with the costs to the region's original peoples, or to reconcile the racism endured by women of color, including within the rights movement, with the gains made by their sex. To move forward, however, Americans must both engage humbly with the tragedies of our shared past and also take heart in its triumphs, including women's ongoing empowerment.

Before the first eastern greenhorns arrived in their covered wagons, the West had changed countless times during the fourteen thousand years of its history that have now been chronicled, just as its political and demographic landscape of red, blue, and purple states continues to shift today. The inspiring legacy of the overlooked westerners who helped redefine "American woman" at home and abroad is an important part of that long record, particularly because it proves that, despite formidable obstacles, change is possible, even for rules once seemingly writ in stone.

NEW WOMEN IN
THE OLD WEST

One

HOME ON THE RANGE

*We were surely taking a wild
and inconsiderate step . . .*

—SARAH JANE CUMMINS,
OREGON SETTLER

O N MAY 4, 1845, Sarah Jane Cummins left St. Joseph, Missouri, a two-year-old frontier town and jumping-off point for the West, to start a grueling migration to the Oregon Territory, and a much longer, unanticipated journey toward greater equality. She and Benjamin Walden, her husband of just two weeks, were seeking a better, more prosperous life in the largely uncharted region, which by 1848 would sprawl across the current states of Oregon, Washington, Idaho, and parts of Wyoming and Montana. After a four-month honeymoon in a wagon train traveling across verdant prairies, arid plains, and the towering Rocky Mountains, they, along with Sarah's family, planned to claim free land in the fertile Willamette Valley. Like other pragmatic young people, they knew that survival there, much less success, required two hardworking, capable partners, and they married before joining the vast enterprise famously defined that very year as America's "manifest destiny to overspread the continent."

Of the thousands of early practitioners of what was later called "manifest domesticity," several hundred, including Cummins, proudly recorded their landlocked westward odysseys. She began her account with a flutter of conflicted feelings. No one had heard from the settlers who had preceded them to the valley the year before, and she admitted that she and her family were taking a "wild and inconsiderate step" into the almost-unknown.

Cummins was just sixteen years old, but she was well prepared to take that wild step, having twice in recent years experienced the rigors of moving west in pursuit of greater prosperity. Agriculture was America's major industry, and her father was one of many men who had profited from developing and selling one farm to buy a larger, preferably cheaper one, sometimes repeatedly. First, he had transplanted her and her siblings from Ohio to Illinois. Then one afternoon, her dazed mother had exclaimed, "What do you think father has done?" No sooner had the family moved to St. Joseph, where Cummins attended its first school, first church, and first lectures on temperance—abstention from alcohol, at least hard spirits—than her father found a lucrative reason to consider migrating again.

In 1843, a provisional government of early settlers tried to encourage development in the Willamette Valley by offering migrants, especially married White men like Cummins's father and their wives (including Native women), a real estate bonanza. These couples could claim 640 acres, or one "section," of land in exchange for living on and improving the property, usually with some cleared fields and a building or two; single men received just 320 acres. (In 1850, two years after the United States officially annexed the Oregon Territory, previously also claimed by Great Britain, Congress passed the Donation Land Claim Act, which legitimized the earlier grants and attracted some seven thousand settlers eager to cash in on the same offer.) In February 1845, Cummins's father and her new suitor decided to join the other ambitious, restless, young and youngish men, many of them farmers and skilled artisans, who saw the 1,800-mile migration from Missouri to Oregon as the royal road to potential rewards well worth the risks.

The footloose men's wives often saw the move differently. Like Cummins's pregnant mother, many were deeply engaged with family, home, and community, and they accurately anticipated a dangerous ordeal leading to an uncertain outcome far from loved ones. Some argued successfully against the move, and many others closely negotiated the terms of their compliance. In patriarchal American society, however, men had the last word in such important matters, and some wives went west under strong protest, including women dragged along by force. Even those who like young Cummins welcomed the move experienced the painful wrench of parting and some degree of homesickness.

Most women soon adjusted to life in their new mobile homes. Once across the Missouri River, Cummins boasted that her covered wagon had "the best accoutrements that the age and inventions of the times produced," but it was just ten feet long and three and a half feet wide and crammed with more than a ton of goods. Practical necessities, such as her husband's tools and bacon stored in barrels of bran, jostled against treasures, including a "Bible, dictionary, arithmetic, grammar, charts and maps, also our diplomas of graduation." For good reason, families lived outdoors in decent weather and suffered when conditions forced them to sleep in or underneath their jam-packed wagons at night.

From sunrise to sunset, the migrants' wagons juddered over the deep ruts and perilous rivers that corrugated the Oregon Trail. Then the West's approximation of an interstate highway, it was just a rough dirt track, based on narrow game paths first used by Native Americans and fur trappers, that only grudgingly allowed for wheeled vehicles. After traversing what was then called the Great American Desert, later the Great Plains, they struggled up an eight-thousand-foot ascent to the South Pass over the ramparts of the Rockies. From there, some parties branched off on secondary trails to California or Utah, and others, including Cummins and her family, continued on to the Pacific Northwest.

The challenges of migration and settlement soon obliged women to become more equal to men by behaving that way, if only by necessity. Early in the trip, most couples stuck to the Victorian era's gender rules: men did the heavy outdoor work, such as driving the wagon and handling the livestock, and women did the domestic chores. As Cummins soon found, however, housekeeping in a canvas-capped "prairie schooner" was rarely smooth sailing. As the migration ground on, it became clear that, far from being secondary, so-called women's work—washing laundry in muddy rivers, gathering dried buffalo dung for fuel, which as Cummins noted, "caused many ladies to act very cross," and cooking three meals a day over campfires—was absolutely essential to their venture. Indeed, their chores were so onerous that most of the relatively few single men who headed west signed on as extra hands to family parties.

Like most women on the trail, Cummins gradually developed a more flexible, western improvisation on her traditional domestic role. After all, to stay safe, fed, and reasonably clean while progressing with the journey, both partners had to do whatever urgently needed doing at any particular moment without considering gender. Some men occasionally helped with cooking and childcare, but many women often cracked the whip over the great teams of oxen or horses, loaded and unloaded the wagons, and did other such men's chores.

Migration showcased the value of women's work and expanded their functional repertoire, but it also offered them opportunities to experience new freedoms and develop new skills. If they rode horses at all, proper women back East used sidesaddles—originally designed to protect virginal hymens—but Cummins anticipated the cowgirl by looping up her skirts and riding "gentleman fashion." She relished the role of scout, jumping on her horse to guide her husband as he drove their wagon through roiling rivers pocked with the hidden boulders that caused many accidents. She proudly noted that while she was leading several girlfriends on a search for pasture for the wagon train's livestock, their route was closely observed by the men, who "profited by our experience" and quickly followed with the horses and cattle.

At a time when girls did not get the same degree of schooling as boys, Cummins also decided to treat the West like a vast coeducational campus. (Indeed, she still fumed over the teacher who had wasted time by making girls practice facial expressions "suited to the occasion of entertaining company.") She enthused over the region's "sermons in stones, books in running brooks," opportunities for geological observations, and spontaneous encounters with wildlife. Thrilled by the sight, she lyrically compared a thundering buffalo stampede to "the undulating movement of a great sea as it rises in regular billows and falls in gently undulating troughs."

As the journey broadened Cummins's experience and encouraged her sense of agency, she grew more independent. When her elders tried to discourage her from helping the men herd the family's cattle over steep mountains, she shrugged off their concern, writing that her "will was not to be swayed in that matter." She and the poorly equipped and provisioned wranglers soon got lost, however, and avoided death from exposure only when her husband shot a gun at a bit of dry coat lining to kindle a fire. Though shaken by the close call, she reminded herself to focus on her future home rather than her present trials and soon rallied to explore on her own. "Seated on eternal snow," she wrote, "looking from over these mountains and hills, across wide valleys into dark glens, above the roar of wind or of waters, I was lost in infinity."

Despite their experiments with women's traditional role, even spirited young wives such as Cummins, who often behaved like what Americans already called "tomboys," clung to their status as proper homemakers for several reasons. Domesticity was, after all, their major source of social identity and power, and throughout the long journey, they proudly continued to wear its symbolic uniform of white aprons, collars, and cuffs, however grimy and ragged they became. Even those who were willing to take on men's chores as need be did not want to add them to their own brutal workload on a routine basis. Sticking to the familiar amid migration's often disorienting circumstances also afforded them certain precious comforts, including some autonomy from men and the solace of the close female ties encouraged by Victorian society's separate spheres.

Cummins was one of many diarists to describe her affectionate bonds and experiences with other "dear good" women on the trail with a warmth conspicuously absent from their reserved remarks regarding their husbands. Influential figures such as Sarah Josepha Hale—editor of the popular *Godey's Lady's Book*, proponent of female education, and promoter of the home-oriented, nationwide Thanksgiving holiday—assured women that as rulers of the domestic domain, they were entitled to amicable unions with spouses of their choosing who shared the goal of a comfortable family life. This was an important advance over traditional arranged marriages, to be sure, but rarely did the proper Victorians make mention of their marital relationships. Even Cummins, a new bride, said little about her ties with the man she primly referred to as "Mr. Walden" or "my husband."

Most women were determined to resume their place in proper homes as soon as possible—on average, establishing a good house and garden took about two years—yet migration also inevitably expanded their sense of their place in the larger world. Over the long months on the trail, whether enthusiastically or not, they had assumed more responsibility, increased their skill sets, boosted their economic status as valued workers, and, perhaps most important showed themselves— and their husbands and children—that they were capable of more than society maintained.

Indeed, that so many women prevailed over the physical and emotional stress tests imposed by migration, even as the medical establishment insisted on their physiological and mental frailty, is one of American history's underremarked ironies. Many diarists boasted about their improved fitness, which they attributed to their strenuous new lives on the trail and the drier, sunnier western climate. (Cummins credited eating buffalo meat, which meant that "for the first time in my life I began to enjoy fairly good health.") Despite the risks of childbirth for the 20 percent of women who were pregnant on the journey, their mortality rate was lower than that of men, whose work was more dangerous.

Like Cummins, most women functioned well during migration, but some were heroic. Following behind her on the Oregon Trail just a year later, Ellen Smith was widowed when her husband died of a heart attack in Wyoming. As the onset of winter and starvation loomed, the mother of nine saw him buried and continued on. After the ordeal killed her sixteen-year-old daughter, already ill with typhus, Smith tied the smallest children and their essentials atop the oxen and set off on foot with the older ones, keeping her offspring alive by feeding them roasted mice. When they reached their intended destination in Oregon, she established her family's homestead as planned—an outstanding economic as well as physical achievement for a woman at a time when very few elsewhere could become landowners.

Migration increased women's sense of competence as well as their economic status, but it also encouraged them to see themselves as patriotic pioneers—a uniquely western identity that powerfully reinforced their later claim to full citizenship, even as it further disadvantaged the region's people of color. In 1836, Narcissa Prentiss Whitman, one of the first two White women to cross the Rockies, set the tone for colonizing maternal "civilizers" charged to create God-fearing homes and families amid the West's "heathens." Back home in upstate New York, the evangelical Presbyterian schoolteacher from a prosperous family had yearned to convert western Native Americans; but as a woman, she could only approximate her ambition by marrying an ordained minister, then serving as his helpmeet. After some matchmaking by the American Board of Commissioners for Foreign Missions, she wed Rev. Marcus Whitman and left for the Oregon Territory. The news that the golden-haired bride had crossed the Rockies—a feat then thought impossible for such a fine lady—and settled at Waiilatpu, near present-day Walla Walla, Washington, helped open the West to migration by women and families.

After Whitman cofounded a mission to serve the Cayuse people, her focus shifted from evangelizing Native Americans to preaching colonization to White women via letters. She duly gave classes in the Bible and domestic skills to the puzzled Cayuse and even adopted three orphans of mixed White and Native blood. Yet she struggled with her new neighbors' difficult Nez Perce language, and soon adopted the patronizing attitude of less virulently racist settlers, who treated Native Americans like children. Her correspondence with family back East reflects her disdain for the Cayuses' communal way of life and ideas about hygiene. As a proper Victorian, she did not comment directly on their sexual mores, but Native societies generally did not believe that unhappy couples should stay together, so they allowed divorce and polygamy. They often permitted premarital sex and accepted intimate ties that benefited the commonweal, such as diplomatic liaisons with important outsiders. Indeed, for nearly two hundred years before Whitman arrived, the Pacific Northwest's lucrative fur trade relied on common-law marriages between White trappers and Native women, which were recognized *à la façon du pays* ("according to the custom of the country").

In letters that were often printed in eastern newspapers as reportage, Whitman glibly assured her readers that "families can come quite comfortable and easy in wagons all the way," and added her own support for colonization: "This country is destined to be filled, and we desire greatly to have good people come, and ministers and Christians, that it may be saved from being a sink of wickedness and prostitution."

Rallying to the federal government's cause of creating a new, transcontinental nation during the Greater Reconstruction, politicians and preachers alike seconded Whitman's nationalistic message with expansionist gusto. To recruit the volunteers needed to secure the West, they did not speak of pawns in a vast federal scheme of cost-effective settler colonization, which largely brought about the conquest of its Native and Hispanic populations by replacing their societies with that of the newcomers. Rather, propagandizers conjured up images of bold, patriotic frontiersmen and angelic civilizers who set out to redeem what Cummins called "wild regions, inhabited by savages and the haunt of wild beasts." Indeed, her first sight of the monumental Rockies rising from the plains evoked thoughts of her own small role in securing "the great beyond, the republic yet to be born, the conquest of the wide, wide West."

Most migrants, including Cummins, were untroubled by the injustice of displacing the West's first inhabitants. They did not know that within two hundred years of Columbus's arrival, much if not most of North America's Native population—guesstimates range between two and ten million—had already succumbed to intertribal warfare and the diseases brought by early colonizers. Nor did they grasp that they were participating in a major global phenomenon of the nineteenth century: the epic exploration of the world and the conquest, displacement, and even decimation of its indigenous peoples by its White minority. For that matter, they did not realize that their own diaspora was just the latest of many that had already shaped the West, from that of the Spanish who arrived in the sixteenth century to that of the Lakota; also known as the Sioux, these Native Americans had migrated from the woodlands of Minnesota, Iowa, and Wisconsin onto the Great Plains, where they in turn pressured the Pawnees, Hidatsas, and other groups.

Like Cummins, most early migrants were White Anglo-Saxon Protestants, many from the Upper South, Illinois, and Missouri, who shared a robust conviction of their racial and cultural superiority that was only confirmed by their ignorance of Native American peoples. Since colonial times, they had been caricatured as brutal "braves," who only bestirred themselves to hunt, fight, and steal horses, and drudge-like, lascivious "squaws," who did all the work. Women in particular had been primed to be fearful by popular "captivity narratives"—interestingly, the first form of American literature focused on female experience. The genre had debuted in 1682, when Mary White Rowlandson, a Massachusetts Puritan, published a bestselling account of her twelve-week ordeal during the so-called First Indian War, in which she cast herself as the godly prisoner of an aggrieved coalition of "murtherous wretches." Such blood-curdling accounts of presumably virtuous White women seized by allegedly savage men of color were not only titillating but also served the important political purpose of rationalizing the injustices wrought by colonization.

The federal government's policy, too, reflected the widespread assumption among Whites that they could not coexist in peace and equality with Native Americans. By the time Cummins went west, many Native peoples had already been segregated on lands called reservations. In principle, they owned and governed these colonies, and in exchange for their freedom, they were to receive adequate food and other goods. In reality, the reservations were usually desolate places, managed by often venal, corrupt "Indian agents," or government representatives, where many Natives sickened and died.

Like many White Americans, Cummins soon distinguished between "good Indians," who were helpful to them, and "bad" ones, who were not. Charged with keeping their loved ones fed and clothed during the long journey, women settlers appreciated Native guides and traders in useful goods, such as buffalo robes, moccasins, and especially food. Still savoring the result of one such transaction, Cummins wrote of turning peas, onions, turnips, potatoes, and "nice, fresh venison" into a fine meal that enabled her grateful family to enjoy "some degree of the comforts of home life." However, she solely blamed the "sullen and wily" Walla Walla and Cayuse men who protested her wagon train's trespass in their homeland for causing a "night of terror," which ended only when the women settlers made "a good supply of coffee" that the "Indians came in hordes to drink" before fading away.

By September 1845, when Cummins crossed into Oregon and turned seventeen, she had expanded her sense of her personal potential and acquired a new identity as a patriotic pioneer in a historic venture—a source of pride for many western women, who used it to their social and political advantage. After attending a Sabbath service with a few settlers' families and a dozen Natives, her family party pressed on to Oregon City, south of what is now Portland, where they passed the winter in a rented house. In the spring, her husband and father traveled to present-day Salem to register homestead claims in the Willamette Valley, near the present-day town of Brooks, and she made the transition from migrant to settler.

The "homestead principle" put forth in 1689 by the English philosopher John Locke stated: "Whatsoever, then, he [a man] removes out of the state that Nature hath provided and left it in, he hath mixed his labour with it, and joined to it something that is his own, and thereby makes it his property." A century and a half later, in the West, Cummins and her husband put Locke's thesis into practice by living on and improving their claimed land. Many women found the time to chronicle migration, but Cummins was one of the precious few who managed to record some details of the hectic process of settlement, when families had to scramble to survive before their new farms could sustain them.

Women were so crucial to the backbreaking process of homesteading that, as with migration, men were reluctant to attempt it alone. Without domestic partners, they would be hard-pressed to get their own work done, whether clearing woods or starting a business. Judging by her diary, both Cummins and her husband considered her contributions to their welfare no less important than his. First, she had to turn what barely qualified as a house—usually a shack or cabin later improved with a sleeping loft, a root cellar, and a lean-to kitchen—into a home. The wherewithal for this project consisted of treasures she had hauled from back East, including a "little chair made of Sugar Maple wood," childhood books, and "calicoes bought during the Revolutionary war."

Then came the homemaker's endless work of cooking three meals a day, mending and sewing clothes from scratch, growing and gathering vegetables and fruit, milking cows, collecting eggs, making butter, and filling the pantry with preserved meats and other foods. Just baking a week's worth of bread and pie for a family could take a whole day, as did doing the laundry—a miserable business of hauling and heating water, then soaping, scrubbing, and rinsing the clothes and hanging them to dry. Some women settlers had to do rough outdoor chores as well.

Agrarian women back East also worked hard, including in the fields if need be, and many earned money from "home production," such as making butter, pies, or poultry for sale. In the West, however, particularly at first, women often virtually supported their cash-strapped families with income derived from their "settler production," whether goods or services. At a time when Oregon had 137 White men for every 100 White women, many of the latter supplied the large, itinerant male population with fresh eggs and bread, mending, and boarding to a degree that might have compromised their respectable status elsewhere. In the all-hands-on-deck West, however, survival trumped such social niceties. Not surprisingly, the women valued their settler production over their quotidian housework.

In 1847, Cummins added childcare to her other duties upon delivering the first of her seven offspring. Settlement was a family affair, and children were desperately needed workers in remote places where both laborers and wages were in short supply. With the rest of White America that year, she also reeled at the news of the "Whitman massacre": a party of Cayuse men had murdered the couple and burned down their mission as revenge for the many deaths among their people caused by the measles brought by the settlers—one of a number of diseases for which Native Americans lacked immunity.

No sooner had Cummins and her husband established their first homestead than the upwardly mobile couple started speculating in real estate—one of the West's earliest and most lucrative industries and soon uniquely accessible to women. Trading up, as her parents continued to do, they sold what she described as "the improvements on our claim" in 1850, then found an even better property near a trading post. "The new claim was alluvial," she wrote, "and we soon had a beautiful home place."

Like most women who went west, Cummins saw herself as a proper wife, mother, and standard-bearer of mainstream American society, not as a rebel or proto-feminist. Yet the Ohio farm girl had honeymooned in a covered wagon, negotiated with Native traders, herded cattle, and flipped homesteads. Although she had seemingly stepped back into the country's old-fashioned agrarian past, just as many women back East fled from farms to the new comforts and conveniences of the Industrial Age's towns and cities, she had retained and even improved upon her foremothers' economic status as coproviders for their families—then as now, an empowering position that many urban easterners forfeited. Despite grave hardships, including the deaths of three of her children, followed in 1887 by that of her first husband, she ended her journal with a late-life note of gratitude for the "marvelous manifestations of the power and goodness of God." She was proud enough of her own story of "one who assists in making a home in a new and practically unexplored region," however, to publish her memoir for future generations. Her repeated hope that they may "never neglect their privilege of honoring the noble founders of our nation—our noble republic" suggests that she numbered herself among them.

In 1848, while the first settlers were still just trickling into the West, three momentous events during the presidency of James Polk, an expansionist Democrat, transformed America in general and the

West in particular. The United States not only officially acquired the huge Oregon Territory but also won the Mexican-American War and with it much of the vast Southwest, including what are now Arizona, New Mexico, and parts of Nevada, Utah, Colorado, California, and Texas. No less important, gold was discovered in California, which turned the West and its mining industry into the country's new economic powerhouse.

Once the gold rush began, the West urbanized with lightning speed. Before the stampede, Native Americans constituted most of the California Territory's population of perhaps 160,000 people, but by 1855 that figure was more than 300,000, and the majority of the newcomers were men. Prospectors desperate for home-cooked meals, clean shirts, and female companionship proposed to "tearful widows of a fortnight and to little girls busy with mud pies." Seizing an economic opportunity available to them nowhere else, some ambitious women, most from the working class, rushed to supply the miners with the domestic skills that husbands got for free.

The iconic pioneer woman may be the proper, bonneted wife on a remote homestead, but Luzena Stanley Wilson, a boardinghouse proprietor in grubby mining towns, has an equal claim to the title. When their husbands joined the gold rush, most women stayed home, but in 1849, Wilson, a Quaker farm wife from Missouri, and her two children tagged along. After barely surviving an especially taxing migration, they arrived in bustling Sacramento tattered and penniless. Founded just the year before, the raw mining capital of north-central California had already attracted some six thousand men afflicted with gold fever; she was one of its three women. One morning, a man paid her $5 for a breakfast—about $168 today—and she noted that "if I had asked ten dollars he would have paid it."

Like the merchants, saloonkeepers, and gamblers who flocked to California in the miners' wake, Wilson and many enterprising cooks, seamstresses, and laundresses saw the lonely, unkempt men eating beans from a can as a gold mine of a different sort. By definition, a respectable wife could not sell her domestic skills beyond the modest limits of home production, but the impoverished mother quickly decided that in the West, needs must. She and her husband sold their oxen for $600 and bought a share in a boardinghouse, which she managed while he mined. According to an oral history recorded by her daughter, this unprepossessing property consisted only of a kitchen and a long room, dimly lighted by dripping tallow candles stuck in whiskey bottles and lined with bunks built from floor to ceiling. On Wilson's first visit, several miners drank at a bar, one lonely man wept over a letter, some invalids slept, and from one bed "stared the white face of a corpse . . . a silent unheeded witness to the acquired insensibility of the early settlers."

Undaunted, Wilson started up a business at a time when few women elsewhere had such a chance. She quickly attracted many rough-hewn but grateful customers, about whom she had few illusions. Surrounded by bags of gold, she wrote, men "plunged wildly into every mode of dissipation to drown the homesickness so often gnawing at their hearts." (That said, she had a soft spot for the well-dressed, polite gamblers: "The 'knights of the green table' were the aristocracy of the town.") At first, her clientele's courtliness amazed the plain, buttoned-up, bespectacled matron, but she soon realized that to the lonely men, any kindly woman was "a queen. . . . Women were scarce in those days."

In 1850, Wilson had to fight hard to maintain her pioneering place in the West's burgeoning hospitality industry. The great flood that swamped Sacramento that year consigned her family to the boardinghouse's top floor for more than two weeks and wiped out her business. In response, she moved her children and her cookstove to

Nevada, settling in a silver-mining camp near the Comstock Lode, then inauspiciously called Coyote Diggings. When her husband joined the family in what soon became the boomtown of Virginia City is unclear.

After surveying her crude new surroundings, Wilson proved her entrepreneurial mettle once again: "As always occurs to the mind of a woman, I thought of taking boarders." Wasting no time, she found two planks (precious in a region short on sawmills), fashioned them into a table, surrounded it with sheltering pine boughs, and bought some overpriced provisions. That night, she attracted twenty diners, each of whom "as he rose put a dollar in my hand and said I might count him as a permanent customer." She quickly expanded her role from rustic restaurateur to hotelier by enclosing her brush shelter and stove under a roof, then gradually adding bedrooms. Her grandly named El Dorado soon accommodated between seventy-five and two hundred customers, who each paid her twenty-five dollars per week.

That Wilson remarked her decision to take her husband "into partnership" makes plain that it was not a foregone conclusion, and that she considered the hotel to be her business—a stunning assumption at the time. Desperate to attract them to the state, the legislature, in its Constitution of 1849, granted women unusual privileges and opportunities, particularly regarding the control of property, that were partly inspired by Spanish-Mexican civil law: "All property, both real and personal, of the wife, owned or claimed by her before marriage, and that acquired afterward by gift, devise, or descent, shall be her separate property; and laws shall be passed more clearly defining the rights of the wife in relation as well to her separate property, as to that held in common with her husband."

Despite her wealth, which at one point amounted to the equivalent of $330,000 today, Wilson hewed to her plain-living Quaker roots and continued to dress simply in a farm wife's calico. In a town of just twenty-three women, she said, "every man thought every woman in that day a beauty." She modestly added that men had come forty miles "just to look at me, and I never was called a handsome woman, in my best days, even by my most ardent admirers." Her one concession to achieving a prosperity that she called "luxurious" was hiring women to do the cooking and housekeeping.

The West's domestic workers often lacked the time or skill to record their experiences, but Mary Ballou, who was employed in a miners' boardinghouse similar to Wilson's, left an eloquent, diary-style letter that testifies to their determination to cash in on the gold rush. Despite time spent "scareing the Hogs out of my kitchen and Driving the mules out of my dining room," she managed to serve three meals a day to ravenous men lined along a thirty-foot-long table. She also produced specialty items on request, including "oisters," a gruel for invalids, and "coffee for the French people strong enough for any man to walk on that has Faith as Peter had."

Despite her daunting workload, Ballou soon branched out to care for babies; nurse the sick (fifty dollars per week); take in laundry; make soap, mattresses, and sheets; and sew flags "both Democrat and Whig." One Fourth of July, she even culled a dollar's worth of gold dust from a stream. When homesick, she turned to her working-class sisters for comfort: "Occasionly I run in and have a chat with Jane and Mrs Durphy and I often have a hearty cry." Friendly by nature and free from the prejudices that most migrants brought west with them, she behaved courteously to the "French and Duch and Scoth and Jews and Italions and Sweeds and Chineese and Indians and all manner of tongues and nations," and in return was "treated with due respect by them all."

Like Ballou, Wilson made the most of the West's economic opportunities for women eager to profit from their domestic skills, if on a grander, entrepreneurial scale. Just as her success seemed guaranteed, however, a fire destroyed the El Dorado, leaving her family homeless and broke once again. Traveling through the fertile Sacramento Valley, they paused at a pleasant spot near Vacaville, where Wilson soon set up shop beneath an oak tree, posted with a sign reading WILSON'S HOTEL. The first customers of yet another successful female enterprise dined atop stumps and slept behind hay bales.

No less than farmers and miners, agrarian settlers like Cummins and urban frontierswomen like Wilson built the American West; indeed, they also made those men's lives and achievements possible. In their different ways, both the homesteader and the businesswoman were equally successful in responding to the challenges of settlement by maximizing their homemaking expertise, assuming more responsibility, and gaining the economic status conducive to political authority—an important refutation of the assumption that women's work is important only when it is not domestic.

At the same time back East, the women's movement was gaining steam, particularly after 1850, when the first of a series of National Woman's Rights Conventions was held in Worcester, Massachusetts. People who can't vote are hard-pressed to change the law, but the activists who attended these crucial meetings began to spread their revolution through powerful if nonelectoral means of exercising political heft, including petitioning, publishing, lecturing, lobbying politicians, and rallying male relatives. Mainstream society responded with decidedly mixed feelings, but the *New-York Tribune* editor Horace Greeley was among those who took a more sanguine, if measured, view. If employers would pay "a capable, efficient woman" at least two thirds of what they paid men to do the same work, they would "very essentially aid the movement now in progress for the general recognition and conception of Equal Rights to Woman."

Most American women never officially joined the rights movement, but many began an incremental pursuit of full citizenship, which is far more complex than qualifying for a ballot. By the mid-nineteenth century, women in the East's venerable towns and villages increasingly stepped out from their homes to join "voluntary associations" that promoted good causes, from social welfare to female education to uplifting lectures and concerts. Despite the grueling challenges of settlement in the West, women moved quickly from establishing new homes to building fledgling communities—efforts that bolstered their claim to more rights.

Two

THE RESPECTABLE
COMMUNITY

Wherever she was, she made civilization,
even when it seemed that she had little
indeed from which to make it.

—KATHARINE HEAD ROYCE,
DAUGHTER-IN-LAW OF CALIFORNIA
PIONEER SARAH ROYCE

W ESTERN WOMEN INCREASED their economic clout by capitalizing on their domestic role, but the "town mothers" who extended it past their doorsteps into their communities also raised women's civic status. On a scale not seen in America since the Puritans—those earlier settler-colonizers who created New England and the classic American town—these westerners used the moral authority derived from society's increasingly expansive, elevated conception of their domestic role to organize schools and churches, libraries and charities in tar-papered mining settlements and near trading posts at remote crossroads.

Most of these pioneers in shifting the traditional model of womanhood based on private domesticity to one that included public service have been lost to history. Women's achievements were generally not considered worthy of inclusion in the public, much less the historical, record. Unless they were criminals, they rarely appeared in newspapers. Since they could not legally incorporate the social institutions they established, men, often their husbands, were listed as founders in official documents and journals and lauded as town fathers.

Sarah Royce, who energetically practiced for the role of town mother in seven raw mining communities before settling down in Grass Valley, California, is one of the exceptions. Her account of stamping an unruly corner of the gold rush with the Puritans' template for a respectable American town was later published by her devoted son, Josiah Royce, a celebrated philosopher and a Harvard colleague of William James. In 1849, the proud graduate of the Albion Female Seminary, in Rochester, New York, her prospector husband, their first baby, and her prized melodeon barely survived a catastrophic migration, during which they were separated from their wagon train and got lost. After arriving in California, they spent the next five years moving between mining towns and settlements largely populated by men. Though far from the "amenities and refinements of home," she wrote, some "showed a consciousness of being somewhat the worse for a long, rough journey." Others were "roughly-reared frontier-men almost as ignorant of civilized life as savages." Determined to maintain standards as best she could, Royce held church services in her "canvas house" whenever possible. On one occasion, she invited a minister—they were often Methodist "circuit riders"—to preach in her "parlor," only to have some local rowdies mock the impromptu congregation's psalm singing, accompanied by her melodeon. Yet other men, she wrote, "appeared very generally to consider it desirable to have some of that sort among them."

———

Respectability was Victorian society's premier virtue, and most women settlers were determined to quickly reproduce the proper homes and communities they had known and loved back East. (Indeed, in the early 1830s, organizers in Boston had founded the American Society for Encouraging the Settlement of the Oregon Territory to "repeat with appropriate variations the history of the Puritan colony of Massachusetts Bay.") In 1854, Royce and her growing family finally put down roots in Grass Valley, where she sparsely furnished their simple but decent house with the few possessions that had survived their many moves. Then she assessed what the new mining community in the Sierra Madre needed to approximate a proper New England town. The Puritans had centered their villages on schools as well as churches, and Royce wanted to follow their familiar example.

Unlike powerless Puritan women, their Victorian sisters vigorously pursued their community-building ambitions armed with their new moral authority. (Not coincidentally, Catharine Beecher, who helped define it, was also a vigorous propagandizer of colonization. In 1832, she had herself migrated to the Ohio frontier to establish the Western Female Institute in Cincinnati; her well-known expansionist views helped position women settlers as nation builders.) Royce was gratified that she and other respectable wives and mothers in the West inspired "in most of the masculine faces, expressions of high appreciation and profound deference," but admiration aside, the men had several practical reasons for encouraging town mothers to roll up their sleeves.

In much of the sparsely populated West, there was a great deal of work to do by whoever was available to do it. Farmers, merchants, and miners like Royce's husband were too preoccupied with getting ahead in business or politics to interfere much with women's plans.

Elsewhere in the country, especially in the South, matrons who participated in even seemingly unexceptionable public activities, such as ladies' aid societies and other charities, could raise eyebrows; but western men could not afford to dismiss capable women who wanted to develop their communities.

Like most women, Royce prioritized a good school for her children, so she turned her modest one-story home into a cozy domestic academy. Her only resources were a Bible, a volume of Milton, several histories, a book of fables, and an encyclopedia that she found in an abandoned wagon, but she was a natural pedagogue. Her initial goal had been to create a school for young ladies, but local boys as well as girls soon joined her three daughters and little Josiah. Their mothers were eager to ensure that their offspring would be safe as well as educated; western children too young for chores often passed the day outdoors, largely unsupervised, while their parents worked. Many suffered from accidents and injuries, but the situation also meant that girls enjoyed an unusual degree of autonomy and adventure.

Royce's home academy was by no means unusual at a time when women who wanted to build an actual schoolhouse or any such physical institution in the West faced steep hurdles, starting with money. Early settlements had to construct, furnish, and heat their own buildings, as well as pay and board their teachers. Many cash-strapped men prioritized investing in their own fledgling farms and businesses over advancing the common good—a sentiment that jibed with the mid-century economy's accelerating shift to me-first industrial capitalism. Thus, some settlements provided only tents, brush shelters, or sod huts to serve as schools; even outhouses might be skipped, should an adjacent stand of trees or bushes be judged sufficient. The management of education was gradually turned over to school boards, whose elected members—by definition, men—controlled funding as well as academic standards. Understandably, then, many western women were more interested in voting, and even running, in those local elections than in the national sort. However, this seemingly commonsensical right was soon regarded as a precursor of women's full citizenship and suffrage, and thus highly controversial.

For his first eleven years, Josiah Royce recalled, his mother and his older sisters were his teachers in philosophy. The scholar who later specialized in the discipline of metaphysics fondly remembered his first encounters with such high matters at his mother's knee, listening to her read Bible stories and explain right and wrong. Expressing a sentiment they strongly shared, he wrote that for "Puritans" like them, the frontier was "the stage for an elemental struggle between good and evil."

One reason why western women were so keen to build schools was that their flexible, open-plan spaces easily doubled as venues for other respectable activities, such as plays, lectures, spelling bees, but especially church. Even though the West was the least religious part of America, sponsoring religious services was among its first and most effective ways to build communities. Congregations that were usually dominated by women provided much wholesome socializing in the form of the suppers, picnics, and musicales that combated isolated settlers' loneliness. Churches also offered desperately needed social services before state and local governments assumed these burdens, which enabled women to organize groups to aid orphans and the sick and provide what was simply called "poor relief" without compromising their propriety.

Leadership in the congregations so important to their communities gave women the chance to enhance their public role, but religion also offered the support and consolation that enabled many to endure the hardships of frontier life, from lingering homesickness and exhaustion to the loss of loved ones. (For the same reason, others sought solace in spiritualism, a contemporary gender-egalitarian movement based on the interaction of the living and the dead that was very popular in the West.) Sarah Royce attributed her own strength to a profound spiritual experience during migration, when the plight of her family, lost, hungry, and exhausted, nearly brought her to despair. Then, she wrote, "He came so near that I no longer simply *believed* in Him but *knew* His presence." She later helped found her community's Disciples of Christ church, but her simple, fervent faith was typical of religion in the distinctly no-frills region. There, denominational affiliations did not much matter, Royce wrote, as long as people "agreed on the great foundation facts and principles of Christianity."

Christianity was the dominant religion among White settlers, but not the only one. The United Hebrew Congregation, the oldest synagogue west of the Mississippi River, was founded in St. Louis in 1837, and by 1851, San Francisco had two shuls. The nineteenth-century western Jewish population was small, however, certainly compared to that of Mormons, or members of the Church of Jesus Christ of Latter-day Saints, who went west to flee religious persecution. By the time pioneers established the sprawling Utah Territory in 1850, Salt Lake City, its capital, already had a population of 6,157. When wagon trains paused there to restock supplies, migrants marveled at its fine temple but often considered the town to be America's Sodom.

Largely because of the Mormon practice of polygamy, most Americans of the era did not regard Mormons as simply believers from another Christian sect but, much like Jews at the time, almost as a people apart. Despite their religious differences, however, Mormon women settlers had much in common with settlers like Royce, including a strong desire for respectable community life and female company, as well as an unshakable belief in a better world to come. Dispatched with her husband and twenty-four other Saints to build a Mormon settlement in the isolated Gila Valley, near present-day Pima, Arizona, Mrs. C. A. Teeples held fast to her faith during many hardships, including sharing her husband's time and affection and a malaria epidemic that killed her son and some neighbors. Thanks to their strong religious convictions, she wrote, she and her community had "weathered it in spite of all the discouragements and trials."

Religious congregations also performed the secular function of discouraging violence and upholding legal and moral norms in places that had little government or law enforcement. (When nine uninvited neighbors, whom they called Gentiles, crashed the Mormons' Fourth of July party and insisted on dancing, the shocked Teeples observed that "each of [the four] women had two revolvers, and the men had one each.") Josiah Royce recalled how easily, in raunchy mining towns such as Grass Valley, "swiftly forming and dissolving, the social sanctions of stable societies disappeared." Sarah Royce noted that women as well as men at times failed to maintain decent standards, allowing that "it was not always the husband that was neglectful and indifferent nor the wife that was faithful." Indeed, one of her neighbors was Lola Montez—aka Eliza Rosanna Gilbert, the Countess of Landsfeld, and the "Spanish dancer"—who took San Francisco by storm in 1853 with her racy Spider Dance, which involved much creative writhing and lifting of skirts; after marrying a Californian, she moved to Grass Valley, where a scandal ensued after the murder of the town doctor, who had been named as corespondent in a divorce suit brought against her.

Considering that her patrons included Alexandre Dumas, Franz Liszt, and King Ludwig I of Bavaria, Montez might have been considered a courtesan; but more pedestrian sex workers were among the first women who went west to towns like Grass Valley to market feminine, if not strictly domestic, services to lonely, homesick men. As one California barroom song put it, "The miners came in '49, the whores in '51. And when they got together, they produced the native son." The great demand for these "soiled doves" soon turned prostitution into a major industry that helped urbanize the West. The law mostly looked the other way as long as the activity was reasonably discreet and did not perturb respectable civic life or depress real estate values. In fact, many cities depended on their red-light districts to boost local commerce, the municipal coffers, and the incomes of police, who were often paid off not to arrest the workers.

Most prostitutes were uneducated girls of various races from poor, troubled backgrounds. They were sometimes listed in official records as "sporting women," but they often pop up in census data in other guises, such as women who had been arrested or had notable amounts of money or property. For the great majority, however, prostitution was a dangerous, downwardly mobile way of life that often led to venereal disease, drug addiction, and alcoholism. Many died from botched abortions, childbirth, and violence, including suicide. The fortunate worked for only a brief interval until a better opportunity arose.

Despite its rough edges, the community that Royce fostered eventually claimed all the hallmarks of Victorian respectability, including several schools, churches, and "social and beneficent societies." But for her famous son's advocacy, the record of her achievements as the founder of a school and church and a pillar of respectable society would have been lost, like those of thousands of other western town mothers who worked like full citizens long before they enjoyed the rights.

In San Francisco, 140 miles to the south of the smaller Grass Valley, women community builders took on more ambitious projects. In 1853, the city's churchwomen united to form the San Francisco

Ladies' Protection and Relief Society, one of California's first philanthropies. The group initially gave "assistance to strangers, to sick and dependent women and children"—primarily the abandoned families of gold-crazed miners—then went on to build a shelter and an orphanage.

As a free state, California attracted Black migrants, including women community builders who also aided San Francisco's civic development. (Other than the sizable enslaved population in Texas—like Oklahoma, considered part of the South by the U.S. Census Bureau—the number of Black people in the nineteenth-century West was small—1.1 percent of the region's total population in 1860; in what became the Midwest, the figure was just under 1 percent, notably in Kansas, where there was considerable support for abolition.) By the 1850s, such women had helped establish three Black churches and a relief society in San Francisco, as well as a branch of the Underground Railroad. One of its leading "conductors," or expediters, was Mary Ellen Pleasant, a staunch Black abolitionist and self-described "capitalist" who helped freedmen find jobs and marriage partners while quietly running her business empire.

As is often the case regarding women, especially those of color, Pleasant's extraordinarily adventurous life is not well documented. According to an autobiography she dictated to a journalist and other accounts, she was born around 1814, either enslaved in Georgia or perhaps indentured in Philadelphia. As a young servant of uncertain legal status, she lived in a wealthy Nantucket household, where she acquired an informal education, polite manners, and a mastery of cookery. She later wed James Smith, an older Cuban abolitionist living in Boston, who left her a sizable inheritance. After marrying a Black man named John Pleasant, she moved to San Francisco in 1849, which is when her second husband disappears from her story.

While learning the ways of her adopted hometown, Pleasant

worked as a cook and listened closely to her wealthy employers. She soon owned and operated boardinghouses and restaurants that catered to well-off men, whose tips informed her shrewd investments in oil, the Wells Fargo bank, and other enterprises. She also formed a business partnership—and perhaps an intimate relationship—with Thomas Bell, an important White banker, who held much of their joint portfolio in his name. Despite whispers about prostitution, voodoo, and a "strange," "mesmeric" air, Pleasant circulated in high society. Newspapers described her variously as a "picturesque Negress" who could pass as White and as "Mammy Pleasant," a moniker she loathed. As the educator and rights activist W. E. B. Du Bois later put it, she was "strangely effective and influential . . . a colored woman who became one of the shrewdest business minds of the State."

The entrepreneur's support of the Underground Railroad is not the only reason why Pleasant is honored as the "Mother of Civil Rights in California." She twice sued a San Francisco streetcar company for not allowing her to ride based on her color. Moreover, she confirmed rumors that she gave $30,000 to John Brown, the abolitionist hanged in 1859 for murder and treason after he mounted an armed insurrection to overthrow slavery. She also asserted that she was the author of the note found in his pocket when he was captured, which read: "The ax is laid at the root of the tree. When the first blow is struck, there will be more money to help." After Bell died from a mysterious fall and his widow won control of his estate, Pleasant lived in reduced circumstances until her death in 1904. The epitaph she requested for her gravestone reads: SHE WAS A FRIEND OF JOHN BROWN.

Like California, liberal-minded Colorado attracted Black migrants, including community-oriented women like Clara Brown, a freedwoman who migrated from Kentucky to the mining town of Central City. At first, she supported herself as a baker, midwife, nanny, and washerwoman. Then, sensing the business opportunity presented by thousands of unkempt miners, she saved enough money to start her own laundry. As her business expanded, she shrewdly invested her profits in mines and real estate in Central City and Denver, eventually accumulating $10,000, then a huge sum. The entrepreneur-philanthropist assisted the needy of all races, donated to the building of both a Methodist and a Catholic church, and helped other Blacks to migrate to Colorado, where their numbers increased after the war. (At the age of eighty-two, after years of searching for her four children, who had been sold away during slavery, Brown finally met with her daughter Eliza Jane, then living in Iowa. On March 4, 1882, the *Council Bluffs Nonpareil* marked the occasion, reporting that the exemplary town mother was "still strong, vigorous, tall, her hair thickly streaked with gray, her face kind.")

Women's efforts to build respectable communities in the West eased their entry into public life, but as settler-colonizers determined to reproduce American models of domesticity and society throughout the region, they also helped to displace its long-established peoples and their cultures. Susan Shelby Magoffin, the privileged eighteen-year-old granddaughter of Kentucky's first governor, was one of the first White women to travel on the eight-hundred-mile-long Santa Fe Trail from Missouri into the Southwest, and her diary offers a rare woman's view of the rich Spanish-Mexican and Native American societies she encountered.

In 1846, Magoffin took up residence in Santa Fe, the charming Mexican provincial capital founded in 1610 by the Spanish, which, in those early days of the Mexican-American War, was occupied by the US Army. Despite her winning enthusiasm for "this new country, its people, my new house," Mexico challenged many of her notions about proper women and respectable societies. She found the ladies' "ciggaritas," décolletage, and comfortable calf-length skirts "truly shocking."

The vibrant mestizo (mixed-race) culture that had been established by early Spanish conquistadors and their Native wives was a stark contrast to color-obsessed America, especially the South, where Magoffin had grown up amid slavery. There were certain distinctions based on degrees of Spanish heritage and wealth, but Mexican society allowed for considerable mobility among racial groups and classes, including intermarriage. A Mexican who considered herself an aristocrat—such as the very grand "dark-eyed Senora" whom Magoffin observed using a servant as a human footstool—might well have some mestizo or Native blood.

Red-haired, bejeweled Doña Gertrudis Barceló, Santa Fe's most powerful woman, might have been sent from central casting to rattle the wide-eyed Magoffin. Although born into a well-educated, prominent family, Barceló owned and operated a posh gambling casino, where she showed off her great skill with cards—monte was her specialty. To Magoffin's amazement, she suffered no sense of womanly shame over her unusual career. On the contrary, the opulently dressed, uncorseted La Tules, as she was called—possibly a diminutive of Gertrudis—was the toast of the town's elite and engaged in unofficial international diplomacy and trade with Yankee newcomers. Magoffin sniffed that wheeling, dealing Barceló was merely a stately dame of a certain age, albeit possessed of a fascinating manner, whose skill was "to allure the wayward, inexperienced youth to the hall of final ruin." Nevertheless, Barceló could and did brag that her great wealth had been "accumulated by my own labor and exertions."

Thanks to more egalitarian Spanish-Mexican civil law, women like Barceló had long enjoyed legal perquisites that many American women aspired to. No powerless femes covert, Mexican wives could sue in court, make contracts, and own, inherit, and control property. Among the landed gentry, some had rights to all-important water as well as land and cattle, and even poor women could write wills to bequeath their humble household goods. Their economic and legal power gave Mexican women a strong say in family affairs and standing in their communities.

Magoffin may have disapproved of the enterprising, theatrical Barceló, but she considered Mexicans "a very quick and intelligent people" and tried hard to learn Spanish. Once the Mexican-American War was over, however, few of the White women arriving in the Southwest followed her example. Indeed, most shared the imperialistic politics of President Polk and his protégée, Jane Storms Cazneau, a journalist and daughter of a US congressman known as the "Mistress of Manifest Destiny."

In an era when women rarely spoke or wrote publicly about national affairs, Cazneau's fiery broadsides in the powerful *New York Sun* confidently applauded Polk's bellicose colonization policy. (The president was one of a series of male mentors, starting with Aaron Burr, the former vice president, who had been among her partners in a Texas real estate scheme in the 1830s; the details of their relationship are unclear, but in 1834, Eliza Jumel, Burr's second wife, named the raven-haired, violet-eyed Cazneau—then Storms, a divorced single mother—as a correspondent in her own divorce case.) During the Mexican-American War, Polk sent the bilingual journalist to Mexico City to serve as a covert diplomat. General Winfield Scott ridiculed her as a "plenipotentiary in petticoats," and Senator Thomas Hart Benton, the great proponent of American expansion, frowned on her "masculine stomach for war and politics," but she was the only journalist behind enemy lines throughout the conflict and became America's first female war correspondent.

Like Narcissa Whitman, Cazneau used a woman's voice to champion western expansion on the racist grounds that it was America's duty to civilize inferior peoples of color. As she put it, Mexico was a "rich and delightful country, soon destined . . . to enrich and be enriched by Anglo-Saxon enterprise and industry." The incoming wave of Yankees who agreed with her quickly colonized the Southwest with their own language, schools, churches, and social institutions. They also imported their national enthusiasm for exploiting fine racial distinctions. Was a mestizo a Mexican, and thus now a US citizen, or a Native American, who was not? On the grounds that they had some indigenous blood, many women and men were swindled out of their property and denied their civil rights. As mining quickly became the Southwest's dominant industry and employer, the American companies' unfair, race-based labor practices further hardened categories of color and class.

Not even the resilient Barceló could withstand the impact of American settler colonization. She had pragmatically sided with the US in the war and even lent money to the cash-strapped army, but once it was over and migration surged, her casino was no longer the place to see and be seen. Barceló had twice gone to the Mexican court to defend her good name against slander, but she could not stop US newspapers from printing articles about Santa Fe's "Queen of Sin." In 1852, as her community underwent the homogenizing, White-washing process later called Americanization, she died at the age of forty-seven, mourned by her own people at a church funeral fit for royalty.

As the American settlement of the Southwest advanced, even privileged women of color, including Hispanicized Native Americans such as Victoria Bartholomea Reid, were forced to contend with the racism inherent in colonization. Born into the Comicrabit people, one of the Native groups in California known as Mission Indians, she lived with her respected family outside Los Angeles, near the Franciscan mission of San Gabriel. When she was six or seven, her parents took their beautiful daughter to be educated at the mission, where she was weaned from her people's ways and tutored in the religion, manners, and domestic skills of a Spanish lady.

At thirteen, Bartholomea was married to Pablo Maria, a much older, prominent Hispanicized Native. In an unusual sign of approval, the Franciscans gave him a sizable property: the 128-acre Huerta de Cuati, a vineyard and orchard near the present-day Huntington Library, Art Museum, and Botanical Gardens that eventually became the childhood home of General George S. Patton. The couple's landowner status secured Bartholomea's acceptance by elite Californios, as members of the territory's wealthy old Hispanic families were called. When Pablo died of smallpox in 1836, in accordance with Spanish-Mexican property law, his twenty-eight-year-old widow, now the mother of four, inherited his estate—a right then generally denied to femes covert.

No picture of Bartholomea survives, but Hugo Reid, a handsome, enterprising Scottish trader who had a deep interest in the region's Native peoples, had fallen in love at first sight during an earlier encounter. Later, upon hearing that she was a widow, he rushed to court her. Before their elaborate wedding in 1837, the twenty-seven-year-old WASP groom converted to his wife's Catholic religion, became a Mexican citizen, and adopted her children—signs of devotion that additionally positioned him to acquire land rights. He also made a strange request of his bride: Would she change her given name of Bartholomea to Victoria, in honor of the British queen and his earlier, long-lost lover?

At first, Doña Victoria prospered as a wealthy matron, known for her fine manners and lavish hospitality as well as her beauty. Her husband dabbled in local politics and, helped by his marriage into Californio society, purchased the thirteen-thousand-acre Rancho Santa Anita, which included the site of what is now the Los Angeles County

Arboretum and Botanic Garden. However, she struggled with her role as an elite Hispanicized Native married to a European in what would soon be the US. Like some other Native American women married to White husbands, she was distressed that her husband's White friends still dismissed her as the "Indian wife."

By 1847, Hugo Reid's distracting outside activities, increasingly poor health, and travels that included two trips to China jeopardized the couple's economic welfare. They were forced to sell Rancho Santa Anita and move into a simple adobe home near the San Gabriel mission. Reid occupied himself in writing scholarly essays about the local Natives for the *Los Angeles Star*; in 1849, he became a signatory of California's first constitution, written the year before statehood. After his death in 1852, his once wealthy, now impoverished widow was forced to sell off her remaining property. In 1855, she returned to the mission, put on Native clothing, and lived quietly until she died of smallpox in 1868. Victoria Bartholomea Reid was buried in an unmarked grave in the mission cemetery.

Whether in the East or West, some men dismissed women's good works and efforts to improve the civic status quo with a patronizing attitude that the social reformer and suffragist Susan B. Anthony paraphrased thus: "That patching business is 'women's proper sphere.'" Nevertheless, while building their cultural institutions and organizing their beneficent associations, they learned how to run meetings, publicize projects, circulate petitions, raise funds, and lobby politicians to make the changes they could not legally effect themselves. These political skills prepared them for their next leap from the community into the realms of social and political reform, including the fight for their own rights.

Opponents of women's legal empowerment expressed a range of

views. Many women feared that if given new rights, they would lose the few they already had, namely their claims to men's support and protection—an evergreen argument that defeated the Equal Rights Amendment more than a century later. Some men insisted that women's small brains rendered them incapable of handling even their own affairs, others that they were too high-minded for base politics. Many more men, however, shared the realistic anxiety that giving women more financial weight within marriage, much less more freedom to leave it, would compromise their patriarchal authority and endanger the age-old double standard regarding what they saw as hard-earned pleasures, such as drinking and gambling, and what women saw as vices.

Presciently realizing that the West—where women settlers were already improving their economic, social, and civic standing—was the right place at the right time to push for equal rights, some talented women organizers left the East behind to bring the battle to the frontier.

Three

"WOMAN RIGHTS"

*The law which alienates the wife's right
to the control of her own property, her own
earnings, lies at the foundation of all
her social and legal wrongs.*

—CLARINA HOWARD NICHOLS, KANSAS REFORMER

A MERICAN WOMEN'S STRUGGLE for rights did not originate with the determination to vote but to own and control property, sue for divorce, and have custody of their children. In 1854, after failing to persuade her state senate to enact women's property rights, Clarina Howard Nichols, a forty-four-year-old, upper-class Vermont journalist and social reformer, left what she had come to consider the reactionary East to devote the rest of her life to promoting progressive causes in the West. She accurately foresaw that its settler society and brand-new legislatures would necessarily be less averse to change and more interested in progress. As she put it, "It was a thousand times more difficult to procure the repeal of unjust laws in an old State, than the adoption of just laws in the organization of a new State."

Like a striking number of prominent activists, Nichols became politicized after a painful personal experience made clear her lack of economic and political rights—and the inextricable tie between those two deficits. Her volatile, spendthrift first husband ran through her large dowry, mistreated her, and threatened to take away their children, but as a feme covert, she could do nothing to protect herself or her family. (Indeed, Susan B. Anthony and many other activists asserted that they remained single because wives could not own property or make legal contracts in their own right.) Reduced to working as a milliner and taking in boarders, Nichols finally returned in shame to her parents' home, where her father pulled strings to secure her a then nearly unthinkable divorce.

Nichols was humiliated by the scandal, but her keen intellect and an unusually fine education for a girl of the era helped her place her personal nightmare in a broader social context. She soon arrived at a stunning conclusion: like her own travails, those of countless women were not just individual misfortunes, as society pretended, but manifestations of systemic injustice rooted in the law—a grave political problem that required a radical political solution.

Once awakened, Nichols began to put her revolutionary realization into practice. After marrying a benign elderly publisher and becoming his newspaper's "Lady Editress," she ran stories about temperance and other controversial women's issues and wrote a series of influential columns on wives' financial insecurity. Despite a concern with Victorian respectability only heightened by her divorce, the tall, striking journalist soon became a popular public speaker on women's rights when lectures were a major form of entertainment. In 1851, she attracted widespread attention at the second National Woman's Rights Convention, in Worcester, Massachusetts. Addressing movement leaders, including Sojourner Truth and Frederick Douglass, she stressed the link between women's economic and political empowerment: "The law which alienates the wife's right to the control of her own property, her own earnings, lies at the foundation of all her social and legal wrongs."

Nichols made her case for women's property rights at the right time. By the mid-nineteenth century, American law was moving from the old British common law's broad principles, including coverture, toward more precision. At the same time, officials and their constituents were forced to confront the Hogarthian spectacle of improvident men's destitute wives and children begging on street corners. As femes covert, married women had no legal protection from the consequences of their husbands' bad judgment or behavior, much of the latter fueled by alcohol during America's epidemic of "dipsomania."

For good reason, temperance, not suffrage, was nineteenth-century women's major social and political cause. On average, men drank seven gallons of hard liquor per year, not counting copious amounts of beer and wine, compared with about two gallons now. Some brutalized their wives and children, made poor business decisions, or squandered their livelihoods on gambling or prostitution, leaving their families homeless. Lawmakers across the country were under increasing pressure to respond to this sobering reality by, at the very least, granting married women a "separate economy" to protect their families from their husbands' follies or vices.

Unlike Nichols's Vermont, some eastern states began to respond to the crisis by increasing women's property rights. In 1848, New York State's Married Women's Property Act became the first law to recognize a wife as an independent individual, able to own, inherit, and control property; enter into contracts; collect rent; file lawsuits; and be free from liability for her husband's debts. In many states, however, efforts to pass similar sensible legislation were balky and incremental. Even New York later walked back some measures, including a wife's right to custody of her children and a widow's control over her late husband's estate.

The national women's movement may have been based in the East, but as Nichols anticipated, much of the progress took place in the West. Where property rights were concerned, eight of its territories would eventually enter the Union as community-property states, of which there are still only nine. Especially in the Southwest, women benefited from the regional influence of the more gender-egalitarian Spanish-Mexican civil law. Indeed, in 1850, when the brand-new state of California gave wives unusually liberal property rights, Oregon's Donation Land Claim Act allowed wives, including Native women married to White men, to claim federal land in their own names—a major precedent—although they could not yet control it.

Nichols was determined to become a true westerner, and because she was also an ardent abolitionist, she chose to settle in "Bleeding Kansas." The territory was then roiled in the violent conflict that raged between 1854 and 1858 over its future as a slave or free state, which made it an ideal venue for supporting emancipation as well as universal suffrage. The huge territory, which stretched west to the Rockies and included much of what is now Colorado, was only sparsely populated by the White settlers just admitted to the homeland of the Osage, Pawnee, and other Plains peoples. Nichols and her husband and four children first claimed land in Douglas County; after her spouse's death, she moved the family from their homestead to what is now Kansas City, Kansas.

Women's rights reformers who hectored rather than cajoled found it hard to have their say, much less get their way, among men who agreed with Thomas Dimsdale, later the editor of the *Montana Post*: "From Blue Stockings, Bloomers, and strong-minded she-males generally, 'Good Lord, deliver us.'" The kindly, humorous Nichols, who often knitted during political events, barnstormed Kansas in the most ladylike way possible.

The Seneca Falls declaration argued for women's rights on the grounds of their equality with men, but Nichols artfully combined the sacred and secular to make a less controversial rationale for their

empowerment. Emphasizing the moral authority, rooted in their capacity for motherhood, that distinguished them from men, she argued that given more freedom, they would use it to nurture society as
they did the family. Reassuring audiences that she would say less
about women's rights than about their responsibilities, sanctioned by
God and country, to shield the home and its community from material and spiritual harm, she also insisted that the law must enable
them to do so. Otherwise, she said, "I am deprived of the power to
protect my children."

Leavening shrewd political and legal arguments with biblical references and heartbreaking stories of powerless, desperate mothers and
widows, Nichols asked: How was a wife to prevent her husband from
losing their home in a risky business deal or a drunken card game?
How could a widow raise her children if she could not claim her dead
husband's property, or even their custody? What recourse did a
mother have if her spouse threatened or abused her or her children?

Nichols never questioned women's domestic responsibilities; rather,
she mildly insisted that they knew best how to manage them: "[Man's]
laws concerning our interests show that his intelligence fails to pre-
scribe means and conditions for the discharge of our duties." She allowed, however, that coping with her own hardships had caused her to
question women's place. "It is only since I have met the varied responsibilities of life, that I have comprehended woman's sphere," she wrote,
"and I have come to regard it as lying within the whole circumference
of humanity."

Nichols was not the only activist and western migrant to promote
women's biologically based moral difference from men as a
strength rather than a deficiency. Eliza Burhans Farnham, a pioneer
in what evolved into the discipline of social work, soon an important

profession for women, went further, insisting that their capacity to bear children made them not just different from but superior to men.

Farnham's interest in women's rights began while homesteading in the 1830s on the Illinois frontier, which she described in *Life in Prairie Land*, her bestselling travel, nature, and homemaking guide. She observed that unlike men—and herself—many women settlers, particularly the gently reared, were unable to experience the "kind of emancipation which so endears the Western country to those who have resided in it." Like the eighteenth-century British reformer Mary Wollstonecraft, Farnham blamed the "artificial and pernicious course of education" and notions of "false social position" imposed on women by society.

After returning to her home state of New York in 1841, Farnham separated from her husband and took up a new career that complemented her interests in women's welfare and education. In 1844, she became the women's matron at Sing Sing state prison, where she tried to rehabilitate her wards with uplifting doses of literature, music, and compassionate treatment. In 1848, after falling out with the jail's authorities over what they regarded as her radical policies, she headed west to California.

Over the next thirteen years spent mostly in the state, Farnham developed an ambitious social-engineering idea, which she elaborated upon in *California, In-doors and Out: How We Farm, Mine, and Live Generally in the Golden State*, published in 1856. She proposed that by migrating west, poor but respectable eastern spinsters could help civilize a state in which the male–female ratio was nine to one, while also finding husbands and fulfilling their maternal destiny. After organizing groups of such hopeful women, she returned to her previous work in 1861 and briefly served as the women's matron at the Insane Asylum of the State of California, in Stockton.

Following an unhappy second marriage, Farnham returned to New York City in 1862, where she immersed herself in writing *Woman and Her Era* (1864). At the time, educated Americans were fascinated by new scientific explanations for human behavior, notably Charles Darwin's theory of evolution, which belatedly debuted in 1859. They were equally if not even more interested in pseudoscientific theories, such as phrenology and Farnham's two-volume explication of women's biologically rooted moral superiority. As she put it, "Life is exalted in proportion to its Organic and Functional complexity; Woman's Organism is more complex and her totality of Function larger than those of any other being inhabiting our earth; Therefore her position in the scale of Life is the most exalted, the Sovereign One."

Like Catharine Beecher, Farnham insisted that women were called to a higher station than mere politics. Indeed, most Americans then agreed with Mark Twain, who wrote that he would be chagrined "to see one of our blessed earthly angels peddling election tickets among a mob of shabby scoundrels she never saw before." Like Nichols, however, she also reinforced the idea of women's moral superiority, which suffragists soon used as a guarantee that, granted more rights, women would use them to foster the homeland as well as the home—a persuasive rationale in a West often regarded as in need of more civilizing.

Back in Kansas, Nichols's campaign for women's rights got a boost from some creative activists. In 1857, equal numbers of women and men in the town of Moneka (from the Lakota term for "morning star") formed the Moneka Woman's Rights Association. The energetic group sponsored programs featuring "such women lecturers as are accustomed to public speaking" and urged every woman in attendance "to convert to her views at least one legal voter."

That same year, Julia Archibald Holmes, a young reformer in the town of Lawrence, Kansas, who had left New England for the more progressive West, fixed on a particularly ingenious way to rally support for women's rights. As she and her husband prepared to join Colorado's gold rush, which boomed between 1858 and 1859, she resolved to demonstrate women's equality en route: she would walk rather than ride in a wagon on the Santa Fe Trail, stand guard duty like the men, and wear the controversial "bloomer costume" associated with suffrage.

Most variations of this "reform dress" featured a calf-length dress or skirt worn over leggings or "Turkish pantaloons." (The best known model was designed by social activist and journalist Amelia Bloomer, who lived in Seneca Falls before migrating to Iowa in 1854.) The costume freed women from the era's restrictive corsets and heavy, trailing skirts, which its advocates regarded as a "male conspiracy to make women subservient by cultivating in them a slave psychology." After wearing the outfit for two years, Elizabeth Cady Stanton blamed much of the "ill-health and temper among women" on the "crippling, cribbing influence" of Victorian garb and praised the reform dress for relieving "little petty vexatious trammels and annoyances every hour of the day," whether climbing stairs or negotiating wet streets. Many women as well as men associated the modest ensemble with radical politics, however, and accused its wearers of being "strong-minded." Other public champions of suffrage followed Stanton in sacrificing comfort to avoid alienating conservative support for the greater cause, but Julia Holmes was undeterred by reactionaries' opinions.

In 1858, Holmes achieved a nationwide public relations triumph for the cause of women's equality by becoming the first woman known to climb Colorado's fourteen-thousand-foot Pike's Peak. In a letter to her suffragist mother composed on the summit, she wrote, "Nearly everyone tried to discourage me from attempting it, but . . . I feel that I would not have missed this glorious sight for anything at all." Her published observations on her western migration turned the "Bloomer Girl on Pike's Peak" into a celebrity and promoted women's rights in a way that no lecture could.

In the West, territories aiming to become states struggled to define voting rules in their new constitutions, which obliged them to debate women's suffrage. In 1859, the Kansas legislators who gathered in the town of Wyandotte for their constitutional convention invited Nichols—also a prominent abolitionist "Free Soiler" and spokeswoman for the new Republican Party—to the major event. Neither she nor the two other women in attendance could vote on the constitution's contents, but she persuaded the fifty-two delegates who could to attend a special address she delivered one evening.

After her moving lecture, Nichols delivered the coup de grâce in the form of 250 petitions that the Moneka association had gathered to support women's equal rights—an impressive indication of public opinion in a huge territory of just 107,000 residents. Persuaded by her argument and the community activists' determined efforts, the delegates ratified the historic "Wyandotte Constitution," which not only prohibited slavery but granted Kansas women long-sought rights regarding property, divorce, and child custody. The constitution, which was adopted by the new state in 1861, limited women's voting privileges to school board elections but was still an important step toward enfranchisement.

Granting wives rights to property was one thing, but enabling them to pick up and leave unsatisfactory husbands—and take their children with them—was something else entirely. Divorce's moral dimension made it anathema in much of Victorian America, but for several reasons, the pragmatic West took a more lenient view.

The western zeal for making progress and becoming prosperous favored companionate marriages of two hardworking partners over obliging unhappy, less productive pairs to stay together. Until the gender ratio leveled off later in the century, White women were scarce in many areas, apt to be choosy, and likelier than men to leave their marriages, especially abusive or onerous ones. (As wits said in Montana, "A man in the mountains cannot keep his wife.") Divorcées were not considered pariahs and often found new husbands quickly.

In gossipy letters to her sister in New Hampshire, Abby Mansur, a boardinghouse domestic worker in California, particularly remarked the heightened value of women and their skills in the region—and the heady effect it sometimes had on their behavior. At a time when women back East were "ruined" by having an affair or divorcing, this shrewd observer of social mores wrote that "it is all the go here for Ladys to leave there Husbands two out of three do it," adding that a single woman "can have her choice of thousands." Despite her numerous threats to stray from her own marriage, she persevered, and her earnings helped secure a family farm and a step up to landowners' status.

Finally, divorce also made sense for thrifty local governments. Women and children who had no means of support had to "go on the county"—live on public funds drawn from "poor levies"—so allowing women to remarry as soon as possible saved money. The party seeking the divorce had to give an accepted legal reason, such as adultery, desertion, or extreme physical abuse, which was as prevalent in the West as in the East. Many courts tacitly acknowledged that the real issue was often incompatibility, however, and added "mental cruelty" to the list. Judges also frequently awarded the custody of children to mothers rather than fathers, which was rare back East. California allowed divorce in 1850 and soon granted the most decrees of any state in America. By the next decade, the Dakotas, along with Utah, were dubbed "divorce mills."

From its first violent rumblings in Kansas, the Civil War and its sequelae had profound effects on a West just beginning to be settled. In Washington, DC, the Republicans, whose base was in the Northeast, and the Democrats, concentrated in the South, had very different designs for the region's future. Since Thomas Jefferson devised the Land Ordinance of 1784 to address the disposition of territory in the public domain, small farmers had griped that the government favored the rich and speculators over average homesteaders and had badgered Congress to sell smaller parcels of land for lower prices. By 1852, they were no longer mollified by half measures—a grievance that had helped fuel the Free Soil Party—which forced Congress to consider free homesteading bills in 1852 and 1854. (That year, Mississippi congressman William Barry—a courageous Democrat—declared that "[if] a female desires to possess a home, and is willing to conform to the requirements of the law, there is no reason why she should be an alien to the justice or the charity of her country.") Congress passed a similar bill in 1860, but it was vetoed by Democratic president James Buchanan. By then, public pressure had made land in the West cheap enough to send the first wave of settlers into the Great Plains. However, it took the Civil War, President Abraham Lincoln, and an abolitionist Republican Congress to pass the unprecedented Homestead Act of 1862.

Intent on furthering their Greater Reconstruction scheme, Lincoln and the Republicans saw the West's new territories and states as a promised land for a free people, whose family farms would soon be united to the rest of America by a great new transcontinental railroad.

The southern Democrats envisioned large western plantations linked by a "great slavery [rail]road" to what soon became the Confederacy. As soon as the war began, however, the Republicans were free to pursue their vision of settlement. In 1862, they passed two ground-breaking gender-neutral laws that recognized women's importance to colonizing the West and had profound consequences for their advancement after the war.

After Lincoln signed the Homestead Act in May, women as well as men who were "heads of households" could aspire to own what was essentially free real estate in the region. Few women elsewhere could acquire land and accumulate equity, but those who were single, divorced, deserted, or widowed could file claims for 160 acres in the western public domain. After they paid a small registration fee of eighteen dollars, the only requirements for "proving up," or finalizing ownership, were improving the property, usually with a small house and some cultivated acreage, then living on it for five years, later reduced to three years; two neighbors had to attest to their fulfillment of these terms. (After a period of six months, claims could also be purchased.) In addition to its economic benefits, the act enabled tens of thousands of women to realize the dream of land ownership that had been bound up with citizenship and status since the agrarian founders' day. This advance, verified by their signatures on government registers, set a powerful precedent for equalizing their legal status.

In 1863, Mary Meyer, a German immigrant who farmed with her children near the present-day town of Beatrice, Nebraska, arguably became the first woman to file for a homestead as a head of household; such individuals are called "independents" here. She and Philip Meyer, her husband, had previously squatted on the property, but following his death about eighteen months after arriving in the US, she enlisted the help of various relatives and a hired man. By the time she proved up her claim, she was by no means the proverbial poor widow but had assets that included a 16×26-foot house and a corral, a corncrib, a chicken coop, and a well; her thirty-five cultivated acres even included some fruit trees and grapevines.

The claimants who filed for their swatches of 285 million acres of homestead land later included the "Exodusters," as the women and men of the first large Black migration from the South after the Civil War were called. Between 1879 and 1881, some twenty thousand of these farmers left states along the Mississippi River to homestead in Kansas, where they established about forty towns. Like many White women homesteaders, Williana Hackman, born in Kentucky, was shocked by her first glimpse of the austere Great Plains. "The scenery to me was not at all inviting," she wrote, "and I began to cry." Far from freeloading, hardworking homesteaders amply repaid the federal largesse by settling great swaths of seventeen western states—45 percent of Nebraska and North Dakota, for example, and about a third of Montana and Colorado—an enormous stimulus to regional and national development.

Just as the Homestead Act increasingly enabled western women to gain an independent stake in real estate, the Morrill Land-Grant Act, passed in July, gave them free or low-cost access to a so-called man's education—and thus a chance at financial independence and an alternative career to marriage. The law granted thirty thousand acres of federal land to each of the states, which were then obliged to build schools with the proceeds from the properties' sale. Most of America, especially the frontier, was still rural and in desperate need of pragmatic professionals to accelerate the development mandated by the Greater Reconstruction. To that end, the act created nearly a hundred tuition-free public colleges and universities that could admit women as well as men. Sixty-seven of these schools were located in the West.

To dodge the controversial issue of whether women and men should share the same campuses, much less classrooms, the federal government left the decision up to the states and territories. In the West, most opted for coeducation for several reasons. As with other controversial policies, such innovations were easier to legislate in a less tradition-bound region already primed for the more egalitarian progressive politics that would peak later in the century. Then, too, by teaching the sexes together, thrifty states and territories were spared the expense of building separate campuses. As quickly as the schools could be built, they offered farmers' and shopkeepers' daughters as well as sons access to a liberal arts education. Like the Homestead Act, the Morrill Act set a powerful legal precedent: women's right to equal treatment from the federal government.

L ike so much of American life, the women's rights movement was interrupted during the Civil War that raged between 1861 and 1865. When the cause reemerged in public discourse, women's lives had changed significantly across the nation. Many had proved that they could take care of themselves and their families while the men were gone for four years. Since the movement began, women had also put in several decades of tireless community service, whether establishing ladies' aid societies and lyceums in the East or building new communities in the West. As they steadily assumed citizenship's burdens, more became interested in claiming its full rights.

In the East, Stanton, Douglass, Anthony, and Lucy Stone, the Boston abolitionist and women's rights reformer, formed the short-lived American Equal Rights Association in 1866 to pursue universal suffrage regardless of gender or color—the only organization in nineteenth-century America that fought for women's and men's rights together. In their petition to Congress, its founders most "respectfully and earnestly pray[ed] that . . . all discriminations on account of sex or race may be removed." As Sojourner Truth said with characteristic directness, "There is a great stir about colored men getting their rights, but not a word about the colored women; and if colored men get their rights, and colored women not theirs, the colored men will be masters over the women, and it will be just as bad as it was before."

Other events suggested that change was in the air. By 1868, 172 women in Vineland, New Jersey, had cast ballots in a separate box during the midterm election, and in Washington, DC, Senator Samuel C. Pomeroy of Kansas had introduced the federal woman's suffrage amendment in Congress. Journalist Jane Croly had founded Sorosis in New York, and in Boston, Caroline Seymour Severance had started the New England Woman's Club—both forerunners of the hugely influential club movement that strongly influenced women's lives and national politics during the late nineteenth century.

In the postwar West, women's experiences changed even more dramatically. Migration significantly increased, and modern technology, particularly the telegraph and the railroad that carried the latest mail and publications, drew the once isolated region closer to mainstream society. Women in Denver and San Francisco now read the same newspapers, books, and magazines as women in Philadelphia and Boston. Like their eastern sisters, they discussed exciting new ideas that affected their lives, including interdependent, companionate marriage, family planning, and women's rights.

The AERA was based in New York City, but after the war, suffrage caught fire in the West. By 1867, Kansas had become such an important battleground for the vote that Anthony, Stanton, and Stone traveled west to help Clarina Nichols rally support for a referendum to enfranchise both women and Black men. Despite the celebrity suffragists' strenuous efforts, voters rejected both causes. Nichols soon completed her own westward migration to California, where she continued to work for suffrage, writing that she was certain that "God is with us—there can be no failure, and no defeat outside ourselves that will not roll up the floodwork and rush away every obstruction."

Like many western activists, Nichols is not as well known as her famous suffragist colleagues in the eastern-centered national movement, but they deeply respected her. She was a true pioneer, as both a westerner and a political visionary whose early argument that women needed the vote to protect and improve both home and homeland became the dominant rationale for the cause. She also helped to seed the West with the progressive politics that soon empowered many of its women, not only as voters but as candidates.

At first glance, Abigail Scott Duniway, a mostly self-educated Oregon homestead wife, and Nichols, an aristocratic Yankee, might seem to have little in common, but both women were radicalized when hardship made clear that a wife was what Duniway called a "nonentity in law." In 1862, her husband had endorsed a loan for a friend without her consent, and when the man later defaulted, her family was forced to surrender their home.

The loss devastated Duniway. She had invested long years of grinding labor as a "servant without wages" while establishing their homestead, and later their second farm—a brutal experience she summed up thus: "To make thousands of pounds of butter every year for market . . . to sew and cook, and wash and iron; to bake and clean and stew and fry; to be, in short, a general pioneer drudge, with never a penny of my own." Yet as a wife, she was incapable of preventing the loss of all she had helped to earn. After her imprudent husband was permanently disabled in an accident, she also had to support their family of six children, first by teaching school, then by opening a millinery shop in Albany, Oregon.

Hat shops were lucrative businesses at a time when White women routinely wore bonnets to shield their complexions and look stylish and refined in public. Because male merchants did not want to compete in that market, they were also among the few commercial enterprises that respectable middle-class women could run without raising eyebrows. The shops became important social hubs, where customers congregated to exchange gossip, examine Butterick dress patterns, and ponder the fashionable, flouncy "Dolly Varden" ensembles, named for a coquettish character from Charles Dickens's *Barnaby Rudge*. Away from male ears, Duniway's clients also candidly discussed their home lives, which opened her eyes to the hard reality of widespread gender-based injustice. As she later put it, "It's odd that men feel they must protect women, since for the most part they must be protected from men."

At the same time, her customers' stories of hardships overcome and goals achieved convinced Duniway of western women's exceptionalism. Most pioneers were average women and men doing the best they could in often difficult circumstances. However, Duniway believed that they emerged from the crucible of life on the frontier endowed with degrees of independence, patriotism, and zeal for progress that distinguished them from other, lesser Americans. Thinking of all that she and other women settlers had accomplished in their remote homesteads and fledgling towns, she wrote, "When women's true history shall have been written, her [*sic*] part in the upbuilding of this nation will astound the world." Unlike Nichols and other suffragists who argued for women's rights based on their moral superiority to men, Duniway, like Sojourner Truth, insisted that they deserved equal rights because the sexes were absolutely equal.

Afire to improve women's lives, starting with securing them the property rights that would spare them the kind of horrific loss she had endured, Duniway moved her family to bustling Portland in 1871, then started the influential *New Northwest*, a women's rights and suffrage journal. The widely read weekly vigorously promoted her argument that all women and men are created equal and thus, according to America's democratic ideal, deserved equal rights. "In looking backward," she wrote later, "it seems strange to me now that I didn't sooner see the need of votes for women."

Four

WYOMING MAKES HISTORY

I am intending to vote this next election [which]
makes Mr. Post very indignant as he
thinks a Woman has no rights.

—AMALIA POST, WYOMING SUFFRAGIST

I N 1869, the Wyoming Territory became the first government in
Euro-American history to enfranchise women. Just one year later,
the Utah Territory took the same bold step. The question of why, a
half century before the Nineteenth Amendment, the West led the
nation—indeed, the world—in thus empowering women has no single, much less simple, answer.

It is often said that Wyoming's male legislators "gave" women the
vote—after all, no one else could—but their complex motivations included pressure from resolute wives, mothers, and daughters. After
turning a small log cabin in South Pass City, Wyoming, into a proper
home for her family, Esther Hobart Morris devoted herself to good
works in the mining community, where her views on women's rights,
supported by her husband, quickly became well known. Like Clarina
Nichols and Abigail Duniway, she had taken up the cause when she
experienced the consequences of her legal powerlessness. After her

first husband's death back East, the widowed young mother had traveled to Illinois to claim some land he owned, but when the state refused to recognize her rights, she became an activist on the spot. After remarrying and migrating to Wyoming, Morris nursed the sick, delivered babies, and preached women's rights and suffrage. Like Nichols, the six-foot-tall, plainspoken woman with the iron-jawed visage of a founding father did not contest women's domestic role but insisted that legal empowerment would enhance rather than threaten it.

In 1869, as the territory's legislature prepared to meet for the very first time in Cheyenne, the public knew that the lawmakers would be forced to debate suffrage, because they had to include voting rules in Wyoming's constitution. One apocryphal story has Morris inviting Republican Herman Nickerson and Democrat William Bright, then the local legislative candidates, to a tea party in her cabin, where women waited to lobby them to sponsor a suffrage bill. In fact, she and Bright only met later, but he was surely aware of the prominent woman's views, and did indeed propose the legislation.

Several personal considerations motivated Bright. He was very fond of his much younger suffragist wife, who, as he later memorably put it, was "as good as any man and better than convicts and idiots." He was also probably inspired by Edward Lee, another territorial lawmaker who, before migrating west, had introduced an unsuccessful suffrage bill while a member of the Connecticut legislature.

Then, too, Bright and the other legislators had many practical and political reasons for enfranchising women. Men outnumbered women six to one in Wyoming's White population of just nine thousand, and officials fervently hoped that such a publicity coup would persuade more women to migrate. Bright was among the many who also wanted to counter the votes of men of color. "Damn it," said one anonymous legislator, "if you are going to let the niggers and the pigtails [the Chinese] vote, we will ring in the women, too." They also knew that passing such a controversial law in their territory would be easier than in a highly regulated state. Then, too, they felt competitive pressure from the Utah, Colorado, and Washington legislatures, which were poised to beat them for the title of the historic "first." Indeed, that very year, Representative Curtis J. Hillyer persuaded the Nevada territorial legislature that women should vote because they were at least as smart as men, paid the same taxes, and would clean up politics, but the bill failed to pass two years later during the constitutionally mandated second vote.

Partisanship played a role, of course. Unsurprisingly, both major parties claimed to revere women. Republicans' first priority, however, was defending two new amendments to the Constitution. The Fourteenth Amendment, ratified in 1868, declared that everyone born in the United States was an American citizen, and that all adult males were entitled to vote. The Fifteenth Amendment, ratified two years later, affirmed that the right to vote could not be denied on account of race but said nothing about gender. After waging these hard-fought battles, Republicans took a one-at-a-time approach to what they saw as women's competing cause.

The Democrats who dominated Wyoming's territorial legislature were even less enthusiastic about suffrage than Republicans. Indeed, the party, particularly in the South, was heavily invested in protecting patriarchal authority from alleged government interference. However, they wanted to vex John Campbell, the Republican governor, by proposing a suffrage bill that they assumed he would veto for partisan reasons, thus annoying its supporters. They also hoped that if for some reason it passed, the women drawn to Wyoming by the prospect of voting would scorn the Republicans and support the Democrats instead.

To the Democrats' chagrin, Governor Campbell did not veto their suffrage bill, allegedly out of respect for his wife—a sentiment shared by many western men impressed by hardworking women's ongoing contributions to settlement. Moreover, of the ninety-three women to cast ballots in Wyoming, twenty-nine voted Democratic and sixty-four Republican. The first was Louisa Ann Swain, described in the local newspaper as "a gentle white-haired housewife, Quaker-ish in appearance," who won her place in history by arriving at the poll in Laramie before it had even opened.

One year later, Wyoming went further and made Morris the na-tion's first woman judge. She performed the duties of the justice of the peace of Sweetwater County so capably that despite her lack of formal legal training, none of the twenty-seven cases she tried were later appealed or reversed by a higher court. Indeed, she was admired by no-frills Wyomingites for not tolerating any pettifoggery from slick lawyers. According to *Frank Leslie's Illustrated Newspaper*, a weekly magazine, she was "the terror of all rogues" and the source of "infinite delight to all lovers of peace and virtue." Not one to be se-duced by celebrity, Morris later wrote that her appointment had been "a test of woman's ability to hold public office" and modestly allowed that "I feel that my work has been satisfactory." As if to silence critics of women's participation in public life, she added, "in performing all these duties I do not know as I have neglected my family any more than in ordinary shopping."

That same year, women in the cities of Laramie and Cheyenne became the nation's first female jurors—itself a radical advance into public life. In a letter to her sister, Amalia Post wrote, "I suppose you are aware that Women can hold any office in this territory. I was put on the Grand Jury. I am intending to vote this next election [which] makes Mr. Post very indignant as he thinks a Woman has no rights." When reporters from the eastern press arrived to satirize the new jurors, the presiding judge rallied the women thus: "You shall not be driven by the sneers, jeers, and insults of a laughing crowd from this temple of justice."

A century and a half later, suffrage still does not confer equality, and women's political progress still comes in fits and starts. After Morris served out her term, which had been vacated by a man who had resigned to protest the suffrage law, she was not elected to another. The territory's judges also rescinded women's right to serve on juries—officially on the grounds that just before suffrage was passed, its constitution had stipulated male jurors. Likelier causes included women's objections to smoking and spitting in court and men's fear that judgments based on stricter female moral standards would result in overly harsh sentences.

The Wyoming legislators' flaws and foibles notwithstanding, every precedent must be set somewhere. While barnstorming through the region with Susan B. Anthony via the new transcontinental railroad, Elizabeth Cady Stanton declared that the territory was a "blessed land, where for the first time in the history of the world, the true idea of a just government is realized, where woman is the political equal of man." In 1890, when Wyoming's statehood was jeopardized by congressional opposition to suffrage, its male legislators held firm: "We will remain out of the union a hundred years, rather than come in without the women." Their loyalty won the day, and later that year, Morris presented the governor with America's new forty-four-star flag, sewn by Wyoming women.

Just a year after Wyoming, Utah became the next government to enfranchise women, and for reasons no less complex, starting with the Mormon religion and its controversial acceptance of polygamy. While passing through Utah on his cross-country stagecoach trip, even Mark Twain could not resist taking an ugly, misogynistic swipe at the practice, writing that he was poised to "make the customary inquisition into the workings of polygamy, until I saw the Mormon women . . ." Where national politics was concerned, Republicans, who considered slavery and polygamy the "twin relics of barbarism," had vanquished the first and were eager to take on the second. They favored enfranchising Mormon women, who they naively assumed must share their view of plural marriage and would vote to outlaw it.

Like the similarly patriarchal South, however, the Utah Territory was dominated by Democrats. They wished to increase their party's electorate to counter both anti-Mormon bias and their Republican neighbors' votes. They also knew that many Mormon women, especially among the educated elite, vigorously supported both plural marriage and suffrage, not least because the vote countered mainstream society's assumption that they were powerless sex slaves. Contrary to the Republicans' expectations, enfranchised Mormon women voted like their husbands, which in turn gave rise to the argument that the vote was wasted on women, who had no minds of their own—a ludicrous assertion that nevertheless boosted opposition to suffrage.

One of her third husband's seven wives, Emmeline Woodward Harris Whitney Wells, an influential journalist and early settler in Salt Lake City, helped shape the Mormon argument that, contrary to public opinion, polygamy and women's equal rights were highly compatible. For thirty-five years, she was the editor of the *Woman's Exponent*, a Mormon bimonthly, which gave her an ideal platform for promoting her defense of polygamy as a form of benign socialism that, by domesticating the male libido, enabled most women to have families.

Always forward-looking, Wells anticipated turn-of-the-century feminists who insisted that sharing household chores and childcare—and for Mormons, even intimate relations—was modern and efficient, and liberated women to pursue the Victorian passions for self-improvement and good works. Employing trendy Industrial Age terminology, she compared the typical Victorian wife, confined to her separate sphere, to a mere "painted doll" or "household deity," while the plural wife was "a joint-partner in the domestic firm."

Wells's dramatic analogy was not entirely farfetched. Mormon women also lived within a patriarchal social structure, but even before the rights movement, they enjoyed what amounted to divorce on demand and certain property entitlements. Men obliged to build the New Jerusalem mandated by God needed capable partners who could function independently and make decisions; many had to support themselves and their children during their husbands' frequent absences on church business or visits to other, sometimes distant families. Accordingly, Mormon girls were raised to be self-sufficient and resourceful rather than dependent on men. Christina Oleson Warnick, a homesteader in Pleasant Grove, Utah, recorded that in addition to her household duties, she dug irrigation ditches, plowed, planted, sheared sheep, cut hay, took in washing, and spun and wove cloth. Lest a moment be wasted, she knitted when walking to a destination.

That Mormon ethos of womanly strength and independence stood Wells in good stead. Like many women's rights reformers, she had problematic relationships with men. After joining the LDS church as a teenager in Massachusetts, she and her first husband had moved west to Nauvoo, Illinois, then the Mormons' capital. When her spouse deserted her soon after she lost her first baby, she supported herself as a teacher, then married again. After the governor issued an "extermination order" against members of the church, she and her older husband joined the mass exodus to Utah, where he died, leaving her with two children. A Mormon woman was not obliged to wait for a man to ask for her hand, and in 1852, she proposed to a prominent elder, married, and bore three more children.

First abandoned, then widowed, Wells next suffered from having to share her chilly third spouse's affections with his six other wives.

Gradually, she redirected her considerable energies to women's rights, journalism, teaching, and the church's extensive charities, and even ran for public office. "All honor and reverence to good men," she wrote, "but they and their attentions are not the only sources of happiness on the earth, and need not fill up every thought of woman."

Not least because it countered the religious stereotype that cast them as powerless, Wells and other Mormon women were particularly proud of their enfranchisement. Although factions of the national movement refused their support as tainted by polygamy, they vigorously promoted a constitutional amendment to guarantee suffrage to all other American women. By the time her husband tried to draw closer, Wells was too busy. Describing a letter full of endearments "that in days past would have filled me with the most infinite pleasure," she compared his sentiments to "*dead sea apples*," adding, "How strange that everything comes too late, when the desire to possess it has gone."

While suffragists in Wyoming and Utah rejoiced over their victories, the national movement experienced a sea change. In 1869, the American Equal Rights Association splintered over the Fourteenth and Fifteenth Amendments, which enfranchised men regardless of race and explicitly defined citizenship as "male." Outraged that the new laws were passed without including women, Stanton and Anthony formed the National Woman Suffrage Association, centered in New York. As Stanton had put it, "if that word 'male' be inserted, it will take us a century at least to get it out." Like many other suffragists, they were also appalled that men whom they considered their social and racial inferiors, including unlettered foreign immigrants as well as millions of new freedmen, could vote but they could not—prejudices within the movement that worsened over time, particularly but by no means exclusively in the South. The NWSA also advocated a range of reforms to secure women's equality, including the rights to divorce and have access to fair employment and full education, and insisted on a constitutional women's suffrage amendment. The organization's weekly journal, called *The Revolution*, boldly proclaimed: "Men, their rights and nothing more; women, their rights and nothing less!"

That same year, Lucy Stone formed the American Woman Suffrage Association, based in Boston, which continued to support the Fourteenth and Fifteenth Amendments on the grounds that including women's enfranchisement would have doomed the great racial advances. Her group, which included prominent men, focused tightly on voting rights, which it beleived should be pursued incrementally, starting with local school board elections, in hopes of amending individual state constitutions, rather than at the federal level. Less radical than the NWSA, the AWSA was also more popular.

Within mainstream society, the issue of women's rights, including suffrage, was still considered controversial but no longer ludicrous, and it increasingly cropped up in the news. In 1871, Victoria Woodhull, the social reformer and soon presidential candidate, stood before the House Judiciary Committee to argue for women's right to vote under the Fourteenth Amendment. During the presidential election a year later, some prominent activists grew tired of waiting for permission and took matters into their own hands. Sojourner Truth was simply turned away at the polls in Battle Creek, Michigan, but Anthony was arrested after casting a ballot for Ulysses S. Grant, then stood trial for the alleged crime in Rochester, New York. Critics took notice of the increased activity and mounted the first organized opposition to suffrage. In 1871, *Godey's Lady's Book* published an antivote petition to Congress composed by nineteen prominent women, and the anti-suffrage movement was born.

The federal government clearly sided with the majority of Americans, who thought voting brassy and unwomanly. In 1875, the US Supreme Court duly considered the case of Virginia Minor, a suffragist from St. Louis who sued for the right to vote in Missouri. Then the justices decreed that although women were "entitled to all the privileges and immunities of citizenship," voting was not one of them: "The Constitution does not confer the right of suffrage upon any one." In 1878, Senator Aaron Sargent of California proposed a suffrage amendment to the Constitution that was based on the Fifteenth Amendment—and identical to the future Nineteenth—but it was rejected, as were similar bills every year thereafter until 1920.

In the West, the women's rights movement underwent major changes of its own. Passing suffrage in Wyoming and Utah had been something of a fluke, made possible by rare conjunctions of favorable circumstances unlikely to occur again. That top-down process, orchestrated by men, was quickly replaced by a grueling, bottom-up slog sustained by indefatigable activists.

Even in the formidable Duniway's own Oregon, legislative progress was slow. In 1873, two years after arriving in Portland and launching the *New Northwest*, she organized the Oregon State Woman Suffrage Association, which claimed for women "every sacred right vouch-safed to every citizen of the United States through the [D]eclaration of Independence and the Federal Constitution." By that point, she had already invited Anthony, a national figure, to make a three-month-long speaking tour of the Pacific Northwest. Enlisting her sons to publish her political journal, Duniway managed the 1871 trip and sold subscriptions and lobbied officials en route. Looking back on their long, difficult, rain-soaked stagecoach travels, she recalled that the experience gave Anthony "a taste of pioneering under difficulties that remained with her as a memory to her dying day."

By the mid-1870s, Duniway, born with the mien and gravitas of a

Supreme Court justice, was poised to become a popular orator and prominent leader in the national as well as regional movement. Despite her gifts and achievements, which included twenty-one didactic novels, however, she could be abrasive. Indeed, she sometimes went out of her way to alienate potential supporters, perversely picking on women quilters by opining that "nobody but a fool" would cut up bits of cloth only to sew them together again, thus "making believe that they were busy at practical work."

Insulting quilters was one thing, but Duniway's belief in western women's exceptionalism also alienated important factions within the national suffrage movement. Even her good friend Anthony noted that her "head is so full of crochets that it is impossible for her to cooperate with anybody, she must simply control." She disdained the eastern leadership for its demure tea parties, flowery rhetoric, and emotional rallies, and developed her own distinctively western modus operandi for campaigning. Her speeches were tailored to what she saw as the West's open-mindedness and skepticism, and her preferred form of lobbying was the "still hunt," in which she privately stalked cautious legislators one by one until they gave their quiet support. "Men like to be coaxed," she said. "They will not be driven."

Perhaps most important from a strategic perspective, Duniway offended temperance supporters—an important suffrage constituency—by vigorously refuting their argument that women must be enfranchised so that they could vote to outlaw drinking. She believed that prohibition, "as necessary as it may be, is only a side issue compared to which the right of suffrage is infinity itself."

Anticipating what arguably became the major obstacle to suffrage in the West, Duniway stoutly insisted that alcohol and enfranchisement were two different issues that, when combined, doomed the latter. She advised activists to explicitly assure men that they were not intending to interfere, in any way, with their rights, but only wanted to be allowed to decide for themselves what women's rights should be. Far from regarding them as the enemy, she insisted that if approached properly, western men would support suffrage out of respect for women's role in settlement and community building: "Nowhere else upon this planet are the inalienable rights of women as much appreciated as on the newly settled borders of the United States."

Finally, Duniway disagreed with the eastern movement's increasing embrace of the rationale for suffrage based on women's moral superiority. Glorified by institutions from the federal government to the new greeting-card industry, the image of the virtuous, nurturing citizen-mother who yearned to uplift and protect the homeland as she did her home fit with the sentimental temper of the times. Unmoved, Duniway insisted that women deserved equal rights because they were equal human beings in a democracy. As she correctly saw, by casting women as different from men, the dubious thesis of their higher morality undermined their equality, reinforced their identification with the home as housekeepers of the nation, and subtly supported patriarchy.

Despite many obstacles, including a chronic lack of funds and a shortage of experienced leadership, western reformers kept on—and on—lobbying legislators to sponsor bills for suffrage and more basic goals, especially full property rights, that were repeatedly raised and defeated. For more than two decades, no western states or territories enfranchised women, but suffragists continued to accumulate experience, resources, and national attention, while other western women continued to make the major social and economic strides that support political equality.

Five

A HOME OF HER OWN

She was a rich mine of life,
like the founders of early races.

—WILLA CATHER, AUTHOR, *MY ÁNTONIA*

As the tremendous disruptions caused by the Civil War subsided, women as well as men rushed to cash in on the offers made earlier by the Homestead and Morrill Acts, which transformed their lives and the West. The homestead law instituted what was essentially a huge, cost-effective antipoverty and development program meant to turn hardworking people of modest means into landowners who would also colonize huge, sparsely populated swaths of the region. Much of the best land in areas that had milder weather and abundant timber, water, and fertile soil, notably California and the Pacific Northwest, had been already claimed or bought by earlier migrants. Agriculture was more difficult and limited in arid, less desirable areas in the Rocky Mountain region, the Southwest, and the westernmost plains and prairies. Wry farmers called homesteading a bet waged by the federal government against them, and of some 4 million claimants, just 1.6 million successfully proved up ownership.

Minnesota was closer to the eastern population centers than many other homesteading locations and initially led the nation in attracting applicants. Most women who settled on its western prairie lived and worked on their husbands' claims; the law's bias against wives made them ineligible to apply for their own land. Between 1863 and 1889, however, a surprising 2,400 women who qualified as heads of households homesteaded in their own names. They are less celebrated and numerous than their successors around the turn of the century, but as documented property owners and taxpayers, they are equally important to history.

In the heyday of the Victorian separate spheres, the early independents challenged conventional notions of women's reliance on men and subordination to their authority with deeds, not just words. Like male heads of households, they supported themselves, controlled their own lives, and developed their own real estate. They also paid their own property taxes, which became an important objective argument for suffrage in a democracy that considered taxation without representation to be tyranny.

Even the barest facts and figures, drawn from a sample of 259 women, portray the Minnesota independents as a redoubtable group. Two thirds of them started out homesteading on their own, not as widows who inherited their husbands' claims and benefited from their initial help. Men generally migrated in youth, but the average age of these "girl homesteaders," as they were often called, was forty-six. Perhaps most impressive, they not only filed but also completed 5 percent of all claims in the region. This stunning proof of their resilience and success was supported by statistics from other states such as North Dakota, where that figure was about 7 percent.

Few single women elsewhere could dream of a home of their own, much less enough land for a farm, but in 1873, Pauline Auzjon, a single fifty-three-year-old Scandinavian immigrant, filed for a homestead in Grant County, a remote spot on the Minnesota frontier. She was an experienced farmer—one of many women who sustained American agriculture during the war—and was as well prepared for homesteading as she could be, but she still faced formidable obstacles. The parents of Laura Ingalls Wilder, the author of the legendary Little House books, claimed land nearby when she was a child, and Wilder described the often harsh conditions in *On the Banks of Plum Creek*, the fourth novel in the series. Broiling summers alternated with arctic winters that produced blizzards of the sort that stranded "Pa" in the outback for a nerve-racking four days. The wildfires and periodic plagues of grasshoppers that Wilder's real and fictional families endured wiped out crops, houses, barns, and gardens in moments.

Despite the challenges, Auzjon persevered to establish the typical independent's claim: a garden, fields for cash crops, pasture for livestock, and a simple dwelling. For her and other such women, homesteading was primarily an economic proposition. They invested their sweat equity in the prospect of a better, more self-sufficient way of life than the alternatives of depending on relatives' charity or working for low wages while paying room and board. Some intended to remain farmers, but like Auzjon, many planned to develop real estate to lease for monthly income or sell at a profit later. Meanwhile, they could live securely in their own rent-free homes and at least partly support themselves by using and marketing what they grew and made.

To eke out a living on the unforgiving prairie at first, most homesteaders, especially the independents, had to be wage earners as well as farmers and homemakers. They either hired men to do brutal, physical chores such as plowing stony fields, chopping down trees, and harvesting wheat—the major cash crop—or bartered their own skills for such services. To pay their expenses, many worked as teachers, nurses, accountants, seamstresses, or servants in nearby settlements. Others periodically took jobs in larger towns, then hurried back to maintain the residency requirements for their claims. As both employers and employees, these independents contributed to the local economy and helped hard-pressed men to support their own farms and families.

Like most settlers, Auzjon had little time or inclination to chronicle her homesteading experience, but census and tax records provide important information. By the time she proved up her claim, she owned eighteen cultivated acres and a 14×15-foot log cabin, as well as cattle, a pig, and chickens. She produced most of what she and her livestock ate, as well as 400 bushels of wheat, dozens of eggs, and 150 pounds of butter for sale. Tax valuations show that her homestead, acquired for elbow grease, steadily appreciated over time until 1887, when she sold it for $1,280—about $33,000 today. To supply income for her retirement years in a snug house in town, she carried the mortgage.

Independent homesteading also attracted many young women. By the age of twenty-four, Emma Setterlund, a Swedish immigrant, was tired of living and working on her parents' farm, and in 1883, she filed her own claim on the Grant County prairie. At least initially, many women on the treeless grasslands had to live in "soddies" built from large bricks of earth or, like Wilder's first dwelling on Plum Creek, dug into a hillside, troglodyte-style. To approximate decent homes, they had to settle for hanging curtains on tiny isinglass widows, tacking fabric on earthen ceilings to catch debris, hardening dirt floors with soapy water, and displaying Bibles and precious bits of carpet and china. Setterlund had grander ideas. She hired carpenters to build her a 12×14-foot house, which she furnished with a bed, cookstove, and table and chairs. As a consequence, she had to spend many winter months away from her property, housekeeping and sewing to earn money for "the necessaries of life and to improve my land."

After five arduous years, during which she hired or bartered for male help in plowing and harvesting her grain, Setterlund, too, owned a prosperous homestead that had appreciated in value. Her ten cultivated acres yielded thirty-nine bushels of wheat as well as garden vegetables for sale. Her chickens produced eggs and meat, and her cows, milk, butter, and cheese, which cut her cash expenses down to salt, sugar, coffee, and tea. In addition to her wood home, which boasted a glass window and even a painted exterior, her assets included a barn, trees "in good growing condition, set out by myself," and "a good well of water worth $10.00 at least."

Auzjon remained single and Setterlund did not marry until the age of thirty-nine, long after proving up, but Anne Gabrielson Skrinde, a Norwegian emigrant who settled near Aitken, Minnesota, became an independent when her husband died in 1882. As cheerful as she was tough, she worked the homestead with the help of her five children, vigorously observed the Sabbath, played music on instruments bought with her egg money, and enjoyed good relations with her Chippewa neighbors, who stopped by for meals while on fishing trips. Her experience as one of the third of the Minnesota independents who began homesteading with their husbands, then continued on alone, offers a sharp contrast to that of most agrarian widows in the East, who generally turned to male relatives. In parts of Nebraska, more than half of the independent women homesteaders between 1878 and 1908 were widows, most in their fifties.

The official documents that outline the prairie women's busy lives fall short in describing homesteading's often overlooked social dimension. Women were crucial to establishing and maintaining the networks of kin and neighbors who shared goods and services, fetched each other's supplies and mail, witnessed the legal validity of each other's claims, and otherwise made the rugged way of life possible. Like other women settlers, they organized schools and churches, visited and hosted neighbors, and gathered the community for musicales, dances, and parties beneath the hard-to-find Christmas tree. Many especially valued the book clubs that expanded their horizons, uplifted family and community life, and prefigured their later concerted social and political action.

Well before the national women's club movement surged around the turn of the century, book groups and literary societies nearly equaled schools and churches as gauges of a western community's respectability. Like Philadelphians and Bostonians, frontier women were immersed in Victorian America's moralistic, sentimental culture, and many shared its obsession with self-improvement. They strove to stay abreast of "the best" in manners and fashion, and even intellectual discourse and the arts. Like their eastern peers, they claimed time away from their domestic duties for what was then called "female improvement," relying on the rationale that if well informed, they were better able to fulfill their womanly mandate to elevate their families and communities.

Just as the Chautauqua Institution, founded in 1874 in New York, began sending prominent speakers, musicians, and other eminences to enlighten rural America, women in western book clubs discussed Mark Twain's novels and Henry Wadsworth Longfellow's poetry. The more ambitious pondered James Russell Lowell's pragmatic philosophy, based on science, progress, and essential moral truths. Determined to tackle the history of civilization, the ambitious women of the Round Table Club of Crete, Nebraska, studied and discussed ancient Egypt, then moved on to Assyria.

Many of the West's small-town libraries—like their post offices, still vital community centers—began as women's book groups. In Powell, Wyoming, one anonymous town mother volunteered to fill some shelves in a corner of her parlor with whatever volumes her friends and neighbors could spare. When the collection and its borrowers outgrew her home, the women formed a club that rented a space nearby that was staffed by members. In time, they staged fundraising events and built a proper library for their remote community. Most of these civic leaders have been forgotten, but the libraries and other cultural institutions they established remain as memorials to their civic devotion and determination to enjoy life's finer things despite the rigors of settlement.

Though records increasingly make clear just how essential women's contributions were to the settlement of the West, wives have frequently been portrayed as beleaguered drudges dragged to the plains and prairies by men. Some were, but others' own accounts often paint a more balanced picture. In 1873, as Auzjon filed her claim, Mary Carpenter, a farmer's wife and mother of three in Rochester, Minnesota, put aside her fondness for "conveniences, elegancies, comforts and all the paraphernalia of civilized life" for prairie homesteading near Marshall, Minnesota. Far from resisting the move, she wholeheartedly agreed with her husband that the venture was a welcome step toward a better life. "We are very 'hard up' for money," she wrote, "but it is best we should go now and have a place of our own if ever." She drove the wagon for most of the two-hundred-mile trip to their claim and was pleasantly surprised that she weathered the journey "better than I feared." Indeed, she added that thanks to her brief migration's effects on her health and appetite, "I can work better than when I started."

As an agrarian woman, Carpenter was well prepared for the grueling labor ahead. "The first two years will be hard very probably," she wrote. "If we struggle through them, then we can stand a chance to do pretty well I think." Even in well-equipped homes, nineteenth-century women's domestic workload was daunting, but she had to perform her chores in a "leaky shanty." On one typical morning, she rose before 4:00 a.m., made breakfast, then skimmed milk, churned butter, did the laundry and ironing, and baked six loaves of bread and seven pumpkin pies, in addition to the usual daily chores. Like other women, she was especially proud of her settler production, which kept her family in cash. During one month, she made a hundred pounds of butter, which, combined with the sale of dozens of eggs, "bought everything we have had."

Some overworked, isolated women homesteaders were susceptible to "prairie madness," a form of depression associated with the vast, windswept environment of the plains and prairies. In *My Ántonia*, Willa Cather, the consummate poet of those landscapes of her Nebraska youth, remarked their way of dwarfing mere human beings and their creations. Describing the experience of watching the "red tip" of the sun set in a field near an abandoned plough, she wrote that as darkness fell, "that forgotten plough had sunk back to its own littleness somewhere on the prairie." Such boundless landscapes can certainly evoke that sense of one's own relative littleness, which psychologists call the "diminutive effect," but social class, too, often influenced which women were likeliest to be negatively affected by the prairie environment.

In 1843, during her own sojourn on the Illinois prairie, then considered the western frontier, Margaret Fuller, soon to be the author of the influential *Woman in the Nineteenth Century* (1845), agreed with Eliza Burhans Farnham that it wasn't that gently reared women didn't like the West but that, because of the limited education and outdoor experience permitted to such "ornaments of society," they couldn't. "When they can leave the housework," she wrote, "they have not learnt to ride, to drive, to row, alone." Fuller might have been describing Annie Green, who reluctantly left her refined circle in Pennsylvania to follow her husband to a utopian community in the high plains near Greeley, Colorado. Unprepared for homesteading's demands or the austere environment, she fell into a years-long melancholy punctuated by frequent bouts of weeping. She sometimes tried to mitigate her spouse's distress over her condition by feigning admiration for the glorious snowcapped Rockies nearby, but wrote that "the sun, moon, or stars never put on that brilliant appearance in my western home as they did in the land of my nativity."

Unlike the genteel Green, Carpenter and many less privileged homesteaders were adept at taking pleasure and comfort where they found them, whether in nature's beauty or human progress. In addition to its spectacular wildflowers, Carpenter enthused over the grassland's "wild geese, and ducks & prairie hens" and "also a very large sandy hill [sic] crane." Gratified that in a single year, nearby Marshall had grown from "one sod house" to "quite a thriving railroad town" about to publish its own newspaper, she added, "I wouldn't go back where we lived before for anything."

Cather captured these protean agrarian wives and mothers in some of her most beloved characters, based on the women homesteaders, often immigrants, whom she met as a girl on her grandfather's Nebraska claim. Ántonia Shimerda, the luminous western Demeter of *My Ántonia*, "had only to stand in the orchard, to put her hand on a little crab tree and look up at the apples, to make you feel the goodness of planting and tending and harvesting at last." In contrast, the entrepreneurial Alexandra Bergson of *O Pioneers!*, who lived like an independent for much of her life, personified the western women who became more equal by achieving as much if not more than many men. When surveying the vast prairie, she saw not only its beauty but also the real estate that would fuel her social and economic ascent: "Under the long shaggy ridges, she felt the future stirring." A farmer rather than a farmer's wife, she turned the claim she inherited from her late father into the engine that pulled her from poverty through drought, depression, and her resentful brothers' animosity into the ranks of the local gentry.

Homesteads such as Auzjon's and Carpenter's on the West's northern prairies became farms that yielded cash crops, but many of those to the south became ranches that produced cattle. By the end of the Civil War, White settlers increasingly displaced Native Americans and the buffalo they hunted on the vast open range: the unfenced grazing land that stretched from Texas to Canada. During the short but storied "cowboy era," which lasted from the late 1860s to the late 1880s and helped define America to itself and the world, ranchers and their hired wranglers drove huge herds of cattle through the grasslands to railroad towns such as Kansas City and Abilene, where the meat was butchered on the spot and shipped east in refrigerated cars.

The cowboy was born in Mexico, but women homesteaders were among the first cowgirls: a new, truly American persona that symbolized western women's can-do agency and independence and soon fascinated the nation. Every pair of hands counted on the West's early, hardscrabble ranches, which created more opportunities for women to develop nontraditional skills and assume new responsibilities. Lily Casey Klasner's unusual account of girlhood on such a homestead begins with her family's 1867 migration from Texas to their impromptu claim in the New Mexico Territory's remote Lincoln County. After surviving an attack by Apaches determined to steal their cattle, they reached their destination, which she and her five siblings felt must be a foreign country. Their first home was a two-room adobe house, their neighbors were Mexicans, and the spicy food was strange but delicious.

At first, six-year-old Klasner's outdoor duties included collecting seeds, feeding the hogs and chickens, and carrying wood and water. Over time, she and her brothers learned to ride, drive a wagon, tend to crops, and care for livestock, until she became renowned as an utterly fearless woman who thought "nothing of riding a horse all day and doing a man's work." Only when the chores were done in the evening did Ellen Casey, her formidable mother, allow time for homeschooling and study.

Klasner had no need to look further for a model cowgirl than Casey, herself the daughter of Texas pioneers. Klasner mildly noted that her mother, despite being partially crippled in childhood, always carried a Spencer—a heavy, double-barreled shotgun. A woman who was both armed and mounted would be a shocking sight back East, but the precaution seemed only prudent in Lincoln County. The area remains best known for the eponymous "war" between rival cattlemen, waged by hired gunmen such as William Bonney, an acquaintance of Casey's who was soon dubbed Billy the Kid. In addition to roving outlaws, the homesteaders feared the local Mescalero Apaches, who once made off with 325 head of the Caseys' cattle and a prized sorrel horse. (Native peoples were robbed of most of their lands, but except for the Dakota and Indian Territories, that tragedy generally had little to do with homesteading claims, most of which were filed after the major damage had been done.)

Like other cowgirls, Klasner and her mother did not see themselves as masculine or radical, but simply as ranch women doing whatever needed to be done, and their western communities agreed. After her husband was gunned down in the street by a White man, Casey became the head of the large family. With the help of Klasner, her older children, and John Chisum, the legendary local cattle baron (played by John Wayne in the eponymous movie), she continued to run the ranch, as well as a general store and mill, and eventually secured the legal title to the homestead her husband had previously claimed under squatter's rights.

Prosperous homestead women such as Klasner acquired what Fuller called the "resources that would fit them to enjoy and refine the western farmer's life." After attending a convent school in San Antonio, however, the bilingual cowgirl had other plans. In the mid-1880s, she became a teacher, then later a telegrapher—an increasingly popular profession for women—just as a long spell of decent weather, the spread of barbed-wire fences, and the regulation of state borders were ending the cowboy era. After leaving an unhappy marriage to Joseph Klasner, she earned a degree in education from Highlands University in Las Vegas, then returned to teaching. She later acquired Chisum's diary in hopes of writing his biography, but that project came to naught. Sadly, the homesteader, cowgirl, telegrapher, and teacher who had lived an early life of remarkable adventure and enterprise died before completing her own memoir, appropriately called *My Girlhood Among Outlaws*.

Perhaps not coincidentally, as independents and other ambitious western women continued to increase their status and claim to equality with equal work, opposition to suffrage mounted. Some opponents argued that women were incapable of handling their public affairs, others that enfranchisement would alienate men and jeopardize their support of the family. As California politician James Caples put it: "Your wife is elected to Legislature and your daughter is elected constable and you are at home taking care of the babies."

Throughout the 1870s, determined activists pressed a number of western legislatures to debate suffrage, only to see the bills rejected, often by narrow margins; in 1875, a bill in the Dakotas lost by a single vote. That same year, the Colorado Territory's lawmakers refused to add enfranchisement to the state constitution, although they gave women the consolation prize of the right to vote in school elections. Then, in 1877, its male electorate rejected, by a ratio of two to one, a referendum to empower what Thomas Brill, a Presbyterian minister, called "bawling, ranting women, bristling for their rights."

In the Washington Territory, when Mary Olney Brown and other feisty suffragists stubbornly headed to the polls for the 1870 election, she wrote that she was "looked upon as a fanatic, and the idea of a woman voting was regarded as an absurdity." Beset by lobbyists during their session the following year, vexed legislators retaliated by declaring, "Hereafter no female shall have the right of ballot or vote at any poll or election precinct in this Territory" until suffrage became "the supreme law of the land."

Despite the activist-publisher Abigail Duniway's relentless efforts, lawmakers in her home state of Oregon kept debating but failing to pass suffrage bills. Mary Beatty, a suffragist in Portland who was described in newspapers as "colored," joined Duniway and two others in attempting to vote in the 1872 presidential election. For Black women living in a state that had codified Black exclusion laws in its constitution, the vote had a special importance, and in the following year, Beatty addressed the first annual convention of the Oregon State Woman Suffrage Association. After failing in 1872 and 1874, women came close to winning full enfranchisement in 1878, but lost by one vote. Female taxpayers were allowed to participate in school elections, however, and the Married Women's Property Act gave wives the right to own and control property. Finally, they were protected from the kind of devastating financial loss that had changed Duniway's life and inspired her to change the law.

Despite the suffragists' political frustrations, western women's other achievements continued to fuel their progress toward greater equality—perhaps less despite than because of the challenges of on-going settlement. More than political speeches or tracts, their boots on the ground, whether on isolated homestead claims or statehouse steps, made the argument that women who bore citizenship's burdens were entitled to its privileges.

Six

A MAN'S EDUCATION

In the adjustment of the new order of things,
we women demand an equal voice;
we shall accept nothing less.

—CARRIE CHAPMAN CATT, SUFFRAGIST AND
GRADUATE OF IOWA AGRICULTURAL COLLEGE

J UST AS THE HOMESTEAD ACT empowered western women to
become landowners, the Morrill Land-Grant Act, which was
also steadily implemented after the Civil War, gave many others access to college, then rare even for men. In 1877, Carrie Chapman Catt, a farmer's daughter from the Iowa frontier who became a
national and international suffrage leader, defied her father by enroll-
ing at the coeducational Iowa Agricultural College. Such young
women soon comprised a remarkable third of the West's college population and also often graduated at higher rates than men.

The conflict between social conservatives such as Catt's father,
who maintained that women's place was only in the home, and equally
adamant rights reformers such as Catt, who insisted that it now included the campus, the workplace, and the great world of affairs, was
not easily resolved. Since colonial days, colleges had been male precincts mostly reserved for the sons of the eastern elite, who received a

"classical education" centered on the Greek and Roman roots of Western civilization and its languages, arts, and sciences. (Dartmouth College, founded to tutor Native men in Christianity and the Yankee way of life, was a notable exception.) Those opposed to allowing women such a "man's education" railed against exposing them to dangerous people and ideas, defined as those that could compromise their virtue or encourage independent interests that undermined their domestic destiny. The influential Harvard physician Edward Clarke even opined that higher education would exact a physical toll by draining their limited energy, taxing their second-rate minds, and harming the "female apparatus," or reproductive organs. If they must attend college, he advised, their workload should be only a third of men's.

In the end, society settled the debate by combining the decorous rationale that educated women made better wives and mothers with the pragmatic argument that a rapidly expanding America urgently needed skilled professionals, particularly teachers. By generating a huge new prosperous class eager to educate its children, the Industrial Revolution fed the rapid growth of free public education, but it also provided the men who had long been schoolmasters with more lucrative careers. The result was a critical shortage of teachers, especially in the West.

By the 1830s, long before Massachusetts became the first state to mandate free public education in 1852, Catharine Beecher had perceived a career opportunity for women and helped resolve the national crisis by turning elementary education into the first female profession. If only women were allowed to deploy in the schoolroom the same lofty, nurturing qualities that fit them to preside over the nursery, she insisted, they would patriotically come to their country's aid. In 1847, while promoting her Board of National Popular Education to Send Women West, which mobilized hundreds of easterners to answer the call for teachers on the frontier, she stressed her belief in their transformative potential: "If all females were not only well educated themselves but were prepared to communicate in an easy manner their stores of knowledge to others . . . the face of society would be speedily changed." The very idea of proper women working for money initially rattled the male establishment—well into the twentieth century, most school districts would not hire wives, who were supposed to prioritize their families—but canny Beecher came up with the winning argument: women would unselfishly work for less than men. (Indeed, by the 1880s, when their wages had climbed to an average of $54.50 per month, male teachers made $71.40.) At last, the respectable single woman who couldn't or didn't want to live as a male relative's unpaid housekeeper, nanny, or nurse now had what Beecher called a "road to honorable independence and extensive usefulness where she need not outstep the prescribed boundaries of feminine modesty."

Many members of America's first generation of college women did in fact become teachers, initially including Catt, but a major regional difference distinguished their campus experiences. In the East, most enrolled in private single-sex schools such as Vassar, founded in 1861. In the West, where the majority of the public land-grant institutions were located, most attended coeducational colleges that were among the world's first.

Catt became a suffragist at thirteen, upon learning that her highly educated mother could not vote. Undeterred by paternal opposition, she paid her own way through college, sometimes by washing dishes. Even such a plucky young woman, however, was nonplussed by the peculiar mix of opportunities and obstacles that the campus presented to women. On one hand, coeducation invited if not required them—and their male classmates and teachers—to test and even blur the boundaries of their separate spheres. Indeed, women spoke and wrote about public affairs, ran and voted in campus elections, and participated in formal political debates, including those on suffrage.

On the other hand, women students were generally not regarded as equal to the men. On the most pedestrian level, the men mailed their dirty laundry back home to their mothers in special postal containers, but the women did their own. Far more seriously, their academic experience was permeated by biased assumptions about women's abilities and futures. For the first two years, they took English, history, biology, and other basic courses with men. When the time came to select a major, some chose disciplines that attracted students of both sexes, such as commerce, bookkeeping, journalism, or like Catt, general science. However, most coeds were pushed to major in a "woman's field" that complemented domesticity.

Regardless of their particular gifts, many talented young women were funneled into either education or what Beecher, one of its founders, called "domestic economy," later home economics. The bias illustrates one of reformer Margaret Fuller's most profound realizations, which accelerated her own transition from philosophy to activism: the same combination of male privilege and limited education that had originally relegated women to a narrow domestic role still prevented many from trying to expand it.

Despite its limitations, however, a college education was a tremendous advance for women and society both. For the first time, graduates had access to self-supporting, socially acceptable professional careers that also benefited the commonweal. Education majors ameliorated the critical teacher shortage and raised the level of instruction beyond what the teenaged graduates of high schools or the "normal schools" that trained elementary teachers could aspire to. Then, too, like Catt, some graduates who began as teachers became superintendents of schools—an important public position—or played other roles in higher education or government service that enhanced women's civic profile.

Its fusty modern image notwithstanding, home economics was a major source of opportunity for women that also revolutionized America's low standard of public health. In keeping with the science-oriented land-grant ethos, the discipline took a technological approach to the homemaking skills that women had traditionally learned from mothers. Cleaning evolved into the exacting field of hygiene, or sanitation, and cooking into the science of nutrition. Interestingly, both "dairy practice," or the technology of butter and cheese production, and horticulture, or the design and maintenance of gardens, were considered domestic sciences and women's fields until later in the century, when men commandeered them.

Home economics was a great boon to a still mostly agrarian nation, much of which lacked clean water, refrigeration, plumbing, and, often, adequate nourishment. At a time when many children were stunted by poor diets, pioneering nutritionists, many of them from land-grant schools, devised the first scientific recipes for healthy, affordable foods, including enriched breads. (By 1875, Catt's college debuted the "test kitchen.") Prevention was still the best cure for many diseases, and graduates educated in modern methods of sanitation trained other women and entire communities on combating rampant food- and waterborne illnesses such as typhoid and cholera.

Now as then, education, nutrition, and public health are vital fields that also provide important positions for women in government and academia. One such pioneer was Professor Margaret Snell, MD—a rights activist known for her unusually comfortable loose dresses and flat-heeled shoes—who ran the Oregon Agricultural College's laboratory for "household economy and hygiene." Her students, who proudly identified themselves with white caps and aprons, were edified by the reproductions of old masters' paintings she hung in their classroom and her lengthy quotations from the Bible, Shakespeare, and her philosopher friend Ralph Waldo Emerson. After graduating from the program, Helen Gilkey earned a doctorate in botany and became a widely published expert in the field. Far from disparaging her domestic science background, she insisted that it "elevated women's sphere" and had helped her realize "the art and beauty in all work."

The western coeds received mixed signals regarding their equality outside as well as inside the classroom. They engaged in a dizzying number of extracurricular activities, some of which, like the Young Women's Christian Association and early sororities such as Catt's Pi Beta Phi, were sex-segregated by choice. They were generally not banned per se from groups such as the literary and debating societies, then popular venues for socializing, but they often had to make compromises to be included. Women were assumed to be naturally domestic, so some clubs expected them to provide the refreshments. Others only allowed them to recite, speak on certain topics, or debate with other women. Her already commanding presence notwithstanding, even Catt had to work up her nerve to join the college's public-speaking society. To her relief, the school paper praised her address on women's rights, in which she stressed that principles "deemed enlightened and infallible in one age" are often later "doomed by the law of progress."

Despite the extracurricular inequities of college life, western coeds made important strides, notably in the improvement of their health and fitness. As Victorian America earnestly debated whether women could be both athletic and feminine, female students were initially excluded from physical education programs or restricted to more graceful, ladylike activities such as archery and tennis. Taking matters into their own hands, many western coeds fervently played sports and joined hiking, fly-fishing, and climbing clubs. Like Catt, some fought to perform the military drills mandated for the land-grant men; after hearing an officer praise the training's benefits, she persuaded him to drill brigades of women, too. Many such groups became highly polished public performers and usually succeeded in getting uniforms, although they sometimes received broomsticks instead of rifles. By the 1880s, women as well as men took up the new, more aggressive team sports, and curious boys watched coeds in bloomers or culottes play field hockey and basketball.

In a significant departure from their often quiet, homogeneous agrarian communities, college women also led expansive social lives. They got to know many different kinds of people from various backgrounds. They met men not just in classrooms but also at dinners, dances, and tête-à-têtes in chaperoned sitting rooms, which prepared them to choose suitable partners for the companionate marriages fostered by the land-grant schools' modern, progressive philosophy.

Housed together in dormitories, western coeds formed the sort of strong bonds with each other that were encouraged by the dogma of the separate spheres. At a time when kissing, hugging, writing love letters, and sharing beds were considered socially acceptable forms of affection between women, some developed "smashes," or the intense romantic friendships that were especially prevalent in single-sex colleges back East. Scholars have documented the passionate, sometimes lifelong attachments that existed between many Victorian women, including a notable number in these pages, but in most cases, very little is known about their sex lives. While attending the University of Nebraska, a land-grant school, Willa Cather had a particularly intense relationship with Louise Pound, a classmate who later became a prominent linguist. Cather herself cut a dashing figure on campus. The journalism major and editor of the college newspaper sometimes styled herself William Cather, Jr., and favored conventionally male haircuts, clothes, and mannerisms. She zealously guarded her privacy throughout her life, however, and scholarly debate about her sexuality continues.

Like Catt and Cather, many coeds met the criteria for the "New Woman," a term coined toward the turn of the century to describe the free-spirited females who were drawn to social experimentation, whether vocational, recreational, or sexual. Caught between the nineteenth century's self-sacrificing domestic model of femininity and the twentieth century's more liberated, self-fulfilling version, the New Woman was determined to control her own life and, above all, not end up like her mother. At home in the world, she was educated, mobile, athletic, and devoted to her own pursuits. Whether she joined the suffrage movement or not, she believed in her legal equality, was interested in careers, and if she did ever wed, expected to do so for love. As the eastern writer and rights activist Mary Heaton Vorse put it, "I am trying for nothing so hard in my own personal life as how not to be respectable when married." Indeed, by the turn of the century, the numbers of both employed and single women rose appreciably.

To critics, the New Woman was a sign of moral decline and a threat to the family, portrayed by one cartoonist as a smoking, pants-clad termagant barking laundry instructions at an aproned man. To others, she was a sign of progress and a breath of fresh air, personified by Henry James's Daisy Miller or Charles Dana Gibson's iconic "girl" in a boy's shirt, tie, and straw boater, swinging a croquet mallet or perching on a bicycle. (Some conservatives fretted that like riding astride, cycling was too sexually stimulating for a proper woman.) In her upswept coiffure, businesslike shirtwaists, and shorter, ankle-length skirts, Ida B. Wells, the journalist and social activist, represented the stylish Gibson archetype popular among young, forward-looking Black progressives.

New Women were generally popular in the West, as long as they went about their pursuits without a fuss and respected flag and family. After all, the region was accustomed to adventurous homesteaders, schoolteachers, and cowgirls and thus open to the advantages as well as the drawbacks of allowing women more freedoms. Many men agreed with the proud father of Thea Kronborg, the future New Woman and opera star who was the Colorado-born protagonist of Cather's *The Song of the Lark*: "A girl with all that energy has got to do something, same as a boy, to keep her out of mischief."

Astonishing liberties such as smoking cigarettes and wearing split skirts or trousers notwithstanding, New Women were by no means as free as men, even in the West. As young adults on campus or elsewhere, they indulged their modern urge to try new things, such as traveling alone by bicycle or train or dating several suitors. As they grew older and the question of marriage grew more pressing, however, they were caught between the push toward independence and the pull of traditional domesticity. Most gave up their careers and adventures to "put family first."

According to census figures, however, 4 percent of the West's unmarried women lived alone, and 3 percent with another woman. Some of them were surely gay or transgender, but such women's personal lives are poorly documented for several reasons. Until the late nineteenth century, when doctors began to theorize about it, sexuality was generally considered to be a behavior, not an identity. Then, too, "maiden ladies" who lived alone or shared a home in platonic "white" or "Boston" marriages attracted no opprobrium, much less attention from the law, as gay men sometimes did.

Migrants went west to start a new life for many reasons, including the desire to experiment with their identity and/or sexuality. At a time when pants signaled "male," some women chose to dress or pass as men in order to get ahead. During the Mexican-American War, Elizabeth Smith adopted the name Bill Newcom and served capably as a Missouri infantryman. After eight months, however, her secret was discovered, and she was discharged. Following her subsequent marriage, she appealed to Congress for her back pay, and after witnesses attested to her competence, she received her wages plus homestead land in her own name in the West.

Other women who dressed and identified as male and are now described as transgender usually appeared in the census as men. The West's live-and-let-live ethos generally discouraged nosy questions, particularly regarding established community members, and most passed unremarked or were tacitly accepted. After Charlotte Parkhurst ran away from a New Hampshire orphanage, she worked at a stable and became a skilled coach driver. At the age of about thirty-eight, she sought her fortune in California, where she became Charley Parkhurst, a cigar-smoking teamster who sported a piratical black eyepatch and drove six-horse stagecoaches during the gold rush. Upon Parkhurst's death in 1879, the long-held secret was finally discovered, which the *Providence Journal* marked by observing that "one of the most celebrated of the world-famed California drivers was a woman. And is it not true that a woman had done what woman can do?" Records later revealed that one Charles Darkey Parkhurst had registered to vote in Santa Cruz County in the 1868 election, and Parkhurst's gravestone in Watsonville, California, reads: THE FIRST WOMAN TO VOTE IN THE U.S.

Tall tales of western women who dressed or behaved in conventionally male ways were also part of the media's over-the-top sensationalism of the frontier. One novel, *The Mustang-Hunters; or the Beautiful Amazon of the Hidden Valley* (1871), featured a "she-male" who mixed "feminine gentleness with masculine firmness." Readers were assured, however, that such women only dressed or acted like men because western circumstances, say, an attack by a grizzly bear or a band of desperadoes, sometimes demanded it.

Native societies in the West as elsewhere generally saw no need for such dissimulation and allowed "two-spirit" girls and boys to grow up according to the sex of their choice and maintain that role as adults. Born in 1806 in Montana, the young girl known as Pine Leaf to her White Clay Gros Ventre people was kidnapped by a man from a rival Crow band, who encouraged her to develop her exceptional skills as an equestrian and a warrior. In her first battle, she killed two Blackfeet opponents and captured many horses, and such exploits eventually earned her the honorific name of Bíawacheeitchish, or Woman Chief.

When her paternal mentor died, Bíawacheeitchish took his place as head of the clan and became the third-ranking member of the Crows' 150-member council of chiefs. She lived with four wives, but whether their relationships were intimate or practical is unclear. In his popular memoir, James Beckwourth, a Black mountain man and explorer, described meeting the great warrior in Montana in the 1840s. He noted that she dressed in female clothing and looked "neither savage nor warlike," but "modest and good natured." In 1845, she was killed by the Gros Ventre while trying to negotiate peace between her two peoples.

Born around 1840 in the New Mexican part of the Southwest's Apacheria Chihenne, Lozen, or Skilled Horse Thief, decided from an early age to follow the path of her older brother, Victorio, the famed Chiricahua Apache war leader. She learned to ride and shoot, then went on to fight as a warrior, first against Mexicans, then against Americans. A young Apache who had fled from US troops with a group of terrified women and children recalled how she had led them across the raging Rio Grande: "I saw a magnificent woman on a beautiful black horse—Lozen, sister of Victorio. Lozen, the woman warrior!" After she guided the party across the river to safety, she addressed the boy's grandmother: "You take charge, now. I must return to the warriors."

Lozen did not marry, have children, or dress as a woman, preferring to serve as what Victorio called "my right hand" and "a shield to her people." After her brother's death, she fought on with Geronimo and the last free Apaches, and in photographs from that era, she is indistinguishable from his male warriors. When the inevitable surrender loomed in 1886, she and Dahteste, a fellow Apache war woman who spoke fluent English, helped to negotiate the terms. In 1889, she died of tuberculosis at the Mount Vernon barracks in Alabama, where she was confined as a prisoner of war.

The violence involved in the military conquest of the West's Native Americans is well documented, but the accounts written by wives of army officers stationed at forts throughout the region offer some sharp, surprising perspectives on both peoples involved. Some were New Women, and the combination of the novel environment and their typically privileged backgrounds encouraged them to test the limits of old-fashioned Victorian propriety. Just as elite women back East were beginning to experiment with skeet shooting and racket sports, they might not only play tennis but also ride out on the grasslands to hunt for game.

The army officers were charged both with keeping unauthorized Whites out of designated Indian country and with protecting settlers—a mandate that effectively forced many Native peoples, already weakened by starvation and exposure to deadly diseases, to choose between confinement on desolate reservations or annihilation. On the Great Plains, the Lakota, Apaches, Comanches, Cheyenne, and other groups often resisted the military, which generated twenty-five to thirty years of organized hell known as the Indian Wars.

Compared to the fighting on the Plains, the conquest of Native Americans in the Pacific Northwest involved relatively little bloodshed, but the worst violence of all, including many acts of genocide carried out by federal troops, state militias, and vigilantes, took place in midcentury California. As Senator John Weller, later the state's governor, had put it back in 1852, "the interest of the white man demands their [the Natives'] extinction." Peoples such as the Paiutes, Modocs, and Mojaves had essentially lived peacefully in the geographically varied, thinly populated region until the arrival of the Spanish explorers in the sixteenth century, followed later by Hispanic colonizers, then by the Americans during the gold rush. Between 1846 and 1873 alone, genocide killed at least sixteen thousand Native Americans, and countless numbers were abused and displaced. In 1862, a White male settler in Red Bluff, California, wrote a letter to the editor of the *Beacon* to protest an incidence of military rape. After the young women had fled from their homes in a "rancheria of peaceful and domesticated Indians," he wrote, "as many as three of the soldiers, in rapid succession, had forced intercourse with the old squaws." By the century's end, disease and starvation had reduced California's Native population from perhaps 150,000 to 30,000.

Considering their husbands' military role, the officers' wives had a surprising amount of interaction with Native Americans, trading with them for rugs, jewelry, and pottery, employing them as nannies, and sometimes socializing with them. When the wife of Iron Bull called on Elizabeth Burt at Fort C. F. Smith, Montana, in 1867, to see Burt's new infant, the important Crow woman wore her best buckskin dress and brought a retinue. Each guest "held the little one . . . and with an admiring smile and comments passed her to the next [woman]." Next, they asked to see Burt's dresses, which she acknowledged as women's universal interest in "clothing and modes of living so different from their own." An eager collector of Native artifacts, Ada Vogdes, stationed at Fort Laramie, Wyoming, observed that although Red Leaf, a leader of the Oglala Lakotas, had killed an army general, he had a "godfatherly looking countenance, one to whom you would go in trouble, were he in different circumstances."

After her marriage in 1873, Martha Summerhayes, a Nantucketer who had studied in Germany, spent much of her life in garrisons on the Southwest's reservations—an experience she described as "glaenzendes Elend," or gleaming misery. She was an astute observer of male and female behavior, both Native American and White, and she understood that the enlisted men who eagerly helped her improve her austere quarters at Fort Apache, in Arizona, were simply expressing "the domestic instinct, so strong in some men's natures." Her husband was apparently not among them. When she complained that they had nowhere to store their things after unpacking, he responded, "What things?"

Summerhayes was among the many liberal-minded White women whose attitude toward Natives was one of maternalistic condescension rather than hostile racism. Indeed, she reserved her contempt for the lower-class White men who often served as Indian agents. Most were equally despised by Native Americans, who, as she wonderfully observed, "know and appreciate honesty and fair dealing, and they know a gentleman when they meet one."

The class-conscious officers' wives were not the only White women in the western forts, although the army laundresses' lives were very different from those of their social superiors. Since 1802, washerwomen had enjoyed a unique official position in army garrisons. Most were married to enlisted men and lived in tents and shanties along a designated Soapsuds Row, often hidden behind the fort's other buildings. Their workload was brutal, but the laundresses could earn up to forty dollars per month from fees, compared to an army sergeant's thirteen; they also received one meal a day, medical services, and bedding. Most of the women were illiterate and rough mannered but amiable, and they often earned extra income as nurses, midwives, seamstresses, or prostitutes.

A number of officers' wives enthusiastically remarked on Native men's physiques with a warmth that undermines Victorian assumptions about women's natural modesty, low libido, and perhaps even horror of "miscegenation." Summerhayes and the other wives looked forward to a twice-weekly military ritual that was also a kind of covert peep show. Swathed from chin to toe in Victorian drapery, they attended a "rather solemn ceremony" during which the Apaches reported to the fort to be counted and given their government rations. While the young lieutenants made eyes at some "extremely pretty" Apache girls, she wrote, "the bucks looked admiringly at the white women . . . Chief Diablo cast a special eye at our young Mrs. Bailey, of the infantry." Of that leader, she wrote, "I was especially impressed by his extraordinary good looks." Vogdes boasted of her sangfroid during an encounter with Red Dog, another Oglala leader, who "had nothing on but the skin in which he was born . . . I never saw such shoulders, arms . . . his legs were equally fine looking."

Some officers' wives' accounts include observations on the government's policies regarding Native Americans. At first, Caroline Winne, a New Yorker stationed at Fort Sidney, Nebraska, in 1874, dismissed the region's Oglalas, Cheyenne, and Arapahos as "dreadful beggars," but only a few weeks later, she wrote, "I do pity these poor wretches. . . . There are some good ones—those who have done good service to the whites. And there is no doubt they are dreadfully imposed upon and cheated by the Indian agents and traders. They don't get half that the Govt. sends them, and they are poor as poverty itself." Katie Garrett Gibson went further. In 1868, eight years before General George Armstrong Custer was defeated and killed by the Lakota at the Battle of the Little Bighorn, his wife, Elizabeth, told Gibson and a group of other officers' wives about the Battle of Washita River, in which he led a massacre of 103 peaceful Cheyenne people, including 75 women and children. Later, Gibson wrote that the account had "confused my sense of justice. Doubtless the white men were right, but were the Indians entirely wrong? After all these broad prairies had belonged to them."

Like New Women, the West's college girls are often criticized for not having been more socially and politically advanced than they were. Yet even coeds who majored in home economics, eschewed the suffrage movement, and gave up their careers after marriage still took advantage of opportunities that were beyond the wildest imaginings of their mothers and grandmothers, and many easterners as well. They devoted themselves to family life by choice rather than from necessity and tapped their liberal arts educations and social graces to uplift their communities as well as their households. Suffragists or not, their democratic experiences of voting and debating on campus prepared them to discuss women's changing role in society and take active leadership roles in civic life, as many did.

In an era when most American girls and boys lacked even secondary educations, the West produced a higher percentage of women college graduates than other regions. Moreover, their example motivated many other girls to persevere through high school or normal school to become teachers, secretaries, accountants, or other skilled workers, fueling women's socioeconomic power.

Seven

WOMEN AT WORK

*Wanted: Young women 18 to 30 years of age, of
good moral character, attractive and intelligent,
to waitress in Harvey Eating Houses on the
Santa Fe Railroad in the West. Wages,
$17.50 per month with room and board.*

—FRED HARVEY,
EMPLOYER OF THE "HARVEY GIRLS"

A S THE CENTURY UNFOLDED, the number of western women in the workforce increased sharply. Between 1870 and 1910, both Dakotas went from having 160 employed women to 19,363 in North Dakota and 29,045 in South Dakota; in Montana, from 171 to 159,896; in Wyoming, from 300 to 6,013. As members of what suffragists soon conceptualized as an unofficial labor union of women workers—whether paid on the job or unpaid at home— they played an increasingly powerful role in the fight for women's full citizenship.

By the 1870s, more than a quarter of all American women had been employed as teachers—testimony to the magnitude of their first major professional breakthrough. Before its land-grant colleges and normal schools could produce the West's own educators, however, staffing its schools was a huge challenge. Her Board of National Popular Education to Send Women West was a stop-gap solution that benefited students and single women looking for respectable work, and likely husbands, but Catharine Beecher also had strong religious and political motives for launching her zealous pedagogical crusade. As a fervent supporter of colonization and the pious daughter and half sister of America's most celebrated clergymen, she wanted to civilize the West not only with education but also with Protestant Christianity. From this perspective, widely shared by the WASP establishment back East, the developing West was spiritually endangered not only by its Native "heathens" and long-resident Catholic Hispanics but also by the influxes of immigrants from Europe, including many more Catholics and some Jews, as well as Mormons. To counter these allegedly dark forces, she wrote, in each "new settlement, the Christian female teacher will quietly take her station, collecting the ignorant children around her . . . opening the book of knowledge, inspiring the principles of morality."

Eastern teachers soon found that frontier education was hard work. Their students needed ample time for agricultural and domestic chores at home, so they had to cram as much information as possible into two short terms in the summer and winter. In order to provide instruction for grades one through eight, they had to focus on fifteen-minute sessions of the basics—reading, penmanship, arithmetic, and history— and relied heavily on memorization, drills, and sometimes corporal punishment. Their obligations extended well beyond the three Rs to include cleaning and filling the school's lamps, carrying the day's water and coal, and sharpening their students' pens. Often their greatest practical challenge was finding even the most basic educational materials. Almanacs, catalogs, and Bibles often did duty for Webster's blue-black spellers, Smith's and Smiley's arithmetic primers, and the McGuffey's readers that Beecher helped to compose.

Even when off duty, teachers were expected to practice the Protestant faith they professed and were forbidden to use tobacco, drink alcohol, or attend public balls. (Male teachers, who were fewer in number, had to restrict courting to one night per week—two for churchgoers; they were prohibited from getting a shave in a barbershop, lest it raise questions regarding their "worth, intention, integrity, and honesty.") In exchange for their dedication, the women received only modest monthly salaries and free room and board with local families, not all of whom were gracious hosts. Yet their work was important, rewarding, and highly valued by their communities, and the region's gender imbalance enabled many to marry. Very few returned to the East.

Unlike Beecher's teachers, Susan "Sue" McBeth was a professional missionary as well as an educator, and her students were not White settlers' children but devout Presbyterian men of the Nez Perce Reservation, located in north-central Idaho. In 1873, she became the first unaccompanied female missionary to arrive in the territory, where she served as a foot soldier in President U. S. Grant's "Peace Policy" campaign to salvage what was left of the West's Native American population. Like many well-intentioned, liberal-minded Whites of the era, including academics, she believed that cultures existed on a scale from savagery to haute civilization, and that "inferior" peoples could ascend the ladder by striving to become like the respectable WASPs at the top. From this perspective, the best chance of survival for those Grant recognized in 1869 in his first inaugural address as "the original occupants of this land" was assimilation into mainstream society—a tactic also long employed by Europe's colonial powers to suppress dissidence.

According to Grant's Peace Policy—devised by General Ely S. Parker, a former aide of Seneca ancestry whom he appointed as Commissioner of Indian Affairs—Native Americans were to be confined on reservations, weaned from their benighted old ways, and reeducated to become monogamous, sedentary farmers and housewives. Corrupt Indian agents were to be replaced by presumably upright military officers and missionaries, many of whom were women such as McBeth; she was later joined by Kate McBeth, her sister, who taught literacy and domestic skills to women. In his second inaugural address, given in 1873, when Sue McBeth arrived in Idaho, Grant underscored his hopes for Native Americans' inevitable assimilation and his intention to follow "a humane course, to bring the aborigines of the country under the benign influences of education and civilization. . . . Wars of extermination . . . are demoralizing and wicked."

The western Natives' crisis created rare professional opportunities for aspirational women such as Sue McBeth. She could not be ordained herself, of course, but she trained Nez Perce men for leadership in the Presbyterian church, including at least ten for the ministry—an elevated duty normally reserved for clergymen who had doctorates in theology. To that end, she mastered her pupils' difficult language, which "facilitates their studies very much & helped my influence with them." In the process, she also produced the two-thousand-word *Dictionary and Grammar of the Nez Perce Language*, a prodigious, much-needed lexicographical resource and an outstanding scholarly achievement, particularly for a woman of the era. When the boat carrying her manuscript on the first leg of its trip to the Smithsonian Institution exploded on the Columbia River, the priceless document was blown overboard into the water. In a seemingly divine intervention, a man found the pages floating in the river, recognized McBeth's handwriting, and dutifully dried and reposted the document to Washington, DC.

The McBeths were widely admired, at least by their White peers, for their attempts to transform nomadic Native Americans into pious Victorian farmers, but Chief Joseph, their legendary leader, must have wondered at the sisters' maternalistic condescension in describing the Nez Perce as "children." As he and some other prescient critics foresaw, the idea of assimilation resonated with Whites, and even many Natives, but it deeply conflicted with their own fundamental traditions, including the communal ownership of land; migratory patterns of hunting, fishing, and foraging; and extended kinship networks.

I n addition to Protestant missionary-teachers such as the McBeths, the West's employed women included between six thousand and nine thousand Catholic missionary nuns, who provided the first non-sectarian social services in many areas. They supported their schools, hospitals, and orphanages through not only charitable donations but also wages from legislatures otherwise hard-pressed to provide help to the poor, sick, and unlettered. Often stationed in remote locations far from clerical authority, the nuns were able to operate with considerable autonomy and faced less anti-Catholic prejudice than in the more sectarian East. Mother Joseph, a Sister of Providence later hailed as the Pacific Northwest's first architect, established some thirty hospitals and schools in the region and, being a skilled carpenter, wore a hammer beside the rosary hung on her belt.

Like their Protestant missionary peers, the nuns parlayed their genuine concern about the West's oppressed peoples into adventurous lives and ambitious careers then unusual for persons of either sex. Sister Mary Baptist Russell, a twenty-five-year-old member of the Sisters of Mercy, left Ireland on a bold quest to become a missionary not in Africa or Asia but in California. In 1863, she and her colleagues left the order's motherhouse in San Francisco for Grass Valley, where they fed the hungry; tended victims of cholera, diphtheria, and smallpox; and taught 120 students at Mount St. Mary's Convent and Academy.

Many children in the mining community had lost their parents from accidents as well as illness, so the "Mercies" next built a large home for sixty-nine orphans as well as twenty nuns. In 1872, they added a Day School for Young Ladies, whose modest fees helped pay the expenses at their two charitable institutions. The rough community was proud of the local girls' mastery of French, German, and music, and the newspaper praised their graduation celebration that year, held in a fine hall adorned with the obligatory lace curtains, as one of the best special events "ever given in this city."

That same year, Sister Blandina Segale, a pretty twenty-two-year-old Italian emigrant and member of the Sisters of Charity, in Cincinnati, first assumed she was headed for the Caribbean when she was assigned to teach in Trinidad. Upon arrival in the small Colorado coal-mining town occupied by many poor Hispanics and immigrants, she was dismayed to find facilities that she compared to "kennels for dogs." She soon hitched up her skirts, climbed onto the schoolhouse's roof, and began dismantling its adobe tiles, until one horrified matron returned with six workers to take over the demolition. Within two months, she and her nuns were running the renovated parish school and the public one, too.

Segale was a jack-of-all-trades and functioned as a nurse as well as a teacher and an administrator. On one occasion, she met the teenage leader of an outlaw gang while treating one of its wounded members. En route to her later posting at Santa Fe—where she shared the dilapidated quarters of Jean-Baptiste Lamy, the cleric who inspired Cather's *Death Comes for the Archbishop*—her stagecoach was surrounded by armed bandits. While her fellow passengers quaked in dread, the nun pushed back her bonnet and stared into the eyes of Billy the Kid. Then, she wrote, "he raised his large-brimmed hat with a wave and a bow," and before riding off, "stopped to give us some of his wonderful antics on bronco maneuvers."

Much of the sisters' work in the Southwest involved the region's oppressed Hispanic population, but Segale was appalled by the injustice of what was increasingly called the "Indian question." She met with Apache and Comanche leaders to support their peoples' civil rights and vocally opposed the common practices of lynching and defrauding Native Americans of their land. "Poor wild hearts," she wrote, "how they feel full of anger and treated unfairly."

Whatever their personal shortcomings and cultural biases, the West's teachers were valued not only as educators but as personifications of women's moral authority and exemplars of civilization on the frontier. These professionals, many of them single, also modeled the resourceful modern woman who supported herself, contributed to her community, and, having assumed more of citizenship's burdens, could reasonably expect to enjoy more of its privileges.

Many educated western women became teachers, but those less advantaged also found new ways to enjoy more prosperous, independent lives. As the Industrial Revolution accelerated throughout the West, agrarian women, like their sisters back East, wanted to make more money doing easier work and have more choices than were afforded by rural life, which for most meant a teenage marriage and years of childbearing and backbreaking chores in outmoded homes. These urban frontierswomen migrated in droves to Denver, Portland, Los Angeles, and other booming cities, where by the 1880s, populations averaged twenty-five women for every twenty men.

Many women became domestic servants, but others found new kinds of jobs in factories, mills, canneries, and offices that had not existed before. The better educated qualified for pink-collar positions as secretaries, salesclerks, printers, and photographers. Some stayed with relatives, but others learned to live independently, perhaps at a YWCA or a boardinghouse, manage their own money, and look after their own affairs. A concerned public worried about the housing, health, and morals of single women living and working in big cities, and especially about the risk of sexual assault, but that danger was probably no greater and perhaps less likely than in the isolated outback.

Some hardworking, adventurous young women found employment in the West's new tourism industry. The railroads' expansion allowed for more travel to and within the region, which now boasted more of its own capitals. Visitors flocked to see the sights in towns such as Pocatello, Idaho, the "Gilded City of the Interior West," which offered theaters, opera houses, and sophisticated shops. In 1878, Fred Harvey, an English-born entrepreneur, saw an opportunity in the West's lack of amenities for tourists that created an opportunity for a new category of respectable female workers. Appalled by a cuisine symbolized by a can of beans, perhaps embellished with some salt pork or bacon, washed down with scalding coffee or rot-gut whiskey, Harvey collaborated with the Atchison, Topeka & Santa Fe Railway to create America's first restaurant chain. A decade after he opened a spotless dining room at the train depot in Florence, Kansas, there was a Harvey House every hundred miles along the tracks, largely staffed by the soon celebrated "Harvey Girls."

Up until then, waitressing had not been considered respectable employment. Indeed, much of America still considered dining out unconventional if not risqué. A young single woman who not only waited on male diners but served them alcohol was regarded as little better than a prostitute. Undaunted, Harvey ran Help Wanted advertisements for intelligent women of good character, aged eighteen to thirty, then carefully trained successful applicants at a monthlong boot camp. They removed their jewelry and makeup, donned black, ankle-length dresses and white bib aprons, and learned about good food and how to serve it. By the end of their training, they could deliver a four-course meal—including delicacies carried in special refrigerated railcars, such as fresh fruit, fish, ice cream, and cheeses—during a thirty-minute train stop.

Known for their propriety as well as their professionalism, Harvey Girls slept in company dormitories supervised by matrons, which protected their good reputations and also allowed them to save their salaries of $17.50 a month, plus room and board, laundry, and travel money. (Male waiters made $48 per month, but much of that went to their living expenses.) They traveled widely, mixed with all strata of society, attracted many suitors, and quickly captured America's heart. According to one popular song, after Katie Casey was unjustly fired from the Harvey House in Winslow, Arizona, her admirer, who ran the town's railyard, simply stopped the trains until she was reinstated:

> *Oh, who would think that Katie Casey owned the Santa Fe?*
> *But it really looks that way . . .*
> *She can hold the freight from Albuquerq' to Needles any day . . .*

Almost seven decades after the first of these waitresses tied on their aprons, Judy Garland starred in *The Harvey Girls*, a hit movie musical based on a popular novel of the same name.

Whether they were teachers or waitresses, women's improved economic position had far-reaching social consequences. A higher percentage of them remained single. Most still married, but they did so later, often in their twenties, and for love and companion-ship instead of mere support. They began family life not as inexperi-enced girls but as self-reliant adults with a nest egg to put toward their next enterprise—more education, a business, or some means of enhancing home production, such as livestock or a sewing machine. The national suffrage movement, long a domain of the prosperous class, began to take notice of this new constituency.

Eight

AN "AMBITIOUS ORGANIZATION OF LADIES"

I feel now and then as if I could not miss.

—ANNIE OAKLEY, SHARPSHOOTER

THAT SO MANY EDUCATED WOMEN became teachers was a sign of progress, but it also indicated their lack of other options, especially in traditionally male professions. In the 1880s and 1890s, American women who wanted to take up law, medicine, or other such careers faced a misogynistic establishment that tried, through various ways, to discourage these potential economic competitors. Nevertheless, western women benefited from the region's desperate need for expertise and mastered unconventional means to become highly trained professionals at nearly twice women's national rate.

Clara Shortridge Foltz, a divorced single mother of five who became the West Coast's first female attorney, began her professional life as a teenage teacher. Upon marrying a dashing if feckless Union soldier turned farmer in her native Illinois, she gave up her job, then bore four children in hardship. After migrating with her extended family, first to Oregon, then to San Jose, California, she gave birth to yet another child in straitened circumstances and soon divorced her philandering, ne'er-do-well husband.

Few could have imagined that the impoverished, twenty-seven-year-old divorcée would soon achieve nationwide celebrity, if not notoriety, as the "Portia of the Pacific," but Foltz quickly showed her mettle. Perhaps inspired by her father, a lawyer and dissident preacher, she first supported her large brood as an orator—a profitable skill before modern media, especially for a young woman with impish good looks and a jaunty cocked chin. After lecturing on the controversial subjects of women's rights and suffrage, she decided to help bring about, rather than just talk about, these political goals by becoming a lawyer.

Women were then not admitted to California's bar, but Foltz studied privately, both with her father and with a local judge, to prepare for the exam anyway. After she passed, the next obstacle was a state regulation that specified that only White men could practice law. Undaunted, she wrote the Woman Lawyer's Bill, which substituted "any citizen or person" for "white male citizens," and in April 1878, persuaded the governor to sign it. Four months later, she became the law's first beneficiary.

Wasting no time, Foltz and her friend Laura de Force Gordon—a former "trance speaker" in the spiritualism movement who became the state's first female newspaper publisher and second female lawyer—fought to include suffrage in California's second constitution, written between 1878 and 1879. They narrowly lost that battle, but they won women the rights of equal access to employment and education—then unprecedented outside the state. At the same time, they also sued the University of California's Hastings College of the Law, in San Francisco, the state's only such school, for expelling them after ten days because their rustling skirts distracted the male students.

The state supreme court eventually upheld their double-barreled argument that as a land-grant institution, Hastings should be coeducational, and that if women could be lawyers they must be admitted to law schools. By then, however, Foltz was too busy with her career to complete the course work necessary for a degree. (In 1991, more than a century after it denied her admission, the college awarded her a posthumous degree of doctor of laws.) She always regretted her catch-as-catch-can legal education, however, and tried to help other women study for the bar. When she later cofounded the Portia Law Club in 1894, its opening event was headlined in a San Francisco paper: "Ambitious Organization of Ladies. Its Object the Establishment of a Law College for Women. Striking Costumes." Foltz archly responded that she planned to wear "the regular Portia mortar-board, the color to harmonize with that of the gown."

Attorney Foltz lived by the adage that "Nothing succeeds like success." She handled many divorces in a state that had the nation's highest rate, but she was also a canny trial lawyer who made headlines as the first woman to prosecute a murder case in California. Of her early appearances in court, she wrote, "I kept my wits fairly well, though I trembled." Her jitters disappeared, however, when taunted about her gender: "I am a woman and I am a lawyer—and what of it? . . . I am neither to be bullied out nor worn out."

Fond of the spotlight and never satisfied with the status quo, Foltz moved her children from city to city in pursuit of what became a multifaceted career. While practicing law in San Diego, she started a daily newspaper. In New York City, she formed the Clara Foltz Gold Mining Company—and also sued a restaurant for the common practice of refusing service to women without male escorts. Back home in San Francisco, she took up oil and gas law and published *Oil Fields and Furnaces*, a trade magazine.

Despite her demanding professional and family life, Foltz remained a linchpin of California's suffrage movement, became the state's first woman deputy district attorney, and served on its influential Board of Charities and Corrections. Her most enduring achievement, however, was the creation of the office of the public defender—then a radical innovation eventually adopted across the nation. Throughout her long life, she was the "first woman" to take on role after role, but not even this human dynamo could realize her dream of a federal judgeship, much less election to the US Senate, as her brother Samuel Shortridge twice achieved.

Sheer necessity inclined the West to accept women doctors more readily than lawyers, but their paths, too, were strewn with hurdles. Bethenia Owens-Adair, an Oregon homesteader's daughter, passed through several careers and colleges before finally graduating from University of Michigan Medical School in 1880 at the age of forty. The enterprising frontier girl, whom her father had admiringly called "my boy," later wrote that until the age of thirty-five, her greatest regret was that she had not been born male, "for I realized very early in life that a girl was hampered and hemmed in on all sides simply by the accident of sex."

Owens had only had a few months of school before marrying a rascal at the age of fourteen, bearing a sickly son at sixteen, and leaving her abusive, hard-drinking spouse at nineteen. As she later wrote, "I was, indeed, surrounded with difficulties seemingly insurmountable." Yet while working as a servant to support herself and her child, she managed to complete her own spotty education and, like so many aspirational women, become a teacher. Soon dissatisfied with her first career, she took out a bank loan to study hatmaking, then, like her fellow Oregon pioneer and milliner Abigail Duniway, opened a shop.

Her customers' laments, especially regarding violent, drunken, or irresponsible husbands, forced Owens to reconsider the hardships she

had endured as a poor teenage mother and confront the systemic nature of the injustices she and other women faced. Already a temperance supporter, she became a rights advocate and suffragist, contributed
articles to the *New Northwest*, and assessed her career options once
more. After working as a nurse for a local doctor and studying anat-
omy, she horrified her friends and relations by announcing that she
intended to leave her successful business to become a physician. Then,
like Foltz and other determined women, she prepared to navigate the
male establishment's obstacle course.

The medical fraternity employed various tactics to discourage
women from becoming doctors. The American Medical Association
simply barred them from membership for nearly seventy years. The
Pacific Medical Journal turned to pseudoscientific jargon, opining that
women were unsuited to many vocations, including medicine, because of "psychological phenomena" connected with ovulation, men-
struation, and birth. Virtually all medical schools refused to admit
them, including Harvard, where men protested that a woman should
not appear "in places where her presence is calculated to destroy our
respect for the modesty and delicacy of her sex."

Like the West's first female lawyers, its first female physicians
had to learn the profession as best they could and often on the job. A
few managed to attend institutions like the Woman's Medical College of Pennsylvania, in Philadelphia, the second such school in the
world, but many others had to settle for alternative health institutes.
These holistic schools were more amenable to accepting women, and
their gentler treatments, such as hydrotherapy, homeopathy, and
physical therapy, had a broad appeal at a time when many physicians
still relied on grisly, ineffective purges and bloodletting. In 1874, after
one year of study at the Eclectic Medical University of Pennsylvania,
also in Philadelphia, Owens graduated with the title of "bath doctor."
Back in Portland, she continued to learn medicine by practicing

quietly with a male physician, while also prudently running a shop that sold hats on one side and medicines on the other.

The era's women doctors, including Owens at first, often specialized in pediatrics or obstetrics and gynecology, which were considered more socially palatable extensions of their nurturing role. The growth of the latter fields, however, also reflected significant changes in women's sexual and reproductive lives. During much of the nineteenth century, most spoke of contraception and abortion in whispers if at all, yet the birth rate halved. In 1873, alarmed political conservatives in Congress who feared a catastrophic population drop passed the Comstock Act. The law banned the sale, advertising, and mailing not only of pornography but also of female pessaries and douches, male prophylactics, and other materials deemed "obscene." Considering contraceptive technology's dubious efficacy at the time, however, America's dramatically declining birth rate most likely reflected women's increasing knowledge about and control over their bodies, including the choice of abstinence. The decision to risk marital tensions by refusing sex testifies to important positive changes in how they saw themselves, as well as their improved standing in society. Not coincidentally, the divorce rate gradually rose to one in twelve couples by 1900, and the number of women who remained single climbed to 10 percent.

After her son graduated from Willamette Medical College, in Salem, Oregon, Owens decided that her holistic degree was not good enough. Determined to have the best credentials in the state, she won admission to the unusually progressive University of Michigan, where she also studied literature and history. After graduation, she made a tour of European hospitals, then returned to Oregon, where she established a practice specializing in diseases of the eye and ear. In 1884, the energetic forty-four-year-old physician married the indolent John Adair, with whom she had a daughter who died in infancy and two adopted sons.

After a life devoted to women's health, suffrage, temperance, and other worthy causes, the highly respected Owens-Adair sadly joined the ranks of women reformers who used their moral authority to advance benighted as well as admirable goals. Like many progressive contemporaries, she endorsed the pseudoscience of eugenics, or selective breeding, to weed out alleged human flaws, and she supported bills that eventually led to the tragic sterilization of thousands of imprisoned, epileptic, and mentally handicapped people.

Among the proverbial "first woman to" figures who competed in a traditionally man's world, Dr. Susan La Flesche Picotte, the nation's first Native American physician and public health reformer, is among the most remarkable. Despite the handicap of race as well as gender, her greatest professional challenge was not admission to medical school but serving afterward as the only doctor for more than 1,200 people in 450 square miles of the West.

La Flesche was raised on the Nebraska reservation of the Omahas by her powerful mixed-race parents, Joseph "Iron Eyes" La Flesche and Mary Gale La Flesche. Both had had White fathers but strongly identified as Omahas. This people had once ranged over tens of millions of acres, dwelling in lodges in permanent villages in the spring and fall, then in portable tipis for the hunting seasons, but the federal government had forced them onto the reservation in 1854. Weakened by competition from the dominant Lakotas and the confinement, starvation, and diseases brought by colonization, they were in desperate straits. Like many aspirational Native Americans, the La Flesches believed that their people's survival depended on assimilation, and they gave their talented children good mainstream educations. "Do you always want to be called 'those Indians,'" their father asked, "or do you want to go to school and be somebody in the world?"

Young La Flesche played the piano, spoke four languages, including French, and graduated with high honors from the Hampton Normal and Agricultural Institute in Hampton, Virginia, which prepared Black and Native American girls to become Christian teachers or homemakers. However, she chose a different vocation after watching an old woman die in agony while the reservation's White doctor sent repeated excuses. In La Flesche's translation, his message was, "It was only an Indian, and it did not matter." In 1889, with the help of her family's influential White assimilationist friends, La Flesche graduated second in her class from the rigorous Woman's Medical College of Pennsylvania. After achieving a feat rare for any woman, much less one of color, she returned home to become both the government physician at the Omaha Agency Indian School and a medical missionary for the Presbyterian Board of Home Missions, for which she received $750 per year.

The gravely pretty, lace-collared Victorian lady was the entire region's only doctor, and she treated many Native and White adults as well as children, often paying house calls by horseback or wagon. The reservation was wracked by malnutrition and alcoholism as well as infectious diseases, including tuberculosis and cholera, all of which were then easier to prevent through education than cure. Like Florence Nightingale, La Flesche leaned heavily on the twinned Victorian ideals of cleanliness and godliness, which on the reservation meant sanitary water and screen doors, church and temperance. "I'm not accomplishing miracles," she wrote, "but I'm beginning to see some of the results of better hygiene and health habits. And we're losing fewer babies and fewer cases to infection."

In addition to her medical practice, "Dr. Susan," like the rest of her family, fought the injustices visited on the Omaha. Her small medical office became a community center and she a de facto social worker who repeatedly tapped her influential connections to help her people. She negotiated their disputes, wrote and translated their documents, and dispensed legal and economic advice until exhaustion and poor health forced her to resign from her positions. After marrying Henry Picotte, a Yankton Sioux man, she resumed practicing medicine in the town of Bancroft, where she treated patients of both races. That the proper matron continued working after bearing two sons bespeaks her community's desperate need of her services.

After her husband died of the tuberculosis and alcoholism that ravaged Native populations, Picotte moved to the reservation town of Walthill and doubled down on community service. She served as president of the local board of health, worked to protect the Omahas' rights to their land, and lobbied for a ban on alcohol in stores on the reservation's borders. She was a superachiever by any measure but was never fully embraced as an equal by her White peers.

In time, Picotte returned to the study of old Omaha legends and even dropped her opposition to the peyote religion, a pro-temperance faith that blended the ritual use of the hallucinogen with elements of Christian and Native spirituality. Despite the hardships she faced, the pioneering doctor and reformer lived to see one dream come true: the Dr. Susan La Flesche Picotte Memorial Hospital, a modern clinic built in 1913 from private donations she solicited, which is now a museum and a National Historic Landmark on the reservation.

Unlike law and medicine, art and literature were generally considered acceptable pursuits for Victorian women. Mary Hallock Foote mastered both in works that, like her own life, counter the stereotype of the macho West with a distinctly female perspective. At a time when artists and writers, including Frederic Remington and Bret Harte, often mythologized lone cowboys and prospectors blazing their way through dazzling scenery, she presented a very different, less heroic West, in which women were just as important, capable, and complex as men.

Born in upstate New York into an elite, progressive Quaker family, Hallock received a then-exceptional education for a girl, culminating with admission to the Cooper Union for the Advancement of Science and Art in New York City. By the 1870s, the early New Woman's fine drawings, engravings, and woodcuts in the popular Pre-Raphaelite style appeared in *Scribner's Monthly* magazine and other prestigious periodicals, as well as in books by Longfellow, Nathaniel Hawthorne, John Greenleaf Whittier, and other prominent authors.

Throughout her single years, Hallock maintained a passionate bond with Helena de Kay, an aristocratic former classmate at the Cooper Union who became a painter involved in New York City's art scene. Whether their tie was ever sexually expressed is unclear, but Hallock's passionate letters testify to its emotional intensity: "Imagine yourself kissed a dozen times my darling." After graduation, the elite bohemian beauties stayed in constant touch, fended off their suitors, and discussed sharing a studio in Manhattan. As they approached their late twenties, however, their families pressured them to settle down into respectable family life. After de Kay married Richard Watson Gilder, a socially prominent editor at *Scribner's Monthly*, later *The Century Illustrated Monthly Magazine*, who was also Hallock's friend and publisher, Hallock wrote to him: "Do you know sir, that until you came along I believe that she loved me almost as girls love their lovers. *I know I loved her so.* Don't you wonder that I can stand the sight of you."

In 1876, after a four-year-long courtship, the twenty-eight-year-old Hallock finally wed Arthur De Wint Foote, a Yale-educated mining engineer, which transformed her life in unexpected ways. His itinerant work took them to the West, mostly California, Colorado, and Idaho, where their marriage soon deviated from the upper-class Victorian norm. He was talented but a poor businessman, and his fluctuating income often barely supported his wife and, soon, three children. Worried by the family's proximity to poverty, Helena Gilder urged Foote to write and illustrate articles about her new life for Richard Gilder's magazine.

Foote responded with a creative surge fueled by not only looming hardship but also the inspiration provided by the West's particular, sometimes disturbing beauty. "Desert did not seem the word for this country," she wrote, "nor was it deserted—it was just coming into being after some long creative pause." In 1878, *Scribner's* published "A California Mining Camp," a feature story that she wrote and illustrated. Readers applauded its fresh, more nuanced female perspective, which included a sensitive depiction of a family of poor Hispanic workers, "brown, ragged, ill-fed, sickly and numerous," whose cheerfulness, "which implied no hope or even understanding of anything better, was the saddest thing in the whole of that warm, sunny desolation."

As Foote understood, part of her appeal as a writer derived from the juxtaposition of her elite social status and her frontier surroundings. She was not just some pioneer wife in a soddy, after all, but the upper-class chatelaine of whatever rough-hewn log castle she graced, who employed an English nanny and a Chinese cook to free up her time for work. Her carefully cultivated persona was publicized by her many visitors, including one traveler who wrote of stumbling upon the isolated cabin of an eastern lady, "and a cultivated one," who shared some of her drawings and "ripped out an intellectual go-as-you-please backed up by good looks and brightness."

Eager to produce more income, Foote added fiction to her professional pursuits. Frontier "dime novels" had been around since *Malaeska; The Indian Wife of the White Hunter* debuted in 1860, but like her artwork and nonfiction, her "Westerns" were distinguished by her clear-eyed, evenhanded treatment of the sexes and her refusal to romanticize the region with conventional tales of handsome cowpokes and damsels in distress. In 1883, Houghton Mifflin published *The Led-Horse Claim*, the first of her dozen novels, initially serialized in *The Century*, which centered on a woman torn between a lover and a brother engaged in deadly competition in the dirty, dangerous Hades of mining.

Much like Foote and her husband, the women and men she created were equalized by their subordination to a spectacular but distinctly unpastoral, sometimes downright menacing Mother Nature. Like her fictional male and female characters in *The Chosen Valley*, who confronted the life-or-death issue of irrigation in the arid West, the anxious husband and wife caught between the endless desert and the lowering sky in "The Coming of Winter," her engraving of 1888, faced forces far greater than themselves that required them to cooperate to survive. As the eastern protagonist of *Edith Bonham*, her most personal and celebrated novel, observed on her isolated desert mesa, "Things may happen any time, but you don't know what, nor where to expect them."

Foote helped educate America about the West from a female point of view, and as a skilled professional and provider for her family, personified its capable women. She enjoyed an unusual degree of prominence for an artist of either sex at the time, and her stories were regarded as equal to those of Harte and other famous contemporaries. She chafed at being segregated in the National Association of Women Painters and Sculptors and lauded as the "dean of women illustrators." However, like some other notable New Women, including Helena Gilder, who became an anti-suffragist—and unlike Sarah Hallock, her rights-activist aunt—she never embraced the women's movement.

A century later, Foote's novels seem dated, but her life of remarkable adventure and achievement, and her account of the West's mining era, remain important resources for historians—as they notoriously were for Wallace Stegner. In 1972, his novel *Angle of Repose*, which relied heavily on her life, letters, and unpublished memoir, won the Pulitzer Prize for Fiction, but his reputation was tarnished by accusations of plagiarism that caused a literary scandal.

The West's most popular women artists, or indeed professionals of any sort, were arguably its singers, dancers, and actors. At first they came from the East, but the region soon developed and exported a unique female entertainer of its own: the cowgirl performer, who personified the two popular romantic ideas of the "Wild West" and the New Woman. Phoebe Ann Moses, or Mosey, later known as Annie Oakley, grew up poor on an Ohio farm, not a Panhandle ranch, but no native-born Texan could match her embodiment of the capable, athletic, self-sufficient western woman. At a time when respectable women were still confined in constricting corsets and their claustrophobic sphere, she electrified audiences by cartwheeling into the arena, vaulting onto her horse, and shooting dimes out of midair—then a nearly unimaginable assertion of female agency. In short order, the cowgirl rivaled the fabled pioneer helpmeet as the iconic western woman in the national pantheon.

Oakley had the rudiments of the cover story necessary to present her traditionally male athletic skills, especially her extraordinary marksmanship, in a socially palatable way. In childhood, she had indeed hunted and trapped to help support her impoverished family. Rarely able to attend school, she seemed destined for a life of the menial domestic work she took up in adolescence. In 1875, however, the servant girl gifted with preternatural hand-eye coordination bested Frank Butler, an older professional sharpshooter, in a local contest.

They soon married, but to preserve her appealingly girlish aura, they performed together in vaudeville shows and circuses as Butler and Oakley. Her sisters already called her Annie, but she chose her own new surname.

Not coincidentally, Oakley transitioned into a glamorous star just as westerners were defining their own cultural identities with the help of the phenomenal showman William Cody. His popular improvisation on the traveling circus, which he called "Buffalo Bill's Wild West," helped create the enduring fantasy that cast White settlers as heroic civilizers who were forced to defend their god-fearing homes from the bloodthirsty "savages" who were in fact their victims. (Propaganda aside, Cody was a former army scout who said, "Every Indian outbreak that I have ever known has resulted from broken promises and broken treaties by the government.") In 1885, Butler persuaded him to hire Oakley as the first of his women performers, and that seemingly unlikely suffragist paid her the same as his male stars.

The Victorian cowgirl soon had pride of place on Cody's sagebrush Olympus of demideities, including George Armstrong Custer, played by a performer, and Sitting Bull, the actual Lakota leader who had trounced the late general in the Battle of the Little Bighorn. Oakley's natural talents notwithstanding, she was a true professional who left nothing to chance. She practiced her routine daily, hitting targets behind her from a reflection on her knife blade and firing pistols, rifles, or shotguns from a galloping horse with either hand, all while wearing a skirt and perched on a sidesaddle. As she modestly allowed, "I feel now and then as if I could not miss."

The perennial ingenue whom Sitting Bull, a genuine friend and admirer, called Watanya Cicilla, or Little Sure Shot, had to work equally hard to maintain her double-sided persona. She explained her jaw-dropping abilities to reporters by artfully blending fact and fiction: they were simply the survival skills of a western maiden who had to help feed and protect her family from ravening beasts, heartless outlaws, and hostile savages. Always mindful of the separate spheres, she took pains to distinguish herself from the likes of the bibulous bullwhacker Martha "Calamity Jane" Cannary, who also joined Cody's show, by daintily serving tea in her tent after the day's riding and shooting were done. But tomboyish behavior acceptable in a girl still raised questions of respectability in a grown woman, and during the sixteen seasons Oakley toured with Cody at home and abroad, she struggled to maintain her maidenly public image. She wore youthful curls that cascaded down her back and a big western hat that crowned her like a halo, but talented younger competitors such as Elaine Smith, sometimes bizarrely billed as the "full-blooded young Sioux girl Winona," pressured her to lower her official age by six years.

As an avatar of the New Woman, western style, Oakley caused a sensation in 1887 when she performed for Queen Victoria and twenty thousand spectators in London while wearing a reform dress that featured a then-shockingly short skirt over leggings and gaiters. For women still hobbled by long skirts and limited ambitions, she was no mere entertainer but the inspirational western representative of modernity and change. By the time she was performing the cowgirl, however, some women in the real West had long cultivated similarly traditional male skills.

In 1863, Martha Maxwell, a well-educated wife and mother, left Wisconsin with her husband and children to join the Colorado gold rush. When the impoverished family was forced to live in a rough mining shack, she became intrigued by the stuffed birds and beasts left there by its previous resident. Taking up a new career, the five-foot-tall homemaker quickly became a highly skilled hunter, naturalist, and taxonomist who modernized the field of taxidermy and popularized the use of dioramas that simulated specimens' natural habitats.

In 1875, Maxwell moved her Rocky Mountain Museum, centered

on the region's natural history, from Boulder to Denver, and in the following year received an important commission that brought her international attention. The wildlife display she created for the "Women's Work" building at the Centennial International Exhibition, held in Philadelphia, became one of the most celebrated attractions at the first world's fair. When criticized for her career, the vegetarian replied, "Which is more cruel? To kill to eat or to kill to immortalize?"

Maxwell was a suffragist, but Oakley, always conscious of public opinion, never officially endorsed the rights movement. She supported equal pay for equal work, however, and even women's participation in the military; indeed, she taught many women how to shoot. As one of the nation's first popular professional female athletes, she also anticipated the turn-of-the-century fitness craze that led women as well as men to exercise and diet for their health. Long after her death, she lives on as an inspirational figure in books, exhibits, and Irving Berlin's popular musical *Annie Get Your Gun*, which absurdly depicts her as deliberately letting a man beat her in a shooting match.

Despite the ordeals they endured to achieve their dreams in a region still engaged in settlement, 14.5 percent of the West's female population worked as doctors, lawyers, and other professionals by 1890, compared to the national rate of 8 percent. Like the region's homesteaders and coeds, they made the case for women's full citizenship by embodying Benjamin Franklin's aphorism: "Well done is better than well said."

Nine

"DO EVERYTHING"

*We must choose. Be a child of the past with all its
crudities and imperfections, its failures and
defeats, or a child of the future, the future
of symmetry and ultimate success.*

—FRANCES WILLARD, PRESIDENT,
WOMAN'S CHRISTIAN TEMPERANCE UNION

T HAT ONLY A RELATIVE handful of women, all in the West, could vote did not mean that the rest had no political power. By the 1880s, many westerners had joined a nationwide movement that weaponized women's moral authority in a war against the vices that threatened the family, including gambling, prostitution, but especially drunkenness. The Woman's Christian Temperance Union—one of the largest, most important political organizations in the nation's history—gave their sex hitherto-unimaginable sway over public policy. Contrary to its later puritanical, reactionary image, the WCTU also gave tens of thousands of its members a respectable path from the home into the larger worlds of women's rights, large-scale social welfare reform, and personal and professional growth.

By 1873, thousands of women across America were fed up with trying to raise families in communities awash in alcohol. As stunned politicians watched from the sidelines, an unprecedented bloc of wives and mothers mounted the Women's Temperance Crusade, which used prayer vigils, petitions, and protest demonstrations to force the closing of hundreds of saloons. In the following year, women of all races, ethnicities, and creeds formed the WCTU, which within three months purged alcohol from some 250 communities and transformed national politics. The nation's first mass women's organization spread quickly from its Ohio headquarters to chapters throughout the West, where the alcohol problem was worst. Even skeptics were forced to recognize the new power of women united by a single cause—a reality soon underscored by the WCTU's alliance with the far smaller, much more controversial suffrage movement.

From their beginnings in the 1830s and 1840s, the temperance, abolition, and women's rights movements had been inextricably intertwined. They were championed by many of the same evangelical and Quaker abolitionists, both Black and White, who regarded slavery, the lack of universal enfranchisement, and alcohol as society's greatest evils. After the Civil War, the temperance movement had accelerated in tandem with the nation's alcohol consumption, which rose as the millions of German, Irish, and Italian immigrants pouring into the cities and the agrarian West increased both demand and supply, notably the beer produced by brewers on the Great Plains.

Well before the WCTU established a chapter in Helena, Montana, in 1883, Elizabeth Chester Fisk, a Connecticut-born exemplar of Victorian womanhood, and her teetotaling evangelical Methodist congregation were mobilized against vice. In the West's informal caste system, Fisk and the other members of Helena's elite "Four Hundred" belonged to the town's respectable, prosperous, "civilized" element, which put down roots, established homes, schools, and churches, and practiced the Victorian era's cardinal virtues of respectability and "keeping up appearances." They were proud that unlike Butte and other grubby mining centers, their gold-plated "Queen City of the Rockies" boasted fine Victorian architecture and even an opera house. One early study that compared the town to Anaconda, the state's crude copper capital, wonderfully noted that the latter had no poodles.

Like San Francisco, Denver, and other regional capitals, however, Helena was organized around providing goods and services to the freewheeling mining, cattle, and lumber industries. These boomtowns attracted a large "sporting class" of young, transient, single, working-class men employed by those major enterprises and the women who catered to them. Indeed, men outnumbered women six to one in Helena's population of three thousand. Fisk could not understand "how any man can be as lost to every principle of manhood as to (seek) in intoxication relief from sorrow," but the members of the sporting class did not share her confusion. No less than elites such as the Four Hundred, such women and men were mainstays of the urban West. Indeed, Josephine Airey, aka Chicago Joe Hensley, a saloon and brothel owner, was Helena's second-largest taxpayer; like other such entrepreneurial women, she mostly stayed out of legal trouble by paying off the police and observing the professional proprieties, starting with discretion.

As the WCTU rapidly expanded into places such as Montana, its leadership recognized America's regional sociological differences by establishing eastern and western divisions. Throughout her tenure, Annie Wittenmyer, its first president, focused tightly on "the entire prohibition of the manufacture and sale of intoxicating liquors as a beverage"—a priority that continued to prevail in the East. However, Frances Willard, who became the union's second president in 1879, regarded prohibition as less an end in itself than as a tool for empowering women to retrofit stale, old-fashioned American society for the progressive modern age. She broadened its goals to address the social evils of poverty, ignorance, and injustice as well—a pragmatic shift in emphasis that was especially popular in the less pious, more forward-looking West.

Willard was a midwesterner herself. She grew up on a farm on the Wisconsin prairie, was mostly homeschooled by her mother, and like Carrie Chapman Catt worked as a rural teacher right after college. Following two years of study and travel abroad, she became president of Northwestern University's women's college in Evanston, Illinois— then an unusual professional distinction; photographs from that time portray a serious academic in wire-rimmed spectacles and a severe coiffure. After an authority clash with the university's president, who was also her former fiancé, she left the school to become the new WCTU's secretary in 1874, then its powerful president until her untimely death in 1898.

Willard quickly established a radical new "Do Everything" agenda for the WCTU. In her thinking, all of society's problems were inter-related, and so stamping out alcohol also called for eliminating pov-erty and ignorance. (She later drolly observed that she had first assumed that people were poor because they drank but came to think the reverse.) Under her visionary leadership, what began as an anti-vice campaign became the command center for a comprehensive social reform platform that included public sanitation, the regulation of adult and child labor, kindergarten education, handicapped facilities, pure food and drug laws, legal aid, the eight-hour workday, the rehabilita-tion of prostitutes—even world peace. In contrast to the agendas of the many male politicians who focused on commerce or foreign affairs, Willard's to-do list prioritized the needs and concerns of women and families, which politicized domesticity and solidified women's shared identity as mothers not only of families but of the nation itself.

Women who couldn't vote but wanted to effect political change had no choice but to persuade men to act on their behalf, and Willard was determined that the WCTU would help change that status quo. Yet persuading the membership to endorse suffrage in its official platform was more difficult than it seemed at first glance. Research done by the union's "franchise department" found that members in the Midwest and West generally favored the vote, but those in the Northeast and South, where the ideal of traditional, apolitical womanhood was stronger, either opposed suffrage or were lukewarm at best.

To win nationwide support, the canny Willard cast suffrage in the least threatening light possible. Soft-pedaling the touchy idea of women's equality as a rationale for the vote, she, like Clarina Nichols, emphasized their moral superiority, which, she asserted, they had objectively proved by waging war on the vices that endangered their families. Mastering the argot of domesticity, the single, highly educated writer, executive, organizer, and lobbyist rallied "citizen mothers" and "municipal housekeepers" under the banner of "Home Protection," then charged them to uplift and defend the homeland itself. Once enfranchised, they must "come into government and purify it, into politics and cleanse the Stygian pool."

By 1881, Willard had won enough support from her membership to add enfranchisement to the WCTU's formal platform. The organization's support, however, was something of a double-edged sword in the battle for suffrage. Just as male voters and legislators often feared, many temperance advocates supported enfranchisement primarily as a means of enacting prohibition—a quandary that Abigail Duniway blamed for the numerous defeats of suffrage bills in the 1880s and beyond.

Fisk had previously considered political activism in general and voting in particular unwomanly and anathema, but upon joining Willard's turbocharged, forward-looking WCTU, she became a suffragist. To her own do-everything list of the Women's Relief Corps, the state's Poor Committee, and the Working Women's Home, she added volunteering at the union's Helena chapter. She circulated temperance petitions, lobbied legislators, helped get supporters elected to the school board, and even traveled to the union's regional conferences. She assured her mother back in Connecticut that she continued to take her duties to her family seriously, but added, "I cannot live wholly within that narrow circle nor do I think it is any woman's duty to do so."

Like suffragists, temperance advocates are often cast as crotchety, prune-faced biddies—despite Stanton's assertion that the former "were a remarkably fine-looking body of women"—but for Fisk and many others, the WCTU was profoundly liberating. Indeed, a number of its leaders led avant-garde personal as well as political lives. The union upheld the ideal of egalitarian companionate marriage, but like a quarter of its elite, Willard remained single. She is often compared to Eleanor Roosevelt, because both were among American history's most powerful women and shared a Do Everything philosophy, but they also had intimate relationships with women as well as men. Unusually for a public figure at the time, Willard specifically affirmed deep female bonds in principle—"In these days, when any capable and careful woman can honorably earn her own support, there is no village that has not its examples of two heads in counsel, both of which are feminine"—and also in her own life, including hers with Anna Gordon, a reformer and composer she called "my loved and *last*."

In the West, the WCTU quickly became another engine that helped drive its burgeoning progressive movement: a broad coalition of citizens who supported reforms to address the Industrial Age's problems of corrupt politics and business, rapid urbanization, surging immigration, and accelerating economic inequality. Indeed, Willard stressed the union's solidarity with kindred organizations, urging her members to "stand bravely by that blessed trinity of movements, Prohibition, Woman's Liberation and Labor's uplift." Accordingly, when the WCTU reached the Pacific Northwest in 1883, its Washington chapters worked to prohibit alcohol and close saloons but also promoted literacy, built libraries and public drinking fountains, housed unwed mothers, and provided day care for working women.

As students in the "WCTUniversity," the union's members were also encouraged to apply the Do Everything principle to their professional and personal as well as political lives. For Catt, Willard, and many prominent westerners, teaching was a starter profession that led to a wider world, but similarly gifted women often remained underutilized in the schoolroom. Willard urged restless teachers to quit their jobs and take up an unusual line of work that forged new vocational paths for women while also freeing up their old positions for other candidates.

One of the most promising of those new professions was social work: an umbrella term for services that aim to improve the functioning of individuals and families, groups and communities. The field's emergence in the late nineteenth century reflected America's increasing openness to a progressive idea promoted by the WCTU and other public-spirited organizations: erstwhile afflictions of the human condition, such as poverty, ignorance, and vice, were problems that, much like slavery, could be analyzed and solved.

Even before it was recognized as a formal academic discipline in 1898 at Columbia University, social work was regarded, much like teaching and nursing, as a natural extension of women's nurturing role, manifested in its concern for children and families, the poor and disadvantaged. In 1889, as immigration surged, Jane Addams and Ellen Gates Starr, both suffragists and pioneering social workers, founded Chicago's Hull House, one of the new "settlement houses" that sprang up to respond to problems caused by rapid urbanization, industrialization, and floods of needy newcomers in America's cities.

Some of the women who served as the West's first de facto social workers were missionaries whose projects had moral as well as practical objectives. In 1879, the Women's Occidental Board of Foreign Missions appointed Margaret Culbertson as the director of the Presbyterian-run Occidental Mission Home for Girls, located in San Francisco's Chinatown. The shelter was one of two such large-scale facilities in the city designed for the rescue and reeducation of Chinese women forced to work as sex slaves.

The heartrending yet rarely mentioned history of prostitution in San Francisco's Chinatown was rooted in its Chinese population's heavily skewed male-to-female ratio, far more extreme than in the rest of the urban West. The laborers recruited by California's railroad industry were too poor to bring their wives and families. By 1860, the city had thousands of Chinese men but only 654 Chinese women, 85 percent of whom were prostitutes; ten years later, those figures peaked at 3,536 and 61 percent. Strict immigration laws that tried to limit the Chinese population to cheap male laborers worsened the imbalance; indeed, the Naturalization Act of 1870 even disenfranchised men who had already met the criteria for citizenship. That slavery was abolished in the US in 1865, followed by indentured labor in 1885, only makes the women's plight the more shameful.

Most prostitutes were young girls who had been either kidnapped or sold by their indigent parents to sex traffickers for as little as fifty dollars. Then they were shipped to the US and auctioned for as much as $1,000 or more. A few were bought by wealthy men and lived as pampered concubines. Some worked in elegant brothels patronized by rich Chinese and White men, the latter intrigued by rumors that Chinese vaginas ran east–west instead of north–south. The rest serviced poor laborers in back-alley joints. *Mui tsai*, or "little sisters," were not prostitutes but young girls sold by often well-meaning parents in China to work as unpaid domestic servants, frequently in brothels; at the age of eighteen, they were free and able to marry.

Brothel owners went to great lengths to protect their human property, and escape was difficult. Some prostitutes gave up and succumbed to drug addiction, madness, or suicide. Others managed to run away, were ransomed by Chinese laborers eager to marry, or contrived to get outside help. Between 1870 and her death in 1897, Culbertson and the city's other missionary-social workers collaborated with law enforcement in conducting raids that released thousands of Chinese women and girls.

Some prostitutes, however, did not want to be rescued. In her legalistic labor contract, Ah Ho, who had indentured herself in order to strive for a better life in America, acknowledged that in exchange for the cost of her passage from China, she "distinctly agrees to give her body to Mr. Yee [Yee-Kwan] for services as a prostitute for a term of four years." After serving her term, she "shall be her own master. Mr. Yee-Kwan shall not hinder or trouble her." Then, too, even women who wanted to be rescued were not exactly free. Many were grateful for the safe harbor, as well as medical care, food, clothing, and vocational training, provided by the missions. This very real aid, however, came at a price exacted by WASP women determined to achieve the two-for-one goal of reforming prostitutes and converting "heathens" at the same time.

The Chinese women had, at the very least, to pay lip service to their hosts' religious and cultural credos. They followed a regimen of attending church and learning English, domestic skills, and a respectable trade such as sewing. They were taken to parks and the beach but were not allowed outside without a chaperone. To advance society's goal of spreading good Protestant families throughout the

West, the Presbyterian home even played matchmaker and introduced the residents to gainfully employed Chinese Christian suitors.

Culbertson enjoyed a highly unusual public career for a woman and was venerated as a near saint, but her obituary in the *San Francisco Call*, headlined "She Gave Her Life to God," hinted at her vocation's darker undercurrents. Although the "gentle matron" eventually subdued even "the most ferocious of the kicking, howling slave girls," the paper allowed that on one deadly occasion, an "especially troublesome" resident gave Culbertson a blow "which caused an internal injury from which she never recovered."

The first Chinese women to arrive in the West were arguably the most ill-fated of its female migrants. In time, however, the number of Chinese prostitutes dramatically decreased. Most women married, found decent jobs that raised their families' economic status, and gave birth to a new social phenomenon: the Chinese American middle class. Few converted to Christianity, but many welcomed the visiting missionary-social workers' practical information on sanitation, health, and basic human rights, including education for girls and the banning of foot-binding.

One Chinese woman enslaved and dragged to the West to be auctioned off as a prostitute was later officially recognized by the state of Idaho as a pioneer homesteader. Fact and fiction are hard to tease apart in her story, but Lalu Nathoy, later known as Polly Bemis, was sold by her impoverished father, then purchased in San Francisco for $2,500 by a wealthy Chinese man who owned a saloon in what is now Warren, Idaho; her role there remains unclear. Somehow, however, she won her freedom, managed a boardinghouse, and married Charles Bemis. The couple became early settlers on the Salmon River, where they built a cabin at a site now called Bemis Point, fished, filed a joint mining claim, and won her legal status as a US resident. Neighbors remembered the tiny woman, whose feet had been bound during childhood, for her love of animals, nursing skills, and sense of humor. Her beloved homestead is now a museum on the National Register of Historic Places, and her astonishing story later inspired a book and a film both called *A Thousand Pieces of Gold*—her recollection of her father's real assessment of her worth.

During the 1880s, whether despite or because of women's increasingly prominent roles in public life, the national suffrage movement won no victories and faced increased opposition. In 1882, a passive-aggressive Senate formed a Select Committee on Woman Suffrage that was charged with considering "all petitions, bills, and resolves" on the matter, which it presumably did until it was disbanded in 1921. In 1887, as the Senate voted on and defeated suffrage for the first time, Congress also passed the Edmunds-Tucker Act. The law disincorporated the LDS church; required voters, jurors, and public officials to take an anti-polygamy oath; prohibited polygamy on the grounds that it was incompatible with democracy; and disenfranchised the Utah Territory's women.

In the West, activists also contended with escalating regional resistance. Listing some of their objections to the vote, the members of the Nebraska Association Opposed to Woman Suffrage, formed in 1882, cited women's unsuitability for the turmoil of politics, insisted that the vote would mean the end of their philanthropic work, and declared that suffragists were "anti-female, anti-family, and anti-American."

Nevertheless, western suffragists took some consolation where they could, starting with partial victories. In the Arizona Territory, activists introduced suffrage bills in 1881, 1883, and 1885 in the legislature, only to see them defeated, but in 1883, women won the right to vote in school board elections. In 1887, Kansas became the first state in the Union to enfranchise women for municipal elections.

Women candidates won all five seats on the city council in the town of Syracuse, and Susanna Madora Salter, of Argonia, was elected as America's first woman mayor.

In addition to these signs of progress, suffragists logged several important near misses. In 1880 and 1882, Oregon's house and senate passed bills that would have enfranchised women. However, temperance activists' insistence that suffrage was the shortcut to prohibition triggered the liquor lobby's robust counteroffensive, which in turn swayed the urban male electorate, and in 1884, voters defeated a referendum by three to one. Washington's territorial legislature achieved an apparent breakthrough in 1883 by passing a bipartisan law granting the vote to all American citizens and "half-breeds"—at least those who "have adopted the habits of the whites"—and even specifying that "his" meant "his or her, as the case may be." Joyous women voted for four years, during which time those who were also temperance supporters joined forces with "law and order" men to close down many brothels and bars. In response, a powerful Saloon League sprang up to persuade the territorial supreme court that suffrage was unconstitutional, and in 1888, women were disenfranchised again. "We have been despoiled of our crown of liberty," lamented one Mrs. Hansen, "and been deprived of our weapon, the ballot, with which we hoped to defend our homes and children."

Despite the suffrage movement's two-steps-forward, one-step-back trajectory, westerners increasingly moved beyond the moral reforms promoted by antivice campaigns to take on new causes in the political arena run by men. Like the abolitionists before them, some influential White women, first rallied by several remarkable Native American women, fought for the equal rights of a people of color before they had secured their own. In the process, they developed unusually influential public careers, changed public policy, and strengthened women's claim to the rights of full citizenship.

Ten

WOMEN AND THE "INDIAN QUESTION"

*Allow an Indian to suggest that the solution of
the vexed "Indian Question" is Citizenship, with
all its attending duties and responsibilities, as
well as the privileges of protection under the law.*

—SUSETTE LA FLESCHE,
NATIVE AMERICAN RIGHTS ACTIVIST

I N 1879, SUSETTE LA FLESCHE, a twenty-five-year-old teacher and
suffragist, became one of the first women of any race to speak out
publicly about the grave crisis facing the West's decimated Native
population. Serving as translator and spokesperson, she helped lead a
delegation of Nebraska's related Omaha and Ponca peoples on a tour
of eastern cities to protest the latter's threatened forced relocation
from their reservation. At the time, most Native Americans were not
US citizens, and the federal government considered many to be merely
its powerless legal wards. The young Omaha woman insisted, however, that their very survival depended on securing equal rights. Only
then would they enjoy "the privileges of protection under the law, by
which the Indian could appeal to the courts, when deprived of life,

liberty, or property, as every citizen can, and would be allowed the opportunity to make something of himself, in common with every other citizen."

The members of her influential, liberal-minded audience in Cambridge, Massachusetts, were predictably moved by the comely, ladylike La Flesche—also called Inshtatheamba, or Bright Eyes—who shed her usual Victorian schoolmarm's garb for traditional tribal dress to deliver her urgent message. (Indeed, Henry Wadsworth Longfellow himself allegedly compared her to Minnehaha, the heroine of "The Song of Hiawatha.") Joseph and Mary La Flesche, her powerful métis parents, had carefully prepared Susette, like her younger physician sister Susan, for assimilation into mainstream society. After graduation from the Elizabeth Institute for Young Ladies in New Jersey, where she wrote an essay published in the *New-York Tribune*, the proper Presbyterian teacher returned to the reservation determined to help her struggling people, who now faced a new threat.

After the Omahas were confined to the reservation, the federal government had put that tribal property in trust for twenty-five years, which made them helpless wards of the US. Roused to activism by the Poncas' looming exile to Oklahoma's inhospitable Indian Territory, the eloquent, bilingual La Flesche, like many Native American women before her, assumed the role of mediator with the White world. She joined forces with Thomas Henry Tibbles, a Methodist minister and journalist at the *Omaha Herald*, who was distressed by the Plains peoples' critical condition, and the pair soon organized a months-long lecture tour to win the hearts and minds of influential easterners.

Alice Cunningham Fletcher, a single, forty-one-year-old suffragist, former teacher, and founder of the career-oriented Association for the Advancement of Women, had what amounted to a secular conversion experience during La Flesche's presentation in Cambridge.

She had recently left her elite social circle in New York City behind to study the new science of anthropology at Harvard's Peabody Museum. Following the lecture, she switched her academic focus from ancient to contemporary Native Americans and took up a groundbreaking career on the Great Plains.

Fletcher's graduate school was the Omahas' reservation, where she spent much of 1881. Accompanied by La Flesche, she also traveled to the Great Sioux Reservation in the Dakota Territory, where she persevered through the rough camping conditions of a six-week-long field trip. The result was "Five Indian Ceremonies," a rigorously scientific report that made her America's first woman anthropologist, Harvard's first woman academic, and a pioneer in her evolving science.

Challenging the status quo came naturally to the bold, privileged Fletcher, and her meticulous ethnographical research disputed the conventional wisdom that Native societies were much alike. *The Omaha Tribe*, her definitive study later compiled with Francis La Flesche, Susette's half brother, and numerous other surveys she conducted throughout the West demonstrated that much like France, Spain, and England, each Native people had its distinct culture, complete with language, politics, arts, and even fashion. She also took pains to stress their humanity and sensitivity. During a bout of "severe illness" in the field, she was comforted by "the Indians coming and going about me in their affectionate solicitude," who "would often at my request sing for me . . . softly because I was weak."

Fletcher's extensive muddy-boots experiences among Native peoples taught her "to hear 'the echoes of a time when every living thing even the sky had a voice,'" and as an anthropologist, she wanted to make that lost realm "audible to others." As a self-appointed mediator between two worlds, however, she soon became fatefully involved in the politics that profoundly affected the subjects she studied.

Fletcher believed that the answer to the "Indian question" was assimilation, and she tried to shape the government's latest iteration of that principle. With her guidance and support, the original goal of reeducating Native Americans in the ways of mainstream society quickly expanded to include a fateful real estate scheme. According to this theory, the collective ownership of tribal land discouraged Natives from adopting the Protestant ethic of hard work, personal initiative, and "keeping up with the Joneses"—a contemporary reference to the wealthy likes of Edith Wharton, the writer and designer, née Jones. From this perspective, the reservation was not a homeland but a piece of real estate that should be sliced into individually owned "allotments" that would enable Natives to become self-sufficient Jeffersonian farmers.

Aided by her authority as one of Harvard's elite public intellectuals, aristocratic social status, and not least a strong resemblance to Queen Victoria, Fletcher made an impressive debut in national politics. In 1881, she coauthored the Omahas' official petition to Congress for the division of their land into allotments; when they received no reply, she appeared at the Capitol in person. In the following year, the federal government granted the Omahas' request, and Republican president Chester Arthur made her a special agent for the Bureau of Indian Affairs, charged with apportioning the Omahas' property in person—unusual federal recognition of a woman's involvement in national affairs.

In 1883, La Flesche married the widowed Tibbles, a father of two, then continued to write, lecture, and testify before government bodies on Native rights and full citizenship. Unlike many reformers, including members of her own family, she shared Chief Joseph's distrust of assimilation and proposed the same remediation for the injustices visited on Native peoples that suffragists sought for women: "Allow an Indian to suggest that the solution of the vexed 'Indian Question' is

Citizenship, with all its attending duties and responsibilities, as well as the privileges of protection under the law."

Fletcher was just one of several high-octane, upper-class women who, once mobilized by La Flesche, found compelling careers that amplified the female voice in public policy. While visiting Boston from her new home in Colorado, Helen Hunt Jackson, a socialite and well-known writer for *The Atlantic* and *The Century*, encountered the Omahas and Poncas, then was unable to "think of anything else . . . from morning to night." Already enthralled by the West, she now became "the most odious thing in the world, 'a woman with a hobby'"—albeit the unusual one of promoting justice for Native peoples.

In 1881, Jackson sent every member of Congress a copy of *A Century of Dishonor*, her comprehensively researched report on the government's shocking history of broken treaties with the first Americans. She hoped that the book would affect policy, but legislators were perhaps discomfited by a woman's righteous indignation, vividly expressed by the quote from Benjamin Franklin on the book's cover: "Look upon your hands: they are stained with the blood of your relations." When they gave her jeremiad a half-hearted reception, she was crushed. While visiting Southern California to restore her spirits, Jackson took up the cause of its "Mission Indians," who had lost the lands granted to them by Mexico after the US won the Mexican-American War. Like Fletcher, she secured an appointment as a government agent, then compiled a fifty-six-page report on the historic injustices these peoples had suffered. A remedial bill based on her research passed the Senate, only to die in the House.

Having twice failed to change the government's policy with

data—her former classmate Emily Dickinson said Jackson had "the facts but not the phosphorescence"—she decided to "set forth some Indian experiences in a way to move people's hearts." In 1884, she wove personal insights from her friend La Flesche and the life of Victoria Reid into the history of the Mission Indians to produce *Ramona*. The novel tells the story of the beautiful, orphaned mixed-race heroine, and Alessandro, the Native American hero, who is driven off his land and eventually out of his mind by American rapacity. Jackson bravely confronted not only the government's wrongdoing but also the reality and complexities of racial intermarriage. Highlighting Ramona's dignity, she wrote, "Her Indian blood had as much proud reserve in it as was ever infused into the haughtiest Gonzaga's veins."

Discriminating readers hailed *Ramona* as the Native Americans' *Uncle Tom's Cabin*. To Jackson's dismay, however, most initially focused on the book's poignant romance and its exotic western setting rather than the heinous politics and prejudice behind the protagonists' tragedy. She was devastated once more: "Not one word for the Indians. . . . It is a dead failure." She died a year later, unaware that her book not only became an American classic, reprinted some three hundred times, but also inspired the remedial legislation on behalf of the Mission Indians that she had hoped for. Like Fletcher, she had put her White privilege and talent in service to another people, changed government policy, and raised women's civic profile.

J ackson had to borrow from the experiences of La Flesche and Reid to create *Ramona*, but Sarah Winnemucca, the first Native American woman to write a book, drew from her own life to produce *Life Among the Piutes: Their Wrongs and Claims*, an account of her people's history and traditions published in 1884. Born Tocmectone, or

Shell Flower, near Humboldt Lake, Nevada, when the Northern Paiutes still roamed throughout the western part of the state and eastern
Oregon, she vividly recalled her first sight of White men, whose pale,
bearded faces reminded her of owls. Like La Flesche, she was an
equal rights activist from a prominent assimilationist family who
made sure she had a good education; for a time, she attended the
Academy of Notre Dame in San Jose, California, until some students'
parents objected to her race. Unlike the proper La Flesche, however,
Winnemucca had the dramatic temperament and colorful biography
that made her a media star.

In 1878, she rescued her father and a party of Paiutes during
the so-called Bannock War; this brief armed conflict involved the
US Army and the Bannock and Paiute peoples in Idaho and north-
eastern Oregon. Impressed by her courage and skill, General Oliver
O. Howard, who maintained good relations with her father, a tribal
leader, made the well-spoken young Winnemucca his translator and
scout, entrusted to race his messages across the desert. A front-page
story in the *New York Times*, headlined "A Brave Indian Squaw," remarked her unusual appointment by Howard and courage in con-
fronting a "renegade horde of Bannocks, Nez Perces, and Shoshones."

When her military appointment ended with the war in 1879,
Winnemucca donned ceremonial tribal dress and became a popular
regional lecturer on the subjects of Native Americans' equal rights
and the reservation system's injustices, including forced relocation.
According to Nevada's *Daily Silver State*, her "quaint anecdotes, sar-
casms, and wonderful mimicry surprised the audience again and
again into bursts of laughter and rounds of applause." In 1880, she
joined a Paiute delegation to Washington, DC, where she argued for
her people's land rights before Secretary of the Interior Carl Schurz
and President Rutherford Hayes. They gave her a sympathetic hearing,
but once again the government failed to honor its promises of help.

By 1883, Winnemucca was acclaimed as "the Indian Princess"—a favorite stereotype for "good" Native American women such as Sacajawea and Pocahontas—and encouraged by General Howard, she undertook a major lecture tour of the East. She gave almost three hundred speeches, testified before Congress, and met with important public figures, including philosopher Ralph Waldo Emerson, Supreme Court justice Oliver Wendell Holmes, and Senator Henry Dawes, the assimilationist and legislative champion of land allotment as "civilization not extermination." Like La Flesche, she also attracted the support of influential White women, including the educator Elizabeth Peabody and her sister Mary Mann, the widow of educational reformer Horace Mann, who aided her efforts to improve reservation schools and helped with the publication of her book.

In *Life Among the Piutes*, Winnemucca insisted that her people's culture was as essential to their survival as food and shelter. To counter stereotypes, she highlighted customs, such as elaborate courtship and marriage rituals, that were the antitheses of Native Americans' supposed savagery. Treading a fine line, she admonished mainstream society for paying lip service to freedom and liberty despite "driving us from place to place like beasts," while also appealing to its sympathies: "My people have been so unhappy for a long time they wish now to *disincrease*, instead of multiply." In 1885, determined to preserve her people's language and culture, Winnemucca opened the Paiute-run Peabody Indian School, in Lovelock, Nevada. Funding was a problem, however, and the school closed in 1888.

Despite the shadows cast by a turbulent personal life that included four marriages and bouts of drinking, Winnemucca worked tirelessly, courageously, and creatively for her people. Like Jackson, she used her literary gifts to thrust the cause of Native rights onto the national stage and in the process amplified women's voices in national affairs.

I n the early 1880s, Mary Bonney, an influential Philadelphia educator who had attended one of La Flesche's earlier presentations in
Boston, became alarmed by the proposed opening of the Indian Territory in Oklahoma to White settlers, which would further worsen
Native Americans' condition there. She enlisted Amelia Stone Quinton, an evangelical reformer and WCTU organizer, to cofound a
group that in 1883 became the Women's National Indian Association, the first nationwide organization to campaign for assimilation
and the wholesale reform of the government's policy regarding Native
Americans. Like the WCTU, the WNIA harnessed the power of
women united by a single cause and illustrated their increased confidence in extending their private moral authority into national politics. As Quinton declared, "the plea of Indian women for the sacred
shield of law" is "the plea of all womanhood."

The WNIA supported full citizenship for Native Americans but
also proposed to alleviate what Quinton called their "great sufferings
from barbarism, to enlighten their physical, mental and spiritual
ignorance" by "uplifting" their homes to the standards of WASP
domesticity through education. Working tirelessly to turn Natives'
welfare and rights into pressing national concerns, she campaigned to
build housing, libraries, schools, and churches on reservations, wrote
articles, gave speeches, and so mastered the art of petitioning Congress that one of her scrolls of signatures was three hundred feet long.
Under her command, the WNIA expanded to eighty-three branches.

Of course, Native American women had their own opinions about
White women's attempts at social engineering. By tradition, the
Southern Ute people regarded women and men as equally involved in
decision making. Quickly mastering the art of selective assimilation,

the women of their large reservation in southwestern Colorado adopted only those White policies that benefited their families and communities. They welcomed sensible advice from home economics, especially the sanitary measures that cut the rate of infant mortality. However, they dismissed the notion that "head of the household" was a male role and continued to earn income on their own. More women agreed to marry, but they rejected the nuclear family household and preserved their extended kinship networks.

The WNIA's greatest beneficiaries were arguably its White leaders and members. Like the WCTU, it was a woman-led organization that proposed political positions that became government policies—a major achievement by those who still lacked full citizenship themselves. Looking back from 1888, Mrs. F. H. Taylor, the organization's recording secretary, declared with satisfaction that until recently, women felt politically powerless to right society's wrongs but now knew that "with united hearts, and God on our side, we can do effective work everywhere for the cause of righteousness."

In 1887, reform-minded women, both Native American and White, were instrumental in successfully pressuring Congress to turn their goal of assimilation into the law of the land—an impressive flexing of political muscle. Indeed, Fletcher was a coauthor of the fateful Dawes Severalty Act, which divided up the reservations into allotments of 160 acres for heads of households and 80 acres for single adults. The law also established special "Indian schools" geared to the reeducation of children and conferred citizenship on land recipients.

Fletcher rejoiced that peoples hitherto "stranded between two modes of life" now had the means to secure economic independence and participate in mainstream society. In 1889, she arrived at the Nez Perce reservation in Idaho to begin the years-long allotment process in person, albeit under the disapproving eye of Chief Joseph, who suspected it was yet another government scheme to rob Native Americans of their land.

Of all the devastation caused by the Dawes Act, Native Americans' sheer loss of real estate is the easiest to quantify. By 1890, the combination of the government's sale of unassigned reservation land to the public—a provision in the bill—and deals made by speculators who plied Natives with alcohol before swindling them out of their property had taken its toll. The 138 million acres that the tribes owned in 1887 was reduced to 104 million; by 1900, to 77 million. By then, families that lost their land and the means of a subsistence living often became fragmented, impoverished, and plagued with chronic illness. Estimates suggest that the Native American population fell to its lowest number in history, from perhaps 600,000 in 1800 to some 250,000 in 1890. By 1934, when the law was revoked, just 34 million acres remained in Native American hands.

More insidiously, the model of assimilation promoted by the Dawes Act used reservation schools, churches, and government agencies to coerce Native Americans into abandoning their ancestral languages, religions, kinship systems, economies, and women's and men's roles. Children were sent to schools, often distant boarding institutions, designed to replace their traditional cultures with English, Christianity, and mainstream society's ways. Dislocated from their homes and families, they were homesick; many were traumatized, and some were physically or sexually abused.

Fletcher never officially acknowledged her grave error in contributing to the Dawes Act, but she soon abandoned politics. She devoted the rest of her life to scholarship and the founding of the Archaeological Institute of America, in Santa Fe, New Mexico. She died in Washington, DC, in the apartment she shared with Jane Gay, her life's partner, and Francis La Flesche, her scholarly collaborator.

The so-called Indian schools' philosophy was deeply flawed, but some of their teachers, nurses, and administrators tried to do the best they could for their pupils. Many belonged to the first generation of Native American professionals. Sixty percent were female, including Elaine Goodale Eastman, a White New Woman par excellence. Her intellectual parents had provided her with an unusually progressive education, and she was already a published poet when she studied to become a teacher of Native Americans at the Hampton Institute. In 1885, New York and Boston newspapers printed the accomplished young woman's account of her first visit to the Great Sioux Reservation in the Dakota Territory.

In 1886, Goodale returned to the reservation's White River camp to teach Lakota children how to assimilate into mainstream society. Proud of her unusual career choice, she wrote, "It was held a distinct adventure back in the demure 1880s for a properly brought-up New England girl to open a day school in a primitive Sioux village." The moccasin-shod teacher who spoke fluent Dakota and rode an "Indian pony" opposed certain government policies, especially trying to purge children of their entire culture and breaking up families by sending the young away to boarding schools. Nevertheless, her supervisors bucked considerable controversy in promoting the young single woman to the managerial position of "Supervisor of Indian Education for the Two Dakotas," responsible for sixty schools—a professional advancement for her even as the welfare of those she served declined.

Goodale genuinely liked and admired the "gifted, lovable, self-reliant" Lakota. During her six years on the reservation, she was "more than content—for most of the time I was enthusiastically happy." She visited with Sitting Bull and witnessed the growth of the Ghost Dance religious movement, which proposed that by performing certain ceremonies and songs, Natives could restore their traditional ways of life that predated colonization. She lived off the land with her friends during a summer-long excursion of hundreds of miles that they called their "Long Hunt" and she called her "pagan interlude." Like other well-intentioned assimilationists, however, she earnestly believed that Native Americans' survival depended on making a "swift transition to another pattern of life altogether," for which education was "the master-key."

In 1890, the lives of Goodale and the Lakota were transformed by the so-called Battle of Wounded Knee, which was actually an avoidable massacre led by the US Cavalry near Pine Ridge, South Dakota. Her eyewitness report of the slaughter that essentially ended the Indian Wars appeared in a New York paper under the headline: "Miss Goodale Blames the Troops for the Killing of Women and Children." While caring for the injured, she met and soon wed Dr. Ohiyesa Charles Eastman, a handsome Santee Sioux graduate of Boston University's medical school.

Approaching the turn of the century, New Women such as Goodale had greatly expanded upon the constrained, homebound lives led by their foremothers, but for most, their freedoms largely depended on staying single or divorcing. Upon becoming Mrs. Eastman, she adopted the staid Victorian domesticity she preached to the Lakota women and pledged to commit herself "wholly in that hour to the traditional duties of wife and mother." She wrote some articles and children's books, as well as *Sister to the Sioux*, her memoir, which was published posthumously in 1978. However, she devoted most of her energy to raising six children and supporting her husband's career, including collaborating on the nine books that made him a celebrated author, expert on Sioux ethnohistory and Native affairs, popular lecturer, and cofounder of the Boy Scouts. After thirty years of marriage, the couple separated but never divorced.

Goodale acknowledged the contradictions between her adventurous single life and her "far from modern" desire to be a proper homemaker. In the end, she blamed her progressive parents for her conflict. Instead of raising her to fit into staid Victorian society, they had educated her according to "ultra-modern theories, which stress individual self-expression at a considerable risk of faulty adjustment to society."

I n the process of championing equal rights for the West's oppressed peoples, some women developed important careers and helped extend women's political influence all the way to Washington, DC. Like the missionary-social workers determined to "redeem" Chinese prostitutes, however, the White reformers' own unconventional, independent lives offered a stark contrast to the model of traditional domesticity they often upheld to others. Moreover, many had a maternalistic, condescending attitude toward people of color that illustrates Victorian women's moralizing impact on public affairs at its worst. Yet history also shows that these women, both Native American and White, worked very hard, and sometimes devoted their lives, to furthering what they and many other well-intentioned people then believed were humane solutions to still-difficult problems. Counseling patience and persistence, La Flesche Tibbles wrote that "Peaceful revolutions are slow but sure. It takes time to leaven a great unwieldy mass like this nation with the leavening ideas of justice and liberty, but the evolution is all the more certain in its results because it is so slow."

Eleven

PROGRESSIVES
AND POPULISTS

Man is man, but woman is superman.

—MARY ELIZABETH LEASE,
KANSAS LAWYER AND POLITICIAN

T HE 1880S AND 1890S were a time of extraordinary physical,
social, and political change in the West. Massive federal
and private investment during and after the Greater Reconstruction had finally connected the region to the rest of society via
five huge transcontinental railroads and the telegraph. Its cities were
the fastest-growing in the nation, and the government continued to
encourage agrarian development by building dams to irrigate semi-
arid areas and promoting homesteading. In a mere eight months
starting in late 1889, six territories became states, which required vigorous debates on the rights of citizenship, including suffrage, in legislatures charged with writing new constitutions.

Energized and educated by their increasing involvement in public
service as community builders and members of reform groups such as
the WCTU, western women held forth in the political arena as never
before. Many were so-called progressives, who were alarmed by the

effects of America's rapid industrialization, urbanization, and surging immigration. Their particular concerns, however, were the corrupt machine politics and big businesses that dominated America in the nineteenth century's last quarter. Nicknamed for the fabulously rich Mughal emperors who once ruled northern India, "moguls" such as railroad titan Cornelius Vanderbilt and industrialist John D. Rockefeller and their giant new corporate monopolies helped turn an economy long based on independent farms, banks, and small businesses into a centralized behemoth. Champions of industrial capitalism who accumulated huge fortunes previously rare in America, these monopolists were determined to maximize profits by any means necessary, and either incorporated their competitors or drove them out of business. Many once self-sufficient citizens had no choice but to become "wage slaves" who toiled in the moguls' factories, railroads, and unsafe mines for low wages. In the West, many farmers lost their homes and livelihoods, which they blamed on the punitive rates exacted by the so-called robber barons' banks as well as their railroads, which were the only means of getting crops to market.

The agrarian West unquestionably faced a crisis, but its origins were more complex than the aggrieved farmers' explanation. The region still reverberated from the great financial panic of 1873, caused by a combination of industrial overexpansion and a drop in consumer demand. That same year, the Republican-mandated return to the gold standard had enriched wealthy capitalists but also reduced the money supply, tightened credit, and raised interest rates for average folk. As mom-and-pop farms struggled to adjust to the challenges of joining the national market economy, they borrowed heavily to buy more land, livestock, and better equipment in hopes of increasing their yield and income. Their overproduction boomeranged, however, dropping the price of a bushel of wheat, say, from a dollar in 1870 to fifty cents by 1895.

After her firsthand experience of the effects on her family of these great political and economic forces, Luna Kellie decided to speak up. In 1876, when she and her young husband and their baby arrived at their 160-acre property, mortgaged to a Boston bank, in western Nebraska's Adams County, they dug their starter home into a frozen hillside and spent their entire fortune of $400 on a stove, fifteen steers, a milk cow, and a plow. During one blizzard, they saved their precious cattle by bringing them inside to weather the storm with the family. That summer, as Kellie worked around the clock beside her husband to establish their first crops, she credited a single sack of flour donated by a compassionate neighbor for saving them from starvation. During the next few years, she was too malnourished to produce adequate milk for two of her babies, who died. When the couple finally managed to turn their homestead into a flourishing farm, all of their hard-earned profits went to the railroad that took their crops to market. As she put it, "the minute you crossed the Missouri River your fate both soul and body was in their hands. . . . [The railroad] robbed us of all we produced."

Some hard-hearted moguls explained away the crisis experienced by families such as hers with the new dogma of "social Darwinism," or the survival of the economic fittest. Kellie and other western women fearlessly broadcast a theory of their own: their terrible new vulnerability was caused by financial and political powers far beyond their control, from which the government failed to protect them. As beneficiaries of women's economic and social advances and as working partners in their family enterprises, they no longer lived in their grandmothers' West and were no longer willing to let the men speak for them in the public debate over the conditions that threatened their families' livelihoods.

After she and her husband started over again on a new farm in Kearny County, Kellie joined the Farmers' Alliance. The organization was the latest iteration of a broad progressive agrarian reform movement that began with the National Grange of the Order of Patrons of Husbandry. Founded in 1867 to offer social support to isolated rural families and to lobby government officials on their behalf, just eight years later, the Grange—an old term for a rustic farmhouse and its outbuildings—claimed 850,000 members. By the 1880s, the much larger pro-democracy, antimonopoly Alliance had hundreds of chapters and several million members, mostly in the interior West and the South. On the local level, the organization provided farmers with affordable co-op stores, mills, and warehouses that competed against the monopolies. Regionally and nationally, the Alliance lobbied for government regulation, if not ownership, of railroads and public utilities, the direct election of senators, a graduated income tax, the free coinage of silver currency to expand the money supply—and women's rights.

Like the 250,000 other western women who joined the Alliance, Kellie saw her work for the organization not as a radical gesture but as a natural extension of her role as an agrarian wife and mother. Somehow, she crammed politics into her already packed schedule of farm chores, care of her eleven offspring, temperance activities, and duties at her Methodist church. She coordinated Alliance speaking tours and publications that educated rural people about necessary reforms, wrote political poetry and songs, and with her children's help, published the progressive *Prairie Home* newspaper on a press in her bedroom.

Just as women such as Kellie supported the Alliance, it supported them. The organization did not officially include suffrage in its national platform for fear of limiting its national reach, particularly in the conservative South. However, women members wrote treatises, gave speeches, lobbied officials, served as officers, and like Kellie even ran for local office. She had been taught that "only the worst class of women would ever vote if they had a chance etc etc." When the men who ran the local school board tried to cut taxes by shortening the academic year, however, she suddenly saw that "a decent mother might wish very much to vote on local affairs at least." With support from her father and husband, she campaigned for and won local women the right to vote in school elections and have a voice in their children's education, and became a strong advocate for universal suffrage.

Later elected the Alliance's state secretary, the now worldly-wise Kellie, distinguished by her heads-up posture and knowing smile, electrified its annual convention with "Stand Up for Nebraska," her famously rousing political poem, which concludes:

> Stand up for Nebraska! Let no foot of her soil
> Be held by the idlers to tax rent from toil.
> Bid the hard-working tenants of other states come,
> And build on each wild quarter section a home.
> And soon the world over the watchword will be,
> Stand up for Nebraska, the home of the free.

By 1890, American progressives increasingly demanded answers to searing questions about the nation's priorities in the Industrial Age: What had gone wrong with the land of democracy and opportunity? Why did they no longer feel in control of their lives? Why did so many average citizens struggle amid the robber barons' grotesque excesses? Why did the government not defend the people's interests against those of Big Business?

Few individuals could answer those questions with the eloquence of Mary Elizabeth Clyens Lease, a western homesteader turned lawyer, orator, and national politician. She began forming her radically democratic political views during her hard youth in rural Pennsylvania, where her genteel Irish immigrant family was consigned to rural poverty after her father and two brothers were killed in the Civil

War. She managed to complete her education, and in 1870 moved west to teach at a school in Osage Mission, Kansas, where she soon married Charles Lease, a local pharmacist.

During the financial panic of 1873, Lease and her husband lost their homestead in Kingman County when they were unable to repay bank loans for farm equipment. They next tried homesteading in Denison, Texas, but again, they lost everything, this time including two babies. In 1883, the couple moved back to Kansas, where Charles found a job in Wichita, and she cared for their their four surviving children and took in laundry to make ends meet.

Already a suffragist and prohibitionist, Lease now focused her formidable intellect on the politics of poverty. She concluded that the government colluded with Wall Street's 1 percent to rig the system against average families, then took up the study of law. In 1885, she was admitted to the Kansas bar—an enormous achievement at a time when women accounted for perhaps half a percent of America's lawyers.

Wasting no time, Lease immediately plunged into the reform politics inspired by the national agrarian and labor movements that sprang up to represent the interests of America's working families. Wielding women's moral authority as a political tool, she addressed meetings of the Alliance, the WCTU, and the Knights of Labor, which included many industrial workers, and discovered a gift for extemporaneous, mesmerizing oratory that earned her the sobriquet "Pythoness of the Plains." Aggrieved farmers, miners, and laborers listened for hours to the rolling rhetoric of the tall, rangy homesteader-attorney with the brogue-tinged contralto voice and regal bearing.

Calling herself merely "an instrument in the hands of a Great Force," Lease accused the government of cooperating with industrial capitalists to render the people powerless. She leavened her jeremiads with biblical references and widely quoted aphorisms, though the one most identified with her—"What you farmers need to do is to raise less corn and more hell"—belonged to Ralph Beaumont, a fellow reformer. She eventually grew tired of denying authorship and simply endorsed the bon mot as "a right good piece of advice."

The homesteader-lawyer called "Queen Mary" by fans and deliberately identified incorrectly in the hostile press as Mary "Yellin'" Lease soon became a national celebrity. Her message especially resonated in the West, where the votes of a vast, disgruntled electorate were up for grabs. Neither the Republican nor the Democratic Party was strongly rooted in the region, where both were widely regarded as corrupt machines more interested in their own hegemony than the people's welfare. The vote was the one power held by average citizens—still mostly men—however, and many westerners were ready to cast theirs for a third party that, like the Prohibitionist Party, founded in 1869, championed a particular nonpartisan cause. The Home Protection Party, established in 1881, focused on temperance, but also agreed with Lease that "no government can be complete without woman any more than can the home," and included suffrage in its platform.

In 1891, Lease helped to found the new People's Party—an extraordinary achievement for a woman. Still the most successful third party in American history, it was strongest in the West and South. These new "Populists" endorsed many of the progressive principles advanced by the Alliance, such as a strong federal government, regulation of transportation and communications, a graduated income tax, increased women's rights, and the free coinage of silver. Their ultimate goal was more ambitious, however. They wanted to democratize capitalism itself to make it work for the people rather than just the rich, say, by giving farmers economic parity with business and industry by providing them with access to the global market. By no means doctrinaire, the Populists embraced modern science, the

Republicans' evangelical morality, particularly regarding prohibition, and the Democratic South's concern for the common folk, as expressed by its agrarian presidents Jefferson and Jackson.

In an unprecedented public forum for a woman, Lease addressed the Populists' national convention in 1892 at the zenith of her fame. She lauded James Weaver, an Iowa homesteader-congressman who was the party's presidential candidate, and others running in local elections, then denounced Big Business, banks, and "intolerant, vindictive, slave-making" Democrats. She saved her harshest words, however, for Washington, DC. The US was "no longer a government of the people, by the people, and for the people," she thundered, "but a government of Wall Street, by Wall Street, and for Wall Street. The great common people of this country are slaves, and monopoly is the master."

Kellie and thousands of agrarian women followed Lease into the Populist Party in such numbers that it sometimes seemed like an extension of the suffrage movement. At a time when both Republican and Democratic clubs segregated their members according to gender, Populists worked together in committees and shared power. Women as well as men voted in its local, county, and state elections, served as leaders and speakers, and ensured that female candidates were nominated for public office. Importantly, they also had an equal say in party policy, which in turn influenced state politics and laws, including voting rights, as Populists and other progressives were increasingly elected to public office.

To compete on the national level, however, the Populists desperately needed to maximize support, especially in the mostly Democratic South, where wary conservatives saw both temperance and suffrage as federal intrusions into their patriarchal private life. Like the Alliance, the party tried to dodge confrontation by throwing suffrage back to the states and territories to decide for themselves.

Despite Lease's insistence that "Man is man, but woman is super-man," not even she could persuade the Populists to include full en-franchisement in their official national platform.

While reformers such as Kellie and Lease continued to rally support for suffrage in the West, the national movement underwent a major structural and ideological transformation. To at-tract the overwhelming support necessary for a constitutional amend-ment, the NWSA and AWSA finally swallowed their differences. In 1890, the two groups merged into the National American Woman Suffrage Association and elected the frail, elderly Elizabeth Cady Stanton as president, supported by Susan B. Anthony. The new or-ganization was determined to focus tightly on getting the vote, state by state, and it sidelined as secondary other issues, such as temper-ance and economic reform, that many suffragists had also supported.

To streamline its message and broaden its appeal to social con-servatives, the NAWSA's leaders definitively downplayed women's equality as a rationale for suffrage in favor of the milder, pragmatic argument that, once empowered, home protectors would tidy up and improve the homeland as well as the home. (Even Stanton was crit-icized for writing *The Woman's Bible*, in which she disputed the tra-ditional religious principle of woman's subservience to man.) The association's municipal-housekeeping rationale proved to have wider appeal, but it also reinforced women's domestic identity, and its strong moralizing tone failed to assuage male fears that once enfranchised, they would overturn the age-old moral double standard.

As immigration surged and American society became ever more diverse, the question of suffrage also became increasingly entangled with explosive issues of race, ethnicity, and class, which led many of the NAWSA leaders to make a devil's bargain. To increase support for the cause, especially but not exclusively in the Jim Crow South, they fatefully assented to the argument that a vote for suffrage was a vote for White supremacy. According to this theory, the ballots of educated, respectable White women would counter those of the men of color and presumably illiterate immigrants whom they considered below them.

The NAWSA leaders and the supporters of the White supremacy argument for suffrage understood full well that the same Jim Crow tactics, including literacy tests and poll taxes, that already effectively disenfranchised Black men in the South would similarly affect Black women, including many of the hundreds of activists who had worked diligently for the national cause. (Even Frances Willard, the suffragist president of the diverse WCTU, indulged in race- and class-based slurs against Blacks, the foreign-born, and Mormons; she also repeatedly declared that enfranchisement should be contingent on passing an educational test.) Despite this grave moral compromise, however, the NAWSA made little headway, even in its home base of New York. In 1894, activists armed with a petition signed by 600,000 supporters could not even persuade legislators assembled at the state's Constitutional Convention to propose a suffrage referendum to the electorate.

For a brief but important moment, Lease and the People's Party upheld the possibility of real systemic political change, from socioeconomic justice to women's rights, but like the NAWSA, the Populists were undermined by their own regional, racial, and class divisions. White farmers in the West and South considered themselves respectable if temporarily cash-poor "real Americans" and looked down on the party's other half, mostly urban workers who were immigrants or people of color. Lease herself was sometimes pelted with eggs in the former Confederate states, which she loudly blamed for her relatives' deaths during the war.

In the presidential election of 1892, the Populists took the West by storm but failed to sweep the nation. Both major parties back East painted them and Weaver, their candidate, as socialists intent on establishing mob rule, and Democrat Grover Cleveland went to the White House. Nevertheless, the democratic, pro-women political ideology of the Populists and other progressives had sunk deep roots in the West, and the dramatic results were soon apparent.

Twelve

SUFFRAGE CENTRAL

Those women did noble work in the East,
but did not accomplish the political
emancipation of a single state.

—CAROLINE NICHOLS CHURCHILL,
COLORADO PUBLISHER

W HILE THE NATIONAL MOVEMENT struggled to gain
ground in the East, western women overcame two decades of legislative stasis to win the vote in Colorado in
1893, then Idaho in 1896. The two states not only gained the distinction of being the only ones to enfranchise women in the nineteenth
century after Wyoming and Utah but also made the American West,
along with the other settler-colonizer societies of Australia and New
Zealand, a nexus of global suffrage.

Where enfranchising women was concerned, Colorado and Idaho
had certain motivations in common. The People's Party failed as a
national movement, but it remained popular in much of the West and
influenced the region's powerful progressive politics, which supported
the rights of farmers, laborers, and women. Then, too, both states
were dominated by the mining industry. Silver miners, and their

employers, were particularly eager to empower women, including their wives, so they could vote to replace the gold standard with the free coinage of silver currency. Both victories also attested to suffragists' increasing success in building coalitions with other groups that needed women's support for their own agendas, including the temperance, labor, and agrarian reform movements. As the number of immigrants surged to 3.5 million between 1890 and 1900 alone, anti-immigrant factions eager to boost the White, American-born electorate played a role as well.

The Rocky Mountain region also boasted a deep bench of talented suffrage campaigners, including Colorado's Caroline Nichols Churchill. After leaving her home in Minnesota for the more salubrious climate of California, she became hooked on the politics of women's rights after protesting a bill that would punish San Francisco prostitutes but not their clients. She later joined the ranks of Victorian women travel writers, but like novelist Abigail Scott Duniway, is best known as a journalist and publisher who helped build western women's crucial political communication networks. Colorado's progressive spirit drew her to Denver, where by the 1880s she published the *Queen Bee*, her popular weekly periodical.

Churchill's self-referentially titled journal rallied women throughout the region with its mix of her own right-between-the-eyes editorials and diverse articles on women's welfare and politics. She dismissed the notion of the separate spheres as "twaddle," and when some male critics tried to embarrass her by attributing her radical views to menopause, she rejoiced that age and experience had made her "fool-proof as well as man-proof."

Unlike many prominent suffragists, Churchill courageously combated the era's accelerating racism, including within the movement. After an anti-Chinese riot in Denver, she wrote, "The Chinaman's greatest crime seems to be his superior industry, sobriety and living within his income." She even drew parallels between the injustices suffered by women and other oppressed groups: "The simple, earnest plaint of the colored people carried an echo of woman's condition. . . . Did we not help to make their [slave-owners] wealth? . . . Why should they now hate us that we are trying to do something for ourselves?"

Although Colorado's state legislature had considered several suffrage bills since the 1870s, the only one to pass had been defeated by the popular vote in 1877, and activists were determined to win the next referendum, scheduled for 1893. In 1892, Elizabeth Piper Ensley, a prominent Black educator, clubwoman, and equal rights advocate, migrated to Denver just in time to help. Born free in Massachusetts to politically oriented parents who had escaped bondage via the Underground Railroad, she had received a good education, including a European tour between 1869 and 1871. She then returned to Boston, where she taught school and established a circulating library before marrying Newell Ensley, a Black college graduate and minister. The couple moved to Washington, DC, where they taught at Howard University's normal school, a teacher-training institute, and then proceeded to Denver, where the state's Black population was centered.

Ensley immediately helped to found Colorado's Non-Partisan Equal Suffrage Association. This grassroots coalition drew support from women's clubs, churches, benevolent associations, labor unions, farmers' alliances, and both Populists and Republicans; it was also one of the few such organizations in which women of different races and classes worked together for the vote. Her executive skills were soon apparent, and Ensley was elected as its treasurer. Determined to rally the state's Black men to vote for women's enfranchisement, she campaigned tirelessly.

In 1893, sixteen years after Colorado activists' last attempt, Ensley,

Churchill, and the members of their diverse association waged a clever, quiet campaign under the noses of saloon owners and brewers. They spread across the big, mountainous state, speaking at rallies, organizing local suffrage groups, distributing pamphlets, winning endorsements, and building coalitions. The NAWSA helped by sending Carrie Catt, who had come a long way since graduating from her frontier land-grant college. She had first worked as a teacher in Mason City, Iowa, then at the age of twenty-four became one of America's first female superintendents of schools—a job she credited for developing her superb administrative abilities. Most New Women gave up their careers upon marriage, but after she wed the town's newspaper publisher, she took up journalism. Following his premature death, she continued to write and also worked for the NAWSA, becoming one of its top organizers and orators. At home in the West, she barnstormed her way through a thousand miles of Colorado, assuring audiences that there were "whole precincts of voters in this country whose united intelligence does not equal that of one representative American woman."

In November, supported by the Populist governor Davis Waite, thirty-three newspapers, and a powerful coalition assembled by the Non-Partisan Equal Suffrage Association, Colorado became the first state to enact suffrage by popular vote, which it did by six thousand ballots. Never guilty of false modesty, Churchill took a bow. Favorably comparing herself to more illustrious, better-funded suffragists such as Susan B. Anthony, she allowed that they did "noble work in the East, but did not accomplish the political emancipation of a single state." Indeed, she declared it unlikely that "another woman on the continent could under the same conditions accomplish as much."

Like other suffragists of color, Ensley had fought hard for enfranchisement to express both her sex's and her people's voices in public affairs. Wasting no time, she founded the Colored Women's Republican Club to encourage Black women to participate fully in civic life.

Abigail Scott Duniway, mother of western suffrage (center), with
national movement leaders Elizabeth Cady Stanton (right) and
Susan B. Anthony (left) at Anthony's home in
upstate New York, circa 1895.

Emmeline Wells, prominent Mormon suffragist and journalist, in 1879.

Clarina Howard Nichols, suffragist-settler who foresaw the West's progressive potential, circa 1854.

Clara Shortridge Foltz, the first woman lawyer on the Pacific Coast, in 1901.

From left to right: Sisters Blandina Segale, Eulalia Whitty, Marcella Heller, and Fidelis McCarthy, who educated and cared for the poor in the mining community of Trinidad, Colorado, circa 1874.

Dr. Susan La Flesche Picotte,
the first Native American physician, center, 1886.

"A pretty girl in the West," an illustration by Mary Hallock Foote,
who portrayed the region from a woman's viewpoint, circa 1889.

Annie Oakley, the sharpshooting star of Buffalo Bill's Wild West show, and unknown actor, circa 1902.

Frances Willard, formidable president of the Woman's Christian Temperance Union, on her bicycle, "Gladys," in 1893.

Polly Bemis, aka Lalu Nathoy, a Chinese American homesteader on Idaho's Salmon River, with her horses Nellie and Julie, in 1910.

Sarah Winnemucca, a Paiute suffragist and activist
for Native American equality, in 1883.

Luna Kellie, agrarian reformer and mother of eleven, in 1900.

Elizabeth Piper Ensley, prominent Colorado clubwoman and advocate for equality for Blacks and women, undated portrait.

Mary Elizabeth Lease

THE DISTINGUISHED
AUTHOR AND LECTURER.
UNDER MANAGEMENT OF
The Western Lecture Bureau,
WICHITA, KANSAS.

Mary Elizabeth Lease, Populist politician and mesmerizing orator, circa 1890s.

Caroline Lockhart, Wyoming's celebrated "New Woman,"
standing behind a bar, undated.

Hallie Morse Daggett, the U.S. Forest Service's first woman fire lookout, on the job in California's Klamath National Forest with her dog, circa 1920.

Elinore Pruitt Stewart, America's most famous "girl homesteader," on a horse-drawn hay mower in 1925.

Mina Westbye (left) at her homestead "villa" in North Dakota, circa 1905.

Jovita Idár, journalist and champion of equality for Hispanics and women, with her colleagues at the *El Progreso*, a newspaper in Laredo, Texas, in 1914.

Dr. Cora Smith King, Treasurer N. C. W. V., Leading
the Delegations from Nine Suffrage States in Suffrage
Parade in Washington, D. C.

Dr. Cora Smith Eaton, a physician, athlete, and suffragist famed for
planting a VOTES FOR WOMEN banner atop Washington's Mount Rainier,
in her role as congressional chair of the National Council
of Women Voters, in Washington, DC, in 1913.

Dr. Esther Pohl Lovejoy, soon to be the director of Portland's Board of Health and president of its Everybody's Equal Suffrage League, washing clothes while mining for gold near Tenderfoot Creek, outside Richardson, Alaska, in 1910. Her husband, Dr. Emil Pohl, stands to the left next to the dog.

Harriet "Hattie" Redmond, a leader of Portland's Black community and president of its Colored Women's Equal Suffrage Association, circa 1912.

MRS. HATTIE REDMOND

One of Portland's progressive wome
n who did much toward winning
the ballot for women in Oregon.

Representative Jeannette Rankin of Montana (left), the first woman
elected to the US Congress, with two unidentified suffragists
in Washington, DC, circa 1917–1918.

Adelina Otero-Warren, suffragist, educator, and the
first Hispanic woman to run for Congress, circa 1910.

In 1894, these new voters helped elect Black politician Joseph Stuart to the Colorado Assembly, where he fostered the passage of an important civil rights bill. Ensley soon became a regional reporter for *The Woman's Era*, the newsletter of the National Association of Colored Women, organized in 1896 by Mary Church Terrell, Ida B. Wells, and other prominent activists to give Black women a platform for pressing for suffrage and racial justice. She patiently compared women's political work to that of the chambered nautilus, "which after completing one house or shell proceeds to make another and so is constantly advancing . . ."

Idaho's politics, like Colorado's, reflected strong mining interests, Populist ideology, and anti-immigrant sentiments, but also added hostility to its powerful Mormon population to the mix. Then, too, after statehood in 1890, its demographics shifted to include many prosperous conservative farmers and their wives, who supported securing prohibition "By pen, by voice, by vote." In 1889, politicians had acknowledged the powerful connection between the causes of suffrage and temperance by taking the highly unusual step of inviting both Abigail Duniway and Harriet Skelton, the president of Idaho's WCTU, to address the delegates at the territory's Constitutional Convention. Seven years later, Idaho women won the vote with little of the usual legislative contentiousness. True to their promise, women prohibitionists later played a major role in making it a "dry state" in 1916.

After the victories in Colorado and Idaho, as American society grew increasingly fretful and conservative, the suffrage movement went through another dry spell, known as "the doldrums," that lasted until 1910. In 1893, historian Frederick Jackson Turner had famously forecast the culture's dark, brooding turn in a speech entitled

"The Significance of the Frontier in American History," delivered to fellow academics at the high-profile World's Columbian Exposition, in Chicago. According to what became known as his "frontier thesis," America's vitality and national character had been forged by stalwart men who continually pushed westward into the challenges of the unknown. Just three years before, however, the director of the US Census Bureau had announced there was no longer a point beyond which the population density was less than two persons per square mile, and declared the frontier closed. Now that men had conquered the West, Turner asserted, "American energy" will "demand a wider field for its exercise."

Turner's frontier thesis reverberated well into the twentieth century. Politicians now had an academic justification for the imperialistic foreign policy soon manifested in the Spanish-American War of 1898. As the leader of that short-lived conflict's fabled Rough Riders, Theodore Roosevelt, then New York's ambitious Republican governor, also capitalized on the era's male nostalgia and anxiety over the loss of the virile pioneer spirit, which he had cultivated as a rancher in the Dakota Territory in the 1880s, while mourning the nearly simultaneous deaths of his wife and mother. Warning of "a crisis in the fate of America," he admonished its now neurasthenic citizenry to take up the "strenuous life," marked by "toil and risk," to save themselves and the nation.

Men's worries about manliness were compounded by major shifts in women's lives and pursuits. Between 1880 and 1910, the ranks of those employed rose sharply from 2.6 million to 7.8 million nationwide. The number of independent-minded women who now made their own money, controlled their own affairs, and voiced their own opinions provoked an inevitable backlash. At the same time, the culture also confronted Freud's theories of sexuality, improved contraception, and other matters related to gender roles, including advice from the new female "efficiency experts" inspired by domestic science. In *Women and Economics*, published in 1898, Charlotte Perkins Gilman, a social reformer and prolific writer, unfavorably compared housework to mass production and advised homemakers to share cooking, cleaning, and childcare collectively—much like Mormon plural wives. Appalled reactionaries already disapproved of allowing women to enjoy the free time away from their domestic duties made possible by new electrical appliances, and they warned of an assault on the family, even socialism. Reflecting society's conservative turn, even some land-grant colleges restricted women from studying "male" subjects such as engineering and shop work, and wary suffragists began to speak of "civic activism" rather than revolution.

Tensions peaked at the approach of the 1896 presidential election. As the ripple effects of the crippling financial panic of 1893 continued to cause high unemployment, violent strikes, and many farm foreclosures, the Populists had high hopes, particularly after the Democratic Party endorsed William Jennings Bryan, their presidential candidate. William McKinley, the Republican presidential candidate, Roosevelt, his vice presidential candidate, and the rest of the eastern establishment, however, warned of mob rule and denounced the silver-tongued "Boy Orator from the River Platte" as a dangerous western radical. Despite strong support in the West and South, Bryan lost the White House by 4 percent of the vote.

Even Lease's bright star was fading. After she unsuccessfully opposed the Populists' alignment with the Democrats she hated and got embroiled in an internecine political dispute in Kansas, she became persona non grata in her home state. In "What's the Matter with Kansas?," a famous editorial written in 1896, William Allen White, the era's quintessential small-town Republican, answered his own question: Populists like the hell-raising Lease. Not only her politics but also her belief in advanced ideas such as evolution and birth control induced other critics to brand her as one of the West's suffragist "harpies" and a "petticoated smut-mill."

After divorcing her husband in 1901, Lease decamped to New York City and took up a new career as a journalist at Joseph Pulitzer's *New York World*. Like many progressives, notably Roosevelt, she was a walking contradiction of altruism and prejudice. Both championed democracy, so they favored suffrage and the direct election of senators; for the same reason, they opposed political machines and the monopolies' stranglehold on the economy. However, they also opposed the great demographic changes that were transforming the nation, especially the foreigners and people of color flooding into its crowded cities and agrarian West in search of opportunity.

More liberal-minded progressives believed that this population of newcomers and the oppressed needed Americanization, as the era's cultural assimilation movement was called, but others supported policies such as immigration restriction, segregation, and even eugenics. In her book *The Problem of Civilization Solved*, published in 1895, just in time for the Spanish-American War, Lease had combined well-reasoned Populist principles for socioeconomic reform with flamboyant racism and xenophobia, including support for the popular idea that the superior White US should colonize Latin America for its own good.

Her racism, biases, and ideological inconsistencies notwithstanding, many of the Populist principles Lease elucidated and helped to mainstream, particularly defending the majority's interests from the 1 percent's, paved the way for the reforms of the Progressive Era and figure strongly in the Democratic Party today. She remained proud that her work in her Populist days had not been in vain, not least because it had helped to make suffrage a national issue.

Like other American institutions, the national women's movement, by then sixty years old, grew increasingly conservative. Elected as the NAWSA's second president in 1900, Catt doubled down on winning the vote state by state, by any means necessary. She even locked horns with the WCTU, which had alienated potential suffrage supporters in large beer-loving immigrant communities in the West, informing its leadership that promoting enfranchisement as a strategic move to secure prohibition threatened the NAWSA's primary goal. She also reinforced the mild argument for empowering citizen mothers to serve as municipal housekeepers and the racist link between White supremacy and the vote. At one of the NAWSA's lowest points, speakers at its annual convention in 1903, held in New Orleans, stoked fears of the "Negro menace," while the shame-faced Anthony traveled across town to appear at a segregated meeting of Black suffragists.

Unlike the elderly Stanton, however, Catt brought a career woman's skills and a midwesterner's perspective to the East-centered organization. Determined to run a flashier, thoroughly modern campaign, she encouraged suffragists' fondness for using spectacle as a means of attracting attention to the cause, such as dressing in white for new, high-spirited public marches and clamorous rallies.

The West, too, grew more conservative during the backlash that followed the empowerment of its women homesteaders, college graduates, professionals, and voters. Even Lucille Mulhall, belatedly anointed by Roosevelt himself as America's first official cowgirl, stuck to the demure, feminine public persona established by Annie Oakley two decades before. Born on an eighty-thousand-acre Oklahoma ranch, the ninety-pound "Champion Lady Steer Roper of the World" often beat cowboys in riding, roping, and shooting competitions. Nevertheless, she was presented as just "a lively athletic young woman" who could also "play Chopin, quote Browning, construe Virgil, and make mayonnaise dressing."

It makes sense that Mulhall and other women who behaved in

unconventional ways would try to keep up appearances in the West, where even a New Woman was expected to go about her personal or professional business without disrespecting male authority. This theme animates Owen Wister's bestselling book *The Virginian*, published in 1902, which sparked a craze for Westerns starring tough, modern male protagonists who rejected tame, industrialized society in favor of the West's freedoms and dangers. He declared that Molly Stark, the novel's heroine, was not a New Woman, but the Vermont schoolmarm who went west to teach in Wyoming certainly plays the part.

The Virginian, the book's strong, mostly silent hero—"When you call me that, smile!"—is both intrigued and vexed by the fetching but "very independent and unconventional" bluestocking who asks lots of questions and wonders why she shouldn't enjoy the same liberty as a man. One day, he writes her a letter that includes a parable about a hen called Emily, whose progressive ideas have distracted her from her proper domestic role: "She was venturesome to an extent I have not seen in other hens only she had poor judgement and would make no family ties. She would keep trying to get interest in the ties of others . . . and she thought most anything was an egg. . . . She died without family ties one day while I was building a house for her to teach school in." Reader, she married him.

Western women suffered physical abuse at approximately the same rate as their eastern sisters, and one individual who defied powerful men famously suffered deadly consequences. In 1886, after divorcing an abusive husband in Kansas, Ellen "Ella" Watson arrived in the town of Rawlins, Wyoming, where she met Jim Averell, a local man of many parts who owned a general store and saloon. They later applied for a marriage license, and in 1889 filed separate but back-to-back homestead claims in Natrona County. She proceeded to improve her land and raise fifty steers, which aroused the wrath of several big cattlemen. These industrial ranchers zealously opposed fences and policed access to water in the vast lands in the public domain where they grazed their huge herds for free.

Watson refused to sell her claim to the cattlemen, and on Saturday, July 20, 1889, they arrived at her homestead, tore down her fences, and let loose her livestock, which they later claimed were mavericks, or young, unbranded animals that she had rustled from their own herds. Then they forced her, and later Averell, into a wagon and headed into the hills, where a witness saw them hanged from a pine tree. On Monday morning, members of a coroner's jury cut them down, and five of the cattlemen were soon arrested for murder. They claimed they had simply taken justice into their own hands to rid the area of two rustlers, however, and were released on bail.

Hanging a woman was a rare event, and Watson's received extensive press coverage. According to the *Cheyenne Daily Sun* and many other papers, she was "Cattle Kate," a prostitute and cattle rustler who traded sex for steers—a thieving, whoring Oakley *noir* who got her just deserts. Both the justice system and the press sided with the powerful cattlemen against the woman homesteader, and by the October trial, the case was dropped for lack of evidence.

D oldrums notwithstanding, members of a new breed of confident, college-educated suffragists, impatient with what they saw as the outmoded, low-key strategies of Duniway and the Old Guard, emerged from the West's progressive and Populist ranks to press aggressively for bills in its holdout states and even run for office before they could vote. In 1888, after a tuberculosis scare sent her to breathe the Rockies' clear, dry air, Ella Knowles set out to become Montana's first female attorney. Women were not even allowed to practice law in the territory, but after studying with a local attorney, the graduate of Maine's coeducational Bates College, where she had been a champion debater, persuaded legislators who had just rejected a suffrage bill to reconsider. To their amazement, she breezed through the bar exam in 1889 and three years later ran for state attorney general on the Populist ticket.

During her arduous 1892 campaign, Knowles traveled over three thousand rugged miles to fulfill her promise to visit every county in the state. The young, pretty "Portia of the People" used charm as well as reason to make her case for controversial Populist policies, as well as suffrage. (The *Atlanta Constitution* later noted that "the most remarkable and successful" of America's perhaps one hundred women lawyers was "not of the aggressive, assertive type that one would naturally expect to find" but was "mild, gentle, womanly, though full of determination, courage and energy.") Unlike the ax-wielding, saloon-smashing prohibitionist Carry Nation, who later told Kansas legislators, "You refused me the vote and I had to use a rock," Knowles appealed to voters' better nature. If Montanans would but "elevate woman, give her full freedom to use the faculties God has given her," they would be celebrated as "a people strong and self-reliant, intellectual, and valiant."

Although she won more than eleven thousand votes, Knowles narrowly lost the election to Republican Henri Haskell. (He promptly appointed her his assistant attorney general, then in 1895 married her.) While busy building an impressive legal career, she redoubled her efforts to secure women's full citizenship and became president of the new Montana Woman's Suffrage Association. In the election year of 1896, she ensured that enfranchisement was included in the Populists' state party platform by bringing a petition signed by three thousand supporters to their convention. The legislature nearly bowed to this pressure, but the WCTU chose that moment to wage an energetic prohibition campaign, and the measure failed by just five votes.

In 1902, Knowles put her career before marriage and divorced her husband when he disagreed with her decision to live and work in Butte. She developed a flourishing practice in mining law, campaigned for the vote, traveled widely, and argued before the US Circuit Court and the US Supreme Court. The suffragist hailed by Catt as "the most successful woman lawyer in the U.S." sadly died prematurely of a throat infection before Montana's women finally won enfranchisement.

Knowles was by no means the only New Woman whose personal life as well as political career were marked by the tension between the traditional and modern models of womanhood. In 1894, Estelle Reel, a single teacher from a socially prominent Democratic family in Cheyenne, Wyoming, took on the major challenge of running as the Republican candidate for the position of the state's superintendent of public instruction, then one of just five such important offices. By rail, stagecoach, and horseback through rugged country, she campaigned with gusto, and voters in the heavily Democratic state gave the lively, stylish teacher a landslide victory that made her an instant national celebrity. Chagrined opponents were reduced to making false claims that she had solicited votes by mailing her perfumed picture to lonely cowboys.

At a time when few women could even get elected to local school boards, Reel was one of the first to win an important statewide office, yet her behavior quickly revealed some ambivalence about her high-profile role. She performed so capably that she was soon spoken of as a potential gubernatorial candidate, but to the dismay of women's rights activists, she quickly ended such talk with a comment to the *New York Sun*: "The idea of a woman running for governor of the state of Wyoming is not worthy of serious consideration."

Considering her social and professional status, ambition, and support for suffrage, Reel's acceptance of the Victorian glass ceiling at first seems contradictory. Yet most Americans of the day believed that if women must have a career, they should confine themselves to seemly fields such as education, nursing, and clerical work while single, then devote themselves to family after marriage. Although she insisted that women should receive the same pay as men in those jobs, Reel declared that they should "not attempt to encroach upon offices which should always be filled by men, one of which is the Governorship." She also opined that suffragists elsewhere should learn from the example of Wyoming's women, who had been "extremely modest in their requests for preferment and power. They essayed no radical reforms and did what they could in politics and legislation in a quite unobtrusive manner." Instead of aiming straight at full enfranchisement, she advised that activists "first get the privilege of voting in school elections," then patiently pursue suffrage in local, state, and national elections, which "will follow in due time."

Reel was a hardworking, popular superintendent of Wyoming's schools, but education was far from the brand-new state's top priority, and her record of actual achievements was mixed. She won more money for the schools, but the male legislature refused her requests to require the certification of teachers and impose a statewide standardized curriculum. As she put it to a friend, "The politicians seem determined to make my office of as little importance as possible." Moreover, despite her strong objections, the system's sixty-seven male teachers earned fifty-eight dollars per month while its three hundred women received just forty-five.

Frustrated, Reel looked beyond Cheyenne to Washington, DC. To prepare herself for the leap, she accumulated valuable experience and credentials by serving on Wyoming's Land Commission and its Board of Charities and Reform. When the Republican Party decided to court both women and western voters, she stepped forward and was appointed as the state's campaign coordinator for William McKinley's presidential bid in 1896. She caused a sensation by attending his inauguration in the capital in a thousand-dollar Parisian gown, then won an impressive share of the victorious party's spoils: an appointment as the National Superintendent of Indian Schools, a significant federal post that came with the honor of confirmation by the Senate and a hefty salary of $3,000 per year.

More than twenty years before most American women could even vote, Reel presided over a busy federal department in Washington, DC, and a $3 million annual budget. To her credit, she worked very hard and even wrote *A Course of Study for the Indian Schools of the United States: Industrial and Literary*, a professional textbook. She also spent much of her time personally inspecting the nation's 250 far-flung Indian schools and their twenty thousand students. Transportation in the western outback was poor, and she often traveled by wagon or horseback; to reach a school at the bottom of the Grand Canyon, she rode a burro.

Despite her strenuous efforts, however, Reel never understood the children she diligently sought to serve. Guided by the conventional pieties regarding assimilation and racist assumptions about the Native students' abilities, she discouraged them from nurturing academic and professional aspirations that she and others thought unrealistic and promoted vocational training instead. Under her tenure, education in the Indian schools actually worsened, which ended whatever progress that William Hailmann, her predecessor, had achieved.

Women's artistry was the one important exception to Reel's blindness regarding Native Americans' creative potential. For all of its devastating costs, reservation life gave women more time to devote to their arts, which became another form of their activism as well as a much-needed source of income for their desperately poor families. Navaho textiles and Pueblo pottery were already prized by the discerning, and Reel vigorously promoted such works because of their aesthetic and historic as well as economic value. "The basketry as woven by Indians for generations past is fast becoming a lost art," she wrote, "and must be revived by the children of the present generation."

Reel persevered in her demanding federal post for twelve years under three presidents before resigning in 1910. Only then did the New Woman allow herself to marry. She settled down with her wealthy rancher in the state of Washington, where she died at the age of ninety-seven, long after many of those who had once thrilled to her trailblazing adventures and achievements.

Thirteen

NEW WOMEN SQUARED

*More independence here than
in any part of the world.*

—EDITH AMMONS KOHL,
SOUTH DAKOTA HOMESTEADER

DESPITE THE LAG IN SUFFRAGE LEGISLATION, a second, much larger surge of independent homesteaders soon fascinated an America trying to come to terms with women's rapidly changing place. Having claimed the equal rights afforded by the gender-neutral Homestead Act, then achieving success as landowners in an allegedly man's West, they were the personification of the individualistic New Woman.

Within the first decade of the new century, the number of independents in many places swelled from as many 10 percent of homesteaders before 1900 to 18 percent or more afterward. Federal stimulus was one major reason. In the Enlarged Homestead Act of 1909, a Congress eager to entice more settlers to sparsely populated parts of the West doubled the size of claims. Then, three years later, the government reduced the residency requirement from five years to three and also permitted filers to spend up to five months away from their homesteads, which allowed them to earn more income elsewhere while finalizing their claims.

The federal government's sponsorship of the twentieth century's massive homesteading revival enabled many more women and men of poor to average means to own land, but as with many Progressive Era policies, its motivations were both enlightened and reactionary. Officials including President Theodore Roosevelt, who occupied the White House from 1901 to 1909, also wanted to offset the nation's increasingly racially and ethnically diverse cities by populating the West with American-born White farming families in the hoary Early Republic mold. Indeed, according to Roosevelt, such young women and men were duty bound to marry and produce at least four children to preserve their race and the nation's identity.

The government might have preferred its western homesteaders to be native-born WASPs, but many were poor European immigrants, who soon made the Great Plains one of the most polyglot places on Earth. German-speakers predominated among the newcomers, who also included Norwegians, Swedes, and Russians. Their often poor English initially estranged them from mainstream society and encouraged them to cluster in insular communities that preserved the old country's ways.

In 1903, twenty-one-year-old Mina Westbye, an industrious Norwegian immigrant, had already learned English and earned enough money as a seamstress and maid in Minneapolis to embark on her carefully planned homesteading enterprise. She and two young female cousins filed adjacent claims on the remote grasslands of Divide County in northwestern North Dakota, sixteen miles from the nearest post office–store. These independents were no outliers but accounted for an impressive 18 percent of their county's claimants and 27 percent of their township's.

Some independents who came from prosperous backgrounds regarded homesteading as a "lark" that enabled them to delay sedate family life, but most had an economic motivation of one sort or another. A few intended to become farmers. Many more, including the four Chrisman sisters of Nebraska's Custer County, claimed homesteads adjacent to relatives' properties to enlarge the extended family's holdings. Still others, including Westbye and her cousins, were real estate speculators who wanted to improve their land, then make a profitable sale that would bankroll their next step up in the world.

Westbye was accustomed to hard work, but like most independents, she saw homesteading as less about doing all the chores herself than about making her own decisions and living in her own home on her own land. Despite the romanticized, eremitical gloss bestowed by the popular press, this rugged, agrarian way of life was still very much a community affair. She quickly hired local men to dig a well, plant ten acres of wheat and flax, and slap together what she called her "villa." Photographs show a hodgepodge, tar-papered shanty with a single small window, but official records approvingly noted its exterior paint and "very nicely furnished" interior, complete with curtains, linens, and a coffee service for entertaining visitors. Snug on her cozy homestead, she read widely, studied botany and theology, and cultivated flowers and a half-acre vegetable garden. At one point, she even enthused that "if I had been a man, I would have been a farmer."

Working-class independents often found local employment as seamstresses, laundresses, or housekeepers, but Westbye was among those who periodically commuted to cities for work. During her first year, she took the train to Minneapolis in December, earned money as a dressmaker during the winter months, then returned to her land in March to prepare for the growing season. On one occasion, an inspector came by during her absence, and she had to prove she had been off working to improve her claim. Making the most of her urban sojourns, she visited Norwegian relatives and friends, including Alfred Gundersen, a Stanford graduate and aspiring botanist, and also mastered photography. Before the art was redefined as a science, a trade, and a male domain, she was one of many women who earned income from taking studio portraits and even shooting photos for local papers.

Although not an independent herself, "Lady" Evelyn Cameron, an aristocratic British-born New Woman who migrated to Terry, Montana, in 1891, took iconic photographs of exuberant women homesteaders in looped-up skirts galloping bareback after cattle. She also made time to teach them useful skills, from plowing fields to the frontier medicine she learned from a Mrs. Kempton, her part–Native American neighbor.

Cameron and her husband left their upper-class life in England to breed polo ponies, but when that plan failed, she ordered a nine-pound camera and learned to operate it. Then she traveled around eastern Montana on horseback, recording family events and scenes of early frontier life, as well as taking the first pictures of North American birds in their natural surroundings. In her day, however, she was especially known for riding astride in pants. After scandalizing a sheriff who threatened to arrest her, she wore a specially made divided canvas skirt instead, which "created a small sensation," she recalled. "After riding into town forty-eight miles from the ranch, I was much amused at the laughing and giggling girls who stood staring at my costume as I walked about."

Well-educated independents had more employment options than their working-class peers. In 1907, after struggling to establish their claim between Pierre and Presho, in South Dakota, Edith Ammons Kohl and Ida Mary Ammons Miller, two sisters from a comfortable Illinois family, decided to go back home. After a posse of local girl homesteaders persuaded them to persevere, Miller found a teaching job, and Kohl was hired by a press that printed public notices. Next, they traded up to a better claim near McClure, close to the Rosebud Indian Reservation of the Lakota, where they opened what became the Ammons post office and general store. Kohl also started a newspaper, called the *Reservation Wand*, and later wrote a memoir called *Land of the Burnt Thigh: One Woman's Conquest of the Wild, Wild West*. The sisters found deep emotional satisfaction in the active homesteading life, which provided, as Kohl put it, "more independence here than in any part of the world. There was a pleasant flow of possession in knowing that the land beneath our feet was ours."

After five years of hard work on her claim and her new career, Westbye sold her homestead for $1,000, then used the proceeds to open a photography studio in Trysil, her hometown back in Norway. Her reverse migration was probably influenced by tensions in her romance with Gundersen, but three years later, he persuaded her to return to the US and marry him. Before finally settling down in New York's Catskill Mountains, the former immigrant servant had used homesteading to become an adventurous New Woman, a landowner on the Great Plains, an artist, a businesswoman, and an erudite vegetarian Unitarian to boot.

Kohl and Westbye were among the many ambitious independents for whom homesteading was a portal into their next personal adventures and professional enterprises, but few could match Elinore Pruitt Stewart in that regard. In 1909, the poor Denver laundress— a widowed single mother who earned two dollars per week—filed an independent claim on land in Wyoming that set in motion an unlikely new literary career.

Stewart's transformation began when she responded to a widowed rancher's Help Wanted ad for a housekeeper, then passed inspection at an interview chaperoned by his mother. She and her small daughter moved to his proved-up homestead in Burnt Fork, Wyoming, sixty miles from the nearest railroad, and five weeks later, she filed a claim adjacent to her employer's property. Many aspiring independents looked to their new way of life for a new identity as well as greater prosperity, and Stewart was eager to shed the poor servant for the self-sufficient frontierswoman.

During a hard youth in the Indian Territory, Stewart had had little education, but she was a naturally gifted writer. She regularly posted lively, often funny letters about homesteading in "blue and gold Wyoming" to her kindly former employer in Denver, who then showed them to a friend who happened to be the editor of *The Atlantic Monthly*. The magazine ran Stewart's correspondence as a series, later published in book form as *Letters of a Woman Homesteader*, illustrated by N. C. Wyeth.

Stewart's epistolary chronicle of homesteading enthralled her prosperous, well-educated readers, who were interested in both women's social evolution and the era's "back-to-the-land" nostalgia. Her engaging accounts mixed tales of a snowy frontier Thanksgiving and the complex marriages of her Mormon neighbors with praise for the new ethos of "rugged individualism." She manifested her particular form of protofeminism in a profound dislike of any efforts to "boss" her and her strong emphasis on women's ability to meet homesteading's challenges.

Positioning herself as her eastern fans' guinea pig, Stewart tested her skills by growing potatoes, beans, and tomatoes, raising poultry, and throwing herself into community affairs, then assured readers, "I can do any of it." She insisted that like her, any self-reliant, nature-loving individual willing to work "as hard as she does over the wash-tub, will certainly succeed, will have independence, plenty to eat all the time, and a home of her own in the end." To be on the safe side, she added that "persons afraid of coyotes and work and loneliness had better let ranching alone."

Most readers did not care that, unwilling to spoil her story, Stewart had initially failed to mention that a week after filing her claim, she married her employer, who then helped improve it. (As to the nature of their romance, she said only that "ranch work seemed to require that we be married first and do our sparking afterward.") Regulations prohibited a married couple from sharing a dwelling while homesteading on adjacent parcels, and though her groom tried to skirt the law by building her a house on her side of their property line, the structure was really just an extension of his. In 1912, Stewart was obliged to relinquish her claim, albeit to her mother-in-law.

By any legal definition, Stewart was not an independent homesteader, but she refused to give up the persona she enjoyed and embodied for many Americans. After achieving literary success, she bore three more surviving children, kept working on her family's ranch, now on the National Register of Historic Places, and continued to write about the experiences that endeared her and women like her to the nation.

Stewart was by no means the only independent whose unconventional career fascinated America and its media. In 1913, Hallie Morse Daggett became the US Forest Service's first woman fire lookout—a summer job in California's Klamath National Forest just ten miles from her homestead. Before being sent off to a female seminary for a proper education, she spent her early years in a remote mining camp in the region, where she acquired the necessary skills and experience to fulfill her duties at the forest's Eddy's Gulch station. The manager who interviewed her described "a wide-awake woman of 30 years, who knows and has traversed every trail on the

Salmon River watershed." He added that she promised to stay at her post faithfully, was "a perfect lady in every respect," and "absolutely devoid of the timidity which is ordinarily associated with her sex."

Tall, handsome Daggett was diligent in performing her duties, she wrote, "for I knew that the appointment of a woman was rather in the nature of an experiment." Three times daily, she scanned the vast forest in every direction from her mountain perch. Many fires were discovered in the evening, "when they look like red stars in the blue-black background of moonless nights," while others caused by lightning required "a quick eye to detect, in among the rags of fog which arise in their wake, the small puff of smoke which tells of some tree struck in a burnable spot." Other than chopping wood for her fire and melting snow for water, she found that there was only "a little—very little—housework to do" in her 12×14-foot cabin. Bears, wildcats, and coyotes abounded, so she added a revolver to her improvised uniform of sturdy knickerbockers, boots, and canvas shirt—a stunning contrast to the proper New Woman garb she wore in most photographs.

Puzzled reporters invariably asked why she had chosen such a seemingly lonely vocation, and Daggett did her best to explain by starting with patriotism. "My interest is kept up by the feeling of doing something for my country," she said, then added that "the very lifeblood of these great foliated mountains surges through my veins." True to her word, she stayed at her post for fifteen seasons, then retired to her nearby homestead.

The media that lionized WASP independents such as Stewart and Daggett skipped over women homesteaders of other races and religions. Despite the competition from outsiders eager to settle on unallotted reservation acreage made available to the public, many Native women managed to keep the land they acquired in their own names through the Dawes Act. Similarly, Hispanic homesteaders in the Southwest maintained the Spanish-Mexican tradition of honoring women's property rights. In Tres Alamos, a settlement in Cochise County, Arizona, Jesus Maldonado de Mejia took advantage of US law both to buy federal land in 1891 and to prove up a homestead claim in 1900. When she died in 1907, she left two hundred acres, two hundred head of cattle, and five horses to Rafaela Mejia, her daughter.

Many European-born homesteaders on the Northern Great Plains were Catholics, and by the mid-1890s, about a thousand Jewish immigrants, including some independent women homesteaders, had settled in the Dakotas. When Rachel Bella Kahn, a poor, eighteen-year-old Jewish mail-order bride from Russia, arrived in Devil's Lake, North Dakota, Abraham Calof, her fiancé, and her prospective in-laws immediately urged her to file for land adjoining theirs while she was still unmarried. Although perhaps abrupt, their request to increase the extended family's property was hardly unusual. While Kahn sewed her bridal dress, her intended arranged for a credentialed Jewish elder to marry them in exchange for two days of his labor.

During her wedding ceremony, the bride showed a Plains homesteader's resilient spirit by diplomatically submitting to what she regarded as her in-laws' "primitive customs." While the women guests sang to the accompaniment of the men beating time on tin pans, her groom covered her eyes with a flour sack, then led her to the huppah. To her dismay, her new relatives insisted that she remain blindfolded during the roast chicken supper. Following the festivities, which included the presentation of gifts—a red felt tablecloth, two chickens, and two undershirts—the bride spent the next months in a tiny shack shared with relatives, a calf, and poultry housed under the beds to prevent them from freezing. Apparently strengthened by adversity, Calof went on to raise nine children on a farm that became a social center for the state's Jewish families.

Most Blacks in the West lived in cities such as Denver, San Francisco, and Los Angeles, but by no means all. Following the Civil War, Agnes "Annie" Morgan navigated a complicated migration from Maryland, where she had been born enslaved around 1844, to join the second wave of independent women homesteaders in Granite County, Montana. She began her journey as a married cook, first on a Mississippi River steamboat, then worked at Fort Meade, in the Dakota Territory, where the Seventh Cavalry was stationed. Rumors that she was employed by General George Armstrong Custer, the regiment's commander, before his death at the Battle of the Little Big Horn remain unsubstantiated, but later evidence suggests that she was a skilled nurse as well as a cook.

In 1892, widowed and impoverished, Morgan made her way to Montana, where she joined about 1,500 Black residents. After she settled in Philipsburg, then a silver-mining boomtown, a prominent lawyer hired her to detoxify and care for an alcoholic relative housed in a cabin on a property in the Rock Creek valley; after his death, she stayed on the land. In 1894, she encountered Joseph "Fisher Jack" Case, a White Civil War veteran from New Jersey, lying beside the creek in the throes of typhoid fever, then nursed him back to health. He repaid her by fencing her still-unofficial homestead, then remained as her common-law husband.

For the next twenty years, Morgan and Case, who had a military pension, also sold their garden produce and hosted hunters and fishermen. She finally filed a homestead claim on her land in 1913, just a year before her death, which he later proved up. Researchers working for the Forest Service on the restoration of her cabin later found a bundle of items in the door frame of her home similar to those carried by the African root doctors who practiced the spiritual tradition called "hoodoo." The Morgan-Case Homestead is listed in the National Register of Historic Places, and in 2013, Annie Morgan was enrolled in the Montana Cowboy Hall of Fame.

Less is known about the intriguing Bertie "Birdie" Brown, a Black woman born in 1871 in Missouri, who migrated to Lewistown, in Fergus County, Montana, in 1898. Nine years later, she filed an independent's claim for land bordering Brickyard Creek, which she proved up by 1912. She raised poultry, kept a garden, cultivated twenty-five acres of wheat, oats, and barley, and lived comfortably in a tidy house shared with a black cat. Like Morgan, she enjoyed warm relations with her neighbors, not least because she produced very high-quality moonshine.

Conservative estimates suggest that about 160,000 independent women homesteaders such as Westbye and Morgan proved themselves in challenging environments to be men's equals, and some did even better. Between the late nineteenth and early twentieth centuries, they accounted for about 12 percent of homesteaders in North Dakota as well as Colorado and Wyoming, where 42 percent of them proved up their claims, versus just 37 percent of men. Thirteen of the sixteen homesteading states west of the Mississippi River enfranchised women before the Nineteenth Amendment, and in 1909, Elizabeth Corey, a teacher and an independent in Stanley County, South Dakota, underscored that connection in a letter to her mother back in Iowa. The woman who styled herself "Bachelor Bess" and prided herself on her financial independence and land ownership was vexed that she had to pay property taxes but could not vote. "Say, I've changed my politics," she wrote. "I'm going to work for 'Woman's Suffrage' tooth and toe nail and then I'm going to have 'em make a law." Based on her contributions to her community as a teacher and her success as a homesteader, fair-minded male neighbors surely found it increasingly difficult to disagree.

The West's independent homesteaders were powerful symbols of the New Woman and her sense of independence, individuality, and agency in an alleged man's world, but they seem almost conventional compared to its fabled female prospectors and miners. In 1898, Lillian Malcolm, a glamorous, thirty-year-old New York City actress, left the footlights of Broadway for the Klondike gold rush. Traveling alone, she drove a dogsled team over the dangerous Chilkoot Trail, nearly freezing and starving to death before finally reaching Dawson, Alaska.

Miners such as Malcolm often had to learn on the job, and her initial efforts at prospecting were disappointing. She slowly built the skills and strength to drill rock, set off dynamite blasts, shovel through debris for ore, and haul out samples, to say nothing of developing the psychological resilience needed to withstand long periods of isolation in harsh environments. Despite the challenges, she resolutely turned down chances to resume acting or marry, and the town's stodgy matrons' scorn only strengthened her resolve: "The day will come when they will not sneer at Miss Malcolm," she wrote. "They will not pick up their skirts when I come around."

Homesteaders found success by hunkering down in one spot, but many miners made their fortunes by moving from place to place. In 1902, when male competitors blocked her from staking claims, Malcolm left the frigid Yukon for new gold and silver strikes in the Southwest's broiling deserts. Tapping her dramatic skills, she earned her traveling expenses en route by telling tales of Alaska. In 1907, she registered a gold claim near Silver Peak, Nevada, then formed a company funded by eastern investors. Impressed, the *Tonopah Bonanza* acknowledged her achievement: "She is a hustler of no mean ability, and has done prospecting on her own account, both in Nevada and in Alaska."

After her celebrated Tonopah strike failed to produce as expected, Malcolm kept trying her luck in various locations in Mexico and California's Death Valley as well as Nevada, where she eventually dropped out of the public record. She never struck it rich, but she left behind another kind of legacy for the era's New Women. Wondering that more of them were "not out in the hills," she wrote, "Woman can endure as much as a man."

A miner's itinerant life was not well suited to marriage and attracted more than twice as many single women, widows, and divorcées as wives. Their disinterest in domesticity did not necessarily extend to sex, however, and Mary Elizabeth "Panamint Annie" Madison was among the few who juggled prospecting with ties to various husbands, lovers, and children. Complex relationships notwithstanding, she shared her colleagues' commitment to the adventurous, independent life. "When you're out on your own by yourself, there's no one to do it for you," she said. "You have to learn to do it yourself."

The women prospectors' rugged vocation apparently agreed with them. At a time when the average life expectancy for a woman was forty-eight, a study of eighty subjects, most of whom worked in the field for several decades, showed that none died young or on the job, and many lived into old age. They generally avoided the binges favored by male colleagues, but there were some notable exceptions. According to her great-grandson, Ferminia Sarras, Nevada's "Copper Queen," "kind of liked the other side of life too . . . the fancy side." She periodically emerged from the desert, headed to Los Angeles or San Francisco, checked into a grand hotel, and bought stylish clothes. Then she proceeded to "dine and wine and everything, just right up to the first class. . . . If she got a little bit lonesome, why she'd go out and get a gigolo." When her money dwindled, she would don her overalls "and take to the hills again and find another mine."

If most prospectors were content to prove their mettle in men's sphere, Ellen "Nellie" Cashman excelled in women's, too. By the late nineteenth century, the industrious Irish immigrant successfully combined prospecting, trading in mines, and running boardinghouses and restaurants with nursing the sick, raising orphans, and establishing schools, hospitals, and churches from Alaska to the Southwest. While in Arizona, she even played angel of mercy during the notorious Bisbee Massacre. When six outlaws killed four civilian bystanders in the course of a robbery, the murderers' hanging was promoted as a public spectacle, but she comforted the doomed criminals and helped tear down the grandstand. Her reputation for sheer goodness was such that legend has it that when gunfighter/deputy marshal Doc Holliday heard a fellow diner criticize the food in Cashman's restaurant, he cocked his pistol, which inspired the man to change his review to "Best I ever ate."

Other miners attributed the religious Catholic's success in mining to divine intervention, but like the independent homesteaders and her sister prospectors, Cashman was a phenomenally hard worker. She spent the early twentieth century in Alaska, where she mined, opened businesses, established another hospital, mushed her dogs, and was covered by the Associated Press. For her extraordinary adventures and prodigious good works, she was later honored by the United States Postal Service with the "Frontier Angel" first-class stamp in its popular Legends of the West series. Cashman, like the independents and prospectors alongside her, personified the West's New Women, including those who were developing a modern lifestyle that the East was moving to emulate.

Fourteen

THE EAST LOOKS WEST

*Petticoats are no bar to progress
in either writing or ranching.*

—CAROLINE LOCKHART,
WYOMING AUTHOR AND CATTLE QUEEN

B Y THE EARLY TWENTIETH CENTURY, the West might have
been more like the rest of America, but it was also becoming
more like the West. As mainstream society increasingly
looked to the region for insights into the future, its next generation of
New Women, from artists and writers to the members of its civic-
minded clubs, demonstrated the inextricable ties between their sex's
social and economic advances and their political progress.

Women played an important role in developing the West's distinctive aesthetics. Julia Morgan, California's first female architect,
and other designers in the trendsetting Bay Area rejected the fussy
Victorian sensibility popular in the East. To develop a home suited
to the fresh, contemporary, western way of life, they borrowed from
the earlier British Arts and Crafts movement. Its designers countered
the Industrial Age's soulless mass production with natural materials,

handwrought details, and simpler forms, such as the bungalow: a low, compact house with veranda that debuted during the British Raj in India (the term derives from "Bengal").

The westerners' most popular creation was America's first modern, low-maintenance, outdoors-oriented home: the Craftsman bungalow. Well suited to California and milder parts of the Pacific Northwest, the house also met the criteria of the region's forward-looking homemakers. Unlike drafty, inconvenient old farmhouses and ornate Victorian honeycombs segmented into numerous rooms for separate functions, the Craftsman combined adaptable, open spaces and the latest mechanical systems with handcrafted cabinetry and cozy fireplaces. Patios and porches took advantage of the region's beauty and climate to blend indoors and outside.

Western women's preference for a more relaxed, casual lifestyle—and for their own pursuits over housework—had historical roots. The nomadic culture of the region's early mining, cattle, and timber towns had long deconstructed domesticity and distributed its elements among boardinghouses, hotels, restaurants, laundries, and tailor shops. As far back as the 1860s, Isabelle Saxon, a Briton who spent five years in San Francisco, had tut-tutted about young couples "averse to the anxieties of housekeeping," who "commonly take up their abode, at least for the earlier years of marriage, at some fashionable hotel or boarding-house."

Morgan designed more than seven hundred buildings, but the first to be celebrated was the North Star House, executed in the West's haute Arts and Crafts style on the grounds of the North Star gold mine, near Grass Valley, California. Far from a bungalow, the ten-thousand-square-foot modern mansion, completed in 1905, included meeting rooms, guest accommodations, and the living quarters of the mine's superintendents. (The first was Arthur Foote, which enabled Morgan to consult with Mary Hallock Foote, an experienced western hostess, on the house's interior design.) Centered on an airy court-yard, the building incorporated local materials, including rocks flecked with gold, that blended with its bucolic setting.

The North Star House was a splashy debut in a career that had been unusual from the start. In 1894, the West still had no architecture school, so Morgan studied engineering at the University of California, Berkeley, under Bernard Maybeck, a wonderful Arts and Crafts architect who recognized her talent. She completed her professional education at the famed École des Beaux-Arts in Paris, then returned to her beloved Bay Area via New York City, where she turned down a job at her cousin Pierre LeBrun's prestigious architectural firm.

Back in San Francisco, Morgan developed her unique blend of Beaux-Arts classicism and California's Arts and Crafts naturalism. As one of America's perhaps fifty women architects, she initially struggled to develop a practice, but she soon found a major patron in Phoebe Apperson Hearst; the prominent mother of William Randolph Hearst, the publishing mogul, helped her secure the North Star commission. Following the San Francisco earthquake of 1906, Morgan restored the elegant Fairmont Hotel and the Merchants Exchange Building, which became her headquarters for more than forty years. A solitary person who never married and vacationed alone, often on tramp steamers, she seemingly had little time for anything but architecture. She even refused to discuss her work, insisting that her buildings speak for themselves.

Morgan designed churches, banks, offices, schools, and homes, but she took a special interest in architecture that fostered women's progress. In 1904, she designed an unusual concrete Mission-style bell tower for Mills College, a women's school in Oakland, followed by six more buildings that showcased her mastery of western light and made the campus a landmark of modern architecture. She later developed an especially fruitful collaboration with the Young Women's Christian Association, which provided housing and recreation for many newcomers flocking to western cities for work or study. Her grand Y buildings, still operating in Oakland, San Francisco, Pasadena, and Salt Lake City, safely sheltered their young, transient residents while also dignifying their ambitious quests with first-class amenities such as handsome courtyards, pools, and chic modern décor.

Morgan went on to design many homes, including the Arts and Crafts–style "hostess houses" that the YWCA later commissioned for army bases. In these homey settings, soldiers could relax with their families, gathered around glowing fireplaces, before their deployments. Her best-known house, however, is by no means cozy. In 1919, she first envisioned what became Hearst Castle, William Randolph Hearst's grand coastal estate high above San Simeon, California, as "a sort of village on a mountain top." For nearly twenty years, she devoted her weekends to working on the vast complex, which included a zoo. Pleased that her patron had chosen a forward-looking western woman architect to design what became a state monument and major tourism site, she paid him high praise for never attempting "to make the buildings themselves other than modern."

Just as Morgan influenced mainstream Americans' ideas about modern women and their homes, Mary Elizabeth Colter shaped their vision of the "Old West," which soon permeated the culture, from the great national parks to suburbia's one-story "ranch house" and its Spanish Colonial and Pueblo Revival cousins. Another very private professional who seemed married to her work, the Stetson-crowned, booted, chain-smoking designer grew up in St. Paul, Minnesota, where she became fascinated by the western rail hub's trains and the local Lakota people's paintings. From 1886 to 1891, she studied at what is now the San Francisco Art Institute, worked as an architectural apprentice, and reveled in California's cultural and physical environment. There were few professional opportunities for women in architecture, however, and she returned to St. Paul, where she taught drafting and mechanical drawing. While vacationing in California in 1901, Colter stopped by a souvenir shop run by the Fred Harvey Company, founded by the creator of the Harvey House restaurant chain, who shared her love of Native arts and railroads; he died that same year. After she informed the management that she disapproved of the way their store displayed artifacts, the firm hired her to help design, decorate, and furnish the hotels, trains, restaurants, and shops that it operated in partnership with the Atchison, Topeka & Santa Fe Railway.

By 1906, the burgeoning tourism industry urged vacationers to "See Europe if you will, but see America first," and people tired of Niagara Falls and the Great Lakes increasingly headed to the West's national parks. Their junkets were promoted as patriotic, historical treks in which covered wagons were replaced by trains, then cars, bound for the federal government's carefully preserved cross sections of a "primitive" frontier from a barely distant past.

Colter shared Harvey's vision of a new cultural tourism that was designed to educate the public about the West's ancient and modern history, and she expressed it in important buildings in the Grand Canyon National Park. (Recent controversy disputes the National Park Service's assertion, shared by many art historians, that she was the principal architect of some of its major projects, but the issue remains to be settled.) The Grand Canyon structures officially attributed to her often share the timeless quality associated with ruins and sacred places, achieved through a combination of traditional craftsmanship and modern engineering. The seemingly archaic stone walls of the seventy-foot-tall Indian Watchtower at Desert View were reinforced with steel by the railroad's bridge builders; inside, the "pre-historic" pictographs and petroglyphs that illustrate the local Hopi people's origin story are ingenious modern reproductions. Designed as a showcase for Native pottery, jewelry, and rugs, the log-beamed interior of Hopi House, one of the park's most admired buildings, shows an extraordinary attention to detail, from its ceiling made from woven saplings and grasses coated with mud to its fireplaces built from broken Hopi pottery.

It seems only fitting that Nampeyo, or Snake That Does Not Bite, a Hopi-Tewa woman internationally recognized as the early twentieth century's greatest Native ceramicist, lived and worked in Hopi House in 1905 during its first year of operation. Born in 1856 at the Tewa village on Arizona's Hopi reservation, she belonged to a people whose "customs and ceremonies and their religion went back to water," wrote Willa Cather, and for whom the women's pottery was "the envelope and sheath of the precious element itself."

After an apprenticeship with her grandmother and many trips to pick up shards of prehistoric Sikyatki ceramics, Nampeyo developed her celebrated, flowing "Hopi Revival" painting style. At first she copied the ancient patterns, she said, "but now, I just close my eyes and see designs and I paint them." By the early twentieth century, her ceramics were sought by museums as well as collectors, and a century later, one of her pots sold for $350,000. Most average tourists were unfamiliar with Nampeyo's artistry, but many nevertheless encountered the beautiful Native woman on the travel posters that Harvey had designed to lure them to the Southwest. In a nostalgic America that mistakenly mourned the demise of "real Indians," who were very much alive, if not always well, the attention and patronage of serious, well-informed connoisseurs such as Colter and Harvey helped create a market for Native arts.

Colter's undisputed mastery of western interior design was famously illustrated by the Super Chief, the AT&SF railway's flagship, which carried movie stars and socialites from Chicago to Los Angeles until airlines dominated long-distance trips. Her fusion of modern Art Deco and the sleek aesthetics of the Southwest's Mimbres people made the elegant passenger train the last word in glamorous travel.

L ike Morgan, Colter, and Nampeyo, female writers continued to shape society's sense of the West and its women's engagement in American life. In the early twentieth century, Zitkala-Sa, or Red Bird, also known as Gertrude Simmons Bonnin, educated the influential readers of *The Atlantic Monthly* and *Harper's Monthly* about the contemporary Native American's struggle to straddle two worlds—the great theme that she explored in literature, music, and politics throughout her life. The daughter of Iyohiwin, a Dakota woman also known as Ellen Simmons, and an absentee White father, she was born on South Dakota's Yankton Indian Reservation. As a small child, she was sent to be reeducated in mainstream American ways at White's Institute, a Quaker boarding school in Wabash, Indiana, where she was called Gertrude. Torn between her own heritage's pull and modern society's push, she had hated being forced to recite Christian prayers at school yet loved developing her intellectual, artistic, and musical gifts. In 1895, while a freshman at Earlham College, she won first prize in the school's oratorical contest with a speech on women's equal rights called "Side by Side"—an egalitarian argument she later made for the relationship between Native and White Americans. Next, the young suffragist and self-described pagan studied violin at the New England Conservatory of Music, in Boston, then taught music for two years at the assimilationist Indian Industrial School in Carlisle, Pennsylvania; in 1900, she toured Europe with its band.

Zitkala-Sa was a talented musician, but her most powerful

instrument proved to be the pen. In a celebrated story called "The Big Red Apples," based on her bittersweet experience of being sent away to school, she drew bold analogies between her eight-year-old self and the biblical Eve, and her reservation and Eden. After all, both the first woman and the little Native girl had been seduced by an apple, whether offered by Satan or a Quaker missionary, and its promise of special knowledge. In "The School Days of an Indian Girl," she contrasted her reservation's outdoor freedoms with her boarding school's "civilizing machine," yet admitted that when back at home, she felt like "neither a wild Indian nor a tame one."

In 1902, Zitkala-Sa married army captain Raymond Bonnin, a man of Yankton Dakota ancestry, then moved to the Uintah-Ouray reservation in Utah, where he was an agent for the Bureau of Indian Affairs. The *Salt Lake Tribune* took notice that theirs was "considered a marriage in high life among their people" and that the bride's "quaint productions are equal to those of Kipling." She missed her previous literary world, but like most New Women, she "put family first" and spent ten years focused on raising her son and only child and participating in reservation life.

Just as Zitkala-Sa used a woman's voice to counter the widespread assumption, reaffirmed by government policy, that Native Americans were meekly relinquishing their cultures and disappearing into mainstream society, Wyoming's Caroline Lockhart subverted the popular characterization of the West as the macho domain of laconic cowboys in blue jeans. Like Owen Wister, Lockhart set her novels in the twentieth century, but the swashbuckling writer and poster girl for the New Woman often featured female characters who, like her, considered themselves entitled to the freewheeling, individualistic way of life traditionally limited to men.

Upsetting the status quo had been second nature to Lockhart since a wild youth spent on horseback and doing as she liked on her indulgent widowed father's Kansas ranch. In 1889, he sent the eighteen-year-old to be tamed at the Moravian Seminary in Bethlehem, Pennsylvania. By the time she graduated a year later, she had a new stepmother she disliked, and armed with an allowance, voluptuous blond good looks, and plenty of nerve, she headed to Boston to launch an acting career. Her theatrical hopes were in vain, but she was the right woman in the right place at the right time to take advantage of another opportunity.

Inspired by the vogue for adventurous "girl stunt reporters" initiated by the *New York World*'s Nellie Bly, Lockhart took up journalism. Explaining a career decision that "came out of clear sky" with characteristic élan, she later wrote, "Nellie Bly was making history at the time so why couldn't I?" Given a chance by the *Boston Post*, she quickly discovered a talent for daredevil journalism. She fearlessly explored the bottom of Boston Harbor in a diving suit, leapt into a fire department safety net, and posed as an addict to uncover abuses at the Home for Intemperate Women. When she wrote a saucy front-page feature on Buffalo Bill Cody, then on tour, that mentioned he had appeared hungover during their interview, he responded by giving her a horse.

In 1901, Lockhart's already eventful life was transformed again when the Philadelphia *Bulletin* sent her to Montana to write about its Blackfeet people. She fell in love with the Rocky Mountain region and its already waning cowboy culture, and three years later relocated to Cody, Wyoming, where she became a town mother, albeit of an admittedly ornery, hard-drinking, philandering sort. In time, she published the local newspaper and also cofounded the famous Cody Stampede, an ongoing annual rodeo and celebration of cowboy culture. The little community was named for and promoted by the showman, but by the turn of the century, even Buffalo Bill, once a near demigod, was in eclipse. The government's robust support of homesteading had spread the sedate farming society, oil was the new gold, and horsepower increasingly came from engines. Even Wyoming showed signs of fusing with the homogenized Midwest.

Determined that Americans would not dismiss what many already nostalgically called the Old West, Lockhart updated its image with contemporary fiction that challenged stale stereotypes of good guys and bad guys, race and gender. The eponymous protagonist of *Me-Smith*, published in 1911, is an especially bad White man who shoots a Native in the back to steal his blanket, then tries to swindle Prairie Flower, the benign Native American widow of a White rancher, out of her property by promising marriage. In Susie, Prairie Flower's mixed-race sixteen-year-old daughter, Lockhart forecasts her later adventurous heroines. No conventional "tawny skinned" shy maiden, she rides her galloping pony "like a cowboy," radiates capability with a "suggestion of boyishness," and undermines the villain until the local Native Americans' sense of justice prevails.

Readers praised Lockhart's page-turners for what they considered her realistic picture of western life, which grew even grittier in *The Lady Doc*. The protagonist is an unscrupulous, unqualified Wyoming practitioner who pursued medicine strictly for the money, performed abortions, and flirted with women. When Lockhart's neighbors read the book, the model for the villainess was among those who unhappily recognized themselves in the alleged fiction. Her success as a writer of such unconventional Westerns is especially remarkable because, unlike Bertha Muzzy Cowan, a master of the genre who went by the ambiguous B. M. Bower, she used her own, obviously female name.

By 1911, a former ranch outside Los Angeles, called Hollywood by its developer, boasted a movie studio on Sunset Boulevard, soon followed by twenty more, and producers took notice of Lockhart's sagas. They admired the western argot that animates *The Fighting Shepherdess*, which she based on the life of Lucy Morrison Moore, the so-called Sheep Queen of Wyoming: "Sence we're speakin' plain, I don't like you nohow. I don't like the way you act; I don't like the way you talk; I don't like the way your face grows on you; I don't like nothin' about you, and ef I never see you agin it'll be soon enough." After that book and *The Man from Bitter Roots* became major movies, she even went to Hollywood to discuss filming *The Dude Wrangler*, her next Western, with Douglas Fairbanks, a screen idol. Although the perennially youthful Lockhart enjoyed unofficial liaisons with various men, including the rodeo star Pinky Gist, she apparently resisted Fairbanks's legendary charms.

Lockhart never joined the suffrage movement, but like her, her unconventional female characters, both admirable and villainous, were powerful personifications of social change. At the age of fifty-four, she declared that "Petticoats are no bar to progress in either writing or ranching" and became a "cattle queen" in her own right on her six-thousand-acre L Slash Heart Ranch on Montana's Bighorn River, where "the drone of the motor car is unknown." Late in life, she wrote, "There are no old timers left anymore. I feel like the last leaf on the tree." When she died at the age of ninety-one, her ashes were scattered over her beloved ranch, which is now a National Park Service tourism site.

Although she became one of America's most popular cowgirls, Tillie Baldwin had not been born in the United States, much less in the West. In 1902, Anna Mathilda Winger left Arendal, Norway, for New York City at the age of fourteen, planning to become a hairdresser. Then she happened to see a performance by Will Rogers, the part-Cherokee cowboy from Oklahoma who began his legendary show business career performing stunts on his pony. The natural athlete was immediately hooked, she recalled, "and after the show I asked him how much he wanted to teach me to ride." He laughed at the idea but put her on his mount, and in a couple of days, she "could pick up a handkerchief with my horse trotting. Before he left Staten Island he had taught me many tricks."

Winger joined the Wild West show of Captain Jack Baldwin, who completed the immigrant's transformation into Tillie Baldwin, a lissome "Oklahoma cowgirl," complete with pistol and lariat, who was supposedly his sister. By 1912, she had won championships in trick and bronc riding at Oregon's legendary Pendleton Round-Up, and later became the first woman to win a Roman race, in which a rider stands with one foot on the backs of two running horses. Jealous beskirted rivals attributed the feat to her radical working costume of capacious bloomers and a middy blouse.

Like the West's writers, artists, and entertainers, the members of its proliferating women's clubs, many of which focused on volunteer community service, exerted a soft but powerful influence on society's ideas of what women could do, especially when united for a cause, be it child welfare or community gardens. Whether they formed a hospital auxiliary or a chorus—such as the one that the members of the Woman's Club of Cripple Creek, Colorado, considered to be the equal of any of the same size in America—they fueled a major nationwide social phenomenon that transformed women's civic role.

When it began in 1890, the General Federation of Women's Clubs, an umbrella organization, represented sixty-three groups; by 1906, that number was five-thousand. That same year, the federation's massive mail campaign ensured the passage of the Pure Food and Drug Act—the first modern consumer protection law. Like the national organization, its affiliates helped politicize domesticity, turn volunteerism into a pathway to professionalism, and greatly improve many communities. Although the GFWC did not officially endorse suffrage until 1914, many of its branches and members worked enthusiastically for the cause.

In the West, progressive women's political clubs joined with labor unions, social welfare organizations, and businessmen's associations to promote the non-partisan "good government" movement, which rose up to combat corruption in Big Business and state and local politics and generally endorsed women's full citizenship. Like their male allies, these activist clubwomen supported policies such as the regulation of workplaces, public utilities, and zoning, but they also pressed a distinctive agenda of family-related issues long championed by the WCTU and other women's groups, including public health measures that addressed substandard housing, polluted food and water, and epidemics of infectious diseases.

In California, prosperous, influential, civic-minded clubwomen had long worked to transform the state with not only playgrounds and libraries but also sewers and medical clinics. In 1900, forty groups formed the California Federation of Women's Clubs, which supported suffrage, scholarships for women's higher education, and, notably, the Child Labor Law of 1906; the federal legislation did not pass that year, but the clubwomen helped to make the industrial exploitation of minors a major national issue. Some western clubs were also concerned by the crisis facing Native peoples and their cultures, and that same year, Colorado's federation, which championed the preservation of ancient Puebloan sites, helped establish Mesa Verde National Park and its precious architecture.

Since the covered-wagon era, women had celebrated the West's natural environment, and many civic-minded clubs took on projects to enhance and protect it. They both built urban parks and preserved the wilderness areas beloved of President Theodore Roosevelt, whose progressive politics and privileged background some of them shared. (While in the White House, he established the US Forest Service, the National Conservation Commission, five national parks, four national game refuges, and over 100 million acres of national forest—an ambitious conservation agenda that not coincidentally increased the federal government's power at the expense of Big Business.) Indeed, the president was accustomed to collaborating with elite women conservationists. Prominent Boston ladies' earlier efforts to stop the destruction of some five million birds per year, caused by the fashion of decorating hats with feathers, anticipated the founding of the Audubon Society and his decision to designate fifty-one bird sanctuaries.

Like Roosevelt, Minerva Hamilton Hoyt, a socialite from Pasadena, California, and an officer in the nationwide, largely female Garden Club, used her private connections to influence public affairs. She was horrified that people were heedlessly stripping thousands of species of cacti, yucca, and other flora from the Devil's Garden, previously an unspoiled natural wonder just south of Joshua Tree. She worked tirelessly with clubwomen on both the national and local level to stop the destruction in the state's High Desert region and to educate Americans about arid landscapes and the need to protect them in parks different from the more familiar green, wooded sort. Finally, in 1936, her efforts were rewarded when President Franklin Roosevelt, Theodore's nephew, designated more than 800,000 acres as the Joshua Tree National Monument.

As the number of immigrants swelled to nine million between 1900 and 1910, the Daughters of the American Revolution, established back East in 1890, were by no means the only clubwomen preoccupied with their patriotic patrimony. In the West, many women, including a large number of Mormons, joined groups that celebrated their members' heritage as freedom-loving pioneers. For women such as Mary Ackley, a frontier pedigree was, like religion, a source of comfort amid life's challenges. After her mother died of cholera during the family's migration to California, her father had settled her and her siblings in a "canvas house" outside Sacramento, where they amused themselves by picking flowers and playing with their calf. In time, the children went to the new school, and the family moved into a proper home, where her father presided as justice of the peace in the parlor. Ackley's pride in her family's rise from a hardscrabble frontier existence to respectability helped sustain her throughout an often difficult life. After an unhappy marriage to a man who ignored her shrewd business advice and left her a widow with young children, she drew upon her past for the strength to support her offspring and see them educated. Then she rewarded herself by moving to San Francisco and cofounding a club called the Association of Pioneers.

Whether they belonged to the National Council of Jewish Women, the National Consumers League, or the Association of Collegiate Alumnae, many clubwomen became politicized when they realized that without the vote, they were powerless to advance their groups' ambitious social goals. Membership in organizations that supported suffrage were especially important for women of color, who wanted to vote to amplify not only their own voices but also those of their oppressed peoples. These activists' impact in the public forum belied their relatively small number in the West.

Women's organizations, including suffrage groups, were often segregated, but racism did not stop suffragist Emma Ray, a freedwoman who made her way to Seattle in 1889 and worked tirelessly among the poor in its jails and slums from founding the city's Colored WCTU. Elizabeth Ensley, Denver's prominent equal rights activist, organized the Colorado Association of Colored Women's Clubs to link groups throughout the state to fight for justice for both Blacks and women. As the group's patriotic theme song put it: "We're Colorado's colored women struggling for a place / We're loyal to our country, we're loyal to our race." Ensley also become a prominent member of the integrated Colorado Federation of Women's Clubs, which opposed racism and supported universal human rights.

Two influential women found a political home in the Society of American Indians, the first such rights-activist group exclusively run by Native Americans, located in Washington, DC. A métis suffragist of mixed Chippewa (or Ojibwe) and French ancestry, Marie Louise Bottineau was fluent in English, French, and the Ojibwes' Anishinaabemowin language. She began her legal career as a teenage clerk in her father's Minneapolis law office, where they defended the land rights of their Turtle Mountain Chippewa nation, back in North Dakota. (At twenty-four she married Fred Baldwin, a White man, but they soon divorced, after which she described herself as a widow.) In the early 1890s, she and her father joined the thriving cadre of Native American intellectuals and professionals in Washington, DC, the better to pursue their people's cause. In 1904, she was appointed as an accounting clerk—a prestigious, well-paid position—in the Office of Indian Affairs, where she joined Francis La Flesche as its second Native employee and first woman of color.

Earlier in her career, Baldwin had been an assimilationist, but by 1911, her perspective began to change after she joined the SAI. A third of these "Red Progressives" were women, including many suffragists like Baldwin, soon a member of the capital branch's executive committee. First and foremost, the organization lobbied for full citizenship for America's 300,000 Native Americans, a third of whom were still powerless wards of the federal government. Definitively securing equal rights for all would end what Baldwin rightly called the "confusion and chaos" that surrounded Native Americans' legal status and strengthen their political voice by adding new voters. (In 1924, Congress finally passed the Indian Citizenship Act, but for more than twenty years, the legislature failed to address the tribes' right to appeal to the US Court of Claims regarding land disputes.) The SAI also supported "Pan Indianism," or the unity of America's far-flung tribes, as well as Baldwin's particular interests: preserving traditional cultures and using public education to counter false assumptions and stereotypes about Native Americans. That said, like some White suffragists, some suffragists of color made disparaging comparisons between their own and other races, as Baldwin did regarding Blacks.

In 1912, Baldwin made a bold professional decision that reflected her dual engagement in the SAI and the suffrage movement. At the age of forty-eight, she became the first woman of color to enroll at the Washington College of Law, graduating with honors at fifty-one. As she had learned while defending the rights of the Turtle Mountain Chippewa, "to a race whose lands and property of other kinds are so valuable," legal expertise is "all-important." Determined to represent both Native American tradition and modern womanhood, she carefully chose her clothing to suit the demands of her complex career. In a 1911 photograph for her government personnel file, she wore Chippewa dress and braids—a very unusual choice—as she sometimes did when campaigning for women's rights. For the huge Woman Suffrage Parade in Washington, DC, in 1913, however, she dressed in contemporary attire and marched with a group of women lawyers.

Baldwin soon became a well-known figure in the capital and a prominent speaker on Native American women's political roles in their traditional societies. "Did you ever know that the Indian women were among the first suffragists, and that they exercised the right of recall?" she asked. "The trouble in this Indian question which I meet again and again is that it is not the Indian who needs to be educated so constantly up to the white man, but that the white man needs to be educated to the Indian."

Involvement with the SAI similarly changed Zitkala-Sa's professional and political life. After joining the organization in 1913 while still in Utah, she began to write again and also collaborated with William Hanson, a Mormon, in creating *The Sun Dance*, possibly the first Native opera; the work premiered in Vernal, Utah, then in New York City. She also became increasingly concerned with the preservation of endangered Native American cultures. Reservations had become the closest thing to homelands, but the maintenance of ancestral traditions was threatened not only by assimilation but also by the exodus of residents forced to look elsewhere for jobs.

In 1917, Zitkala-Sa and her husband joined their fellow Red Progressives in Washington, DC, where she served as the SAI's secretary, edited its magazine, and lectured, wrote, and organized on behalf of its causes. At first, Baldwin welcomed the beautiful, charismatic newcomer, who shared her interests, including advocacy for the modern Native American woman. The two leaders soon engaged in a power struggle, however, and tensions mounted when Zitkala-Sa moved the society's office to her own comfortable apartment. She also strongly opposed the Native American Church's ritual use of peyote—an issue on which the SAI was divided. By comparing the hallucinogen to alcohol, however, she forged important connections with the WCTU and other women's groups.

Zitkala-Sa continued her political work after the SAI was disbanded in 1920. Under the auspices of the General Federation of Women's Clubs, she formed the Indian Welfare Committee, then later founded the National Council of American Indians, which worked to shore up tribal cultures and protect Native lands for the future. In addition, she published *American Indian Stories, Legends, and Other Writings*, in which she wrote, "Now the time is at hand when the American Indian shall have his day in court through the help of the women of America." With Charles Fabens and Matthew Sniffen, she also coauthored *Oklahoma's Poor Rich Indians*, which exposed the corrupt policy of giving unscrupulous interlopers "legal guardianship" of Native lands that happened to be rich in oil and gas.

The New Woman, writer, musician, suffragist, and a founding mother of the modern Native American rights movement was eventually laid to rest at Arlington National Cemetery, an honor accorded not to her exceptional achievements but to her husband's military service. She lies under a tombstone engraved with his name, a tipi, and the words HIS WIFE / GERTRUDE SIMMONS BONNIN / ZITKALA-SA OF THE SIOUX INDIANS.

Where working for equal rights for her people and her sex was concerned, Jovita Idár, a Hispanic activist, suffragist, and journalist from a prominent family in Laredo, Texas, also discovered the strength in numbers of like-minded women. As the first president of La Liga Femenil Mexicanista, or League of Mexican Women, founded in 1911, she argued for women's enfranchisement and equal access to employment and education. After becoming frustrated by the "Juan Crow" laws that limited Hispanics' rights in Texas, and especially her inability to change the biased system that denied them decent schools, she had switched her career from teaching to journalism and activism. She urged women to take the responsibility for their own and their children's schooling into their own hands, "so that we are not devalued and humiliated by the strangers who surround us." A proud Methodist in a largely Catholic community, she criticized the Roman Church as well as the US government for its misogyny. "Women are no longer servants," she wrote, "but rather the equals of men, companions to them."

Idár's fiery editorials for the journals *La Crónica* and *El Progreso* also protested lynchings, land seizures, and the Mexican-American War's other dire, ongoing sequelae. During the Mexican Revolution, which began in 1910 and continued for more than a decade, she infuriated the army and the Texas Rangers by publicly criticizing President Woodrow Wilson for deploying troops to harass desperate Mexican refugees at the border. On the first occasion that the Rangers stormed the office of *El Progreso* to shut down the newspaper, she barred the door, but they returned in her absence the next day and broke the printing press. Far from being silenced, Idár and her brother launched the journal *Evolución*, which strongly promoted women's rights as well as their people's. After marrying, she settled in San Antonio, where she and her husband started the town's Democratic Club. She also edited *El Heraldo Christiano*, a Methodist newspaper, taught childcare classes, and started a free kindergarten. "Educate a woman," she said, "and you educate a family."

As immigration surged at the turn of the century, society in the East and West grew increasingly preoccupied with pressing questions first raised during abolition: Who is a real American? Who is a full citizen? Suffragists nationwide pointed out that as the model of womanhood expanded from private domesticity to include public service, women had already made major contributions to their communities for decades. They asked why they, patriotic, dutiful Americans of long standing, should not have equal rights—especially when those privileges were enjoyed by immigrant men who couldn't even speak English and others whom many women considered their inferiors?

The "real American" rationale for suffrage had a special resonance in the West, where the population of eight million in 1890—a quarter of which was already foreign-born—surged to eleven million by 1900. White women had long been portrayed as patriotic civilizers who worked unselfishly to build local governments, schools, and other social institutions, often side by side with men. Many in the younger generation added their achievements as independent home-steaders, college graduates, and professionals, as well as their involvement in progressive politics. Increasingly joined by women of color, they wondered why they, as loyal Americans, still could not vote.

That question particularly resounded among the members of the West's progressive women's clubs. In California, they had relentlessly lobbied state legislators to pass a suffrage bill in 1893, only to see the governor declare it unconstitutional and veto it. As activists geared up for the 1896 campaign, Laura Gordon, the accomplished newspaper publisher and lawyer, devised a trendy slogan: "The American woman citizen is becoming alarmed for the safety of the National household." The suffragists garnered support from good-government groups, including Republican businessmen worried by competition from the Populists and those same Populists, whose candidate, Adolphe Sutro, had just been elected mayor of San Francisco. Despite the NAWSA's racist bent, Naomi Anderson, an eloquent Black suffragist, graciously agreed to appear on a stage with Anthony to urge Union Army veterans of both races to give women the vote. Nevertheless, the referendum was defeated by opposition in the state's northern cities, where influential liquor interests were strongest and large populations of immigrant workingmen were worried by the prospect of temperance.

As preparations for the elections of 1910 began, clubwomen and other activists added to the momentum for the vote then building in the West's holdout states. Moreover, many legislators, eager to increase the electorates in their still thinly populated states and region, were increasingly sympathetic. Male voters could see for themselves that enfranchised women in Wyoming, Utah, Colorado, and Idaho had not abandoned their families, much less grown beards, as some antisuffragists predicted; as westerners, they also wanted to uphold their reputation for being modern and forward-looking. As *Votes for Women*, a popular monthly journal published in Seattle, crowed, the West had long been peopled by "free souls who gladly gave up the luxuries of the East in order to escape its slavery," whose zeal for suffrage would hopefully be "washed back over the East with the returning tides of humanity."

Keenly aware of the implications for the national amendment, the NAWSA energetically lobbied in the West at the state and local levels. As in decades past, however, homegrown suffragists' relentless efforts were essential to winning over their resistant states. Their previous four victories had been won in legislatures, but now they faced the tougher prospect of winning over male voters one by one in referendums, starting in Washington.

Fifteen

THE ENFRANCHISED WEST

Every honest, intelligent and sane person who
has considered the subject carefully is a suffragist.

—ESTHER POHL LOVEJOY, OREGON PHYSICIAN

I N 1906, Cora Smith Eaton, North Dakota's first woman doctor, fell in love with the Pacific Northwest's natural beauty and moved to Seattle, Washington, just as the state's suffragists were gearing up for yet another campaign. The outdoorsy physician-athlete established her medical practice, cofounded the city's Mountaineers Club, and joined the Washington Equal Suffrage Association. President Emma DeVoe and its other members recognized the attractive, active, educated Eaton as the ideal representative of savvy third-generation western suffragists and soon elected her as treasurer and unofficial game planner.

To prepare for the referendum to be presented at the 1910 election, Eaton and DeVoe deployed three major strategies that finally broke the suffrage logjam not just in the West but in the nation. First, instead of preaching to the converted, they reached beyond barriers of race, class, and gender to build mutually beneficial coalitions with other progressive, nonpartisan organizations that needed women's votes to further their own agendas. Adopting the slogan "Unity in Diversity," they won support from good-government groups fighting corrupt business and politics, agrarian organizations, labor unions seeking fair wages, women's clubs pursuing public health, and churches battling vice. To reduce friction, they downplayed controversial issues such as temperance and women's equality and heeded the advice of Mary O'Neill, a journalist from Butte, Montana: "Give them all the dope you can about the influence of women on behalf of children and appeal to the higher standard of motherhood. . . . That's the gush that gets the public."

In addition to coalition building, Eaton and DeVoe highlighted an emerging theme that helped democratize and unify a movement long dominated by bourgeois WASPs: American women as workers, whether paid or unpaid. This shared identity, the activists insisted, joined all women in a huge if unofficial labor union whose members would vote for government that benefited their homes and homeland. As Washington's population doubled between 1900 and 1910, that informal guild included not only the ladylike graduates of its three teachers' colleges but also young urban waitresses, clerks, cannery workers, and industrial seamstresses—a hitherto neglected constituency less interested in gender ideology than in voting for an eight-hour day, a minimum wage, and a safe workplace.

The new suffragist symbol of the working woman, whether a homemaker or a secretary, who was ready to join forces with her sisters to improve America was well received in Washington and throughout the West. When Margaret Quinn, a poor servant in the town of Everett, was shot dead by her jealous, drunken husband in 1908, angry women of all classes, united by outrage over domestic violence and their political powerlessness, attended her funeral—a stunningly democratic display of support for women's rights.

Eaton and DeVoe were also among the first suffragists to mount a creative mass-media public relations operation, which transformed the American political campaign altogether. In the summer of 1909, the NAWSA deliberately scheduled its national convention, which attracted thousands of attendees, to coincide with the Alaska-Yukon-Pacific Exposition, which brought 3.7 million visitors to Seattle. In addition to boosterish buttons, posters, shopping bags, and electric signs, the local activists propagandized this vast captive audience with a dirigible that pulled a suffrage banner across the sky and a special suffrage train that started in Chicago and picked up supporters en route. On one theatrical parade float, a costumed "Goddess of Liberty" stood ready to remove a Washington woman's shackles, while other august female deities representing the region's four suffrage states looked on approvingly.

Eaton also made two personal, much-publicized contributions to the 1909 summer campaign. She coauthored the *Washington Women's Cook Book: Votes for Women, Good Things to Eat*, which cleverly reinforced the compatibility of domesticity and enfranchisement. To appeal to a wide readership, she published tempting recipes for special-interest groups, including sailors and vegetarians, alongside health advice, beauty tips, and inspirational material about women's rights. A half century after Julia Holmes scaled Pike's Peak, Eaton, an experienced climber who had summited on all six of the state's major mountains, also led a party of bold NAWSA delegates and their male supporters on a three-week camping trip to the top of Mount Rainier. (Enrollees were advised that skirts were forbidden and that knickerbockers were more practical than capacious bloomers.) Although the wind prevented her from planting it upright, Eaton and the cause garnered much publicity when she deposited a VOTES FOR WOMEN banner in a crater on the mountain's peak.

Despite the Washington suffragists' heroic efforts, tensions remained high leading up to the 1910 election, including within their own ranks. The genteel DeVoe, supported by Eaton, found the aggressive lobbying tactics of May Arkwright Hutton, their wealthy, much-married suffragist colleague, to be pushy and coarse. After an ugly power struggle, complete with threats of blackmail regarding her allegedly shady past, Hutton left to form her own organization, named the Political Equality League, and DeVoe was reprimanded by the NAWSA.

More seriously, uneasiness over women's empowerment increased along with its seeming likelihood, which fueled the antisuffrage movement across America. Many women still clung to their traditional role in the home, and many men, who felt their authority diminishing there, defended their own sphere, now materialized as popular new fraternal lodges. Responding to this widespread anxiety, both the Democratic and Republican Parties became more conservative and patriarchal. In the West, Ruth Wilson Patton, the daughter of a prominent rancher outside Los Angeles and the future general's mother, advised husbands that once enfranchised, their wives would be too busy cavorting with strange men on juries to attend to their homes and children. However, antisuffrage sentiment was strongest in the Northeast, where supporters ingeniously blended humbug and realpolitik. Amid dire warnings of women voters' masculinization, these conservatives appealed to regional loyalty with a shrewd political observation: so far, support for the vote had been limited to the West, where progressives and Populists of the "crude, raw, half-formed commonwealths of the sagebrush and the windy plains" generated "in endless procession foolish and fanatical politics and policies for a generation or two."

Despite the opposition, on November 8, 1910, Washington's male electorate enfranchised the state's women with a resounding 64 percent majority. Wasting no time, Seattle's new voters cast the ballots needed to recall Hiram Gill, the corrupt mayor who had allowed prostitution and gambling to flourish in the city, then repelled his attempted comeback in 1912.

Energized by Washington's great victory, suffragists in other western states adopted its winning strategies of coalition building, working women's solidarity, and splashy, inventive campaigns to suit their different political climates. Since the gold rush, wealthy, populous California had had an outsize impact on public opinion, and its long-awaited adoption of suffrage was crucial to building momentum for a national amendment. In 1911, the state's voters once again faced a referendum.

Suffragists were encouraged by the previous year's midterm elections, which swept progressive, good-government Republicans into power, but they anticipated the usual urban, antitemperance opposition that had foiled their previous efforts. Heeding their Washington colleagues' strategic lessons, they lofted the banner of women's unity as workers and built powerful coalitions across social, racial, and gender boundaries. In the more Hispanic south, activists distributed tens of thousands of pamphlets in Spanish, and Maria de Lopez, a prominent Los Angeles clubwoman, campaigned and translated at rallies. In San Jose, Sarah Massey Overton, an influential educational reformer, rallied fellow Black suffragists and worked with White ones in the inter racial Suffrage Amendment League and the Political Equality Club. To appeal to the working class, the state's Wage Earners' Suffrage League added Chinese, Black, Italian, and Hispanic chapters. Determined to avoid antagonizing the male electorate, movement leaders even asked the state's very active WCTU to lie low before the election. Most important, the campaign cleverly offset northern opposition by maximizing support in the huge state's rural south, where the vast network of the California Federation of Women's Clubs soon thrummed with an urgent message: members must lobby their local newspaper editors, business leaders, and clergymen as well as their male relatives to empower women as municipal housekeepers as well as home protectors.

The suffragists' geographical strategy paid off. They failed in the Bay Area and almost lost Los Angeles, but after an agonizingly long count, rural voters carried the day, if only by some four thousand ballots. On October 10, 1911, after writing the state's Women's Vote Amendment, Clara Foltz, California's first woman lawyer and one of the few original suffragists able to rally, accepted congratulations all night long.

Born to a poor family in San Francisco's Chinatown in 1887, Tye Leung became the first Chinese American woman not only to vote but also to be employed by the federal government. After her parents tried to force her into a loveless teenage marriage, she ran away to the Presbyterian Mission House, founded to rescue Chinese prostitutes, where Donaldina Cameron, Margaret Culbertson's successor, gave her a safe home and a good education. The bright teenager soon became her mentor's translator and interpreter. When the state's women were enfranchised, she explained that she had diligently studied the candidates and issues before casting her ballot, because "we women are more careful than the men. We want to do our whole duty more. I do not think it is just the newness that makes use [*sic*] like that. It is conscience."

Tye Leung was free to vote but not to marry Charles Schulze, her White fiancé, who like her was employed at the city's Angel Island Immigration Station. California's antimiscegenation laws banned such unions, so in 1913, they wed in Washington. When they returned to California, however, both were forced to give up their jobs.

After her husband's untimely death, she raised their children, worked as a bookkeeper and telephone operator, and served her Chinese community, which also esteemed her as an unlikely pinball wizard.

Like Washington and California, Oregon had a long history of seesaw suffrage legislation. Voters had defeated referendums in 1894, 1900, and 1906, but Dr. Esther Clayson Pohl Lovejoy was among the young suffragists, tired of Duniway's "still hunts," who were determined that things would be different in 1912. As a physician and director of Portland's Board of Health—the first woman to hold that important position in a major American city—she had learned how to unite diverse women as workers, both paid and unpaid, to improve their communities. Now, she intended to harness their power to win the vote.

Despite appearances, the beautiful young physician had firsthand knowledge of working-class women and their struggles. Raised by poor parents in a logging camp, she decided early to become financially independent and modeled herself on the woman doctor who delivered her youngest sister. After her family moved to Portland, she received her first real schooling, then clerked in a dry-goods store to earn tuition money for the University of Oregon's medical school. As one of its three women students, she "rejoiced that none of the boys threw eggs at us," excelled in her studies, and in 1894, graduated as an obstetrician-gynecologist.

Like Eaton, Lovejoy was a physician-adventurer who embodied the bolder third-generation suffragists. After she married Emil Pohl, a surgeon, they practiced medicine in Portland until 1898, when they joined the gold rush in Skagway, Alaska. They paid house calls by dogsled and helped establish the area's Union Hospital, but Lovejoy soon moved back to Oregon, thereafter joining her husband only for the far north's short summers. In 1902, she gave birth to their son in Portland, then enlisted her mother to care for him.

While juggling her medical practice and motherhood, Lovejoy also threw herself into progressive politics and the Oregon State Woman Suffrage Association's fight for the vote. Between 7 and 8 percent of the state's doctors were women—twice the national average—and as one of them, she spoke with special authority about public health and welfare. Emphasizing the municipal-housekeeper argument, she asserted that once enfranchised, women could force the government to improve substandard housing and sanitation in their communities. In 1905, Portland's progressive mayor appointed her to its Board of Health, then made her its director.

Once in public office, Lovejoy tapped the collective might of diverse working women—whether mothers at home or bookkeepers, clerks, and seamstresses—once united to fight for their families' well-being. Supported by municipal housekeepers in Portland's Woman's Club, the Council of Jewish Women, the Women's Medical Club, and other groups, she achieved her goals of purifying the milk supply, sending nurses to public schools, and improving garbage collection. With their backing, she even protected the city from an outbreak of the bubonic plague in 1907 by cleaning up the waterfront and exterminating the flea-infested rats that spread the disease. Her dedication to turning Portland into one of the nation's healthiest and most sanitary cities was the more remarkable considering the personal tragedies she endured while pressing forward. In 1908, her little boy died of peritonitis. Three years later, her husband succumbed to encephalitis in Alaska. Even her second marriage proved to be unhappy and ended in divorce.

In 1912, faced with Oregon's sixth suffrage referendum—the most of any state—Lovejoy adopted the strategies that had succeeded in Washington and California, starting with devoting her managerial and political skills to coalition building in earnest. She united Portland's twenty-three suffrage organizations across lines of race, class, and gender into the Everybody's Equal Suffrage League. This new umbrella organization boasted that it was "free from all cliques and class distinctions and open to all" and scorned "any rules and regulations"; its dues were a quarter, and all members were vice presidents. The league's dizzyingly eclectic membership included chapters for stenographers, men and boys, Quakers, and every conceivable special-interest group, for whom Lovejoy's democratizing message was the same: "Every honest, intelligent and sane person who has considered the subject carefully is a suffragist."

With the support of Harriet "Hattie" Redmond, a longtime leader in Oregon's suffrage struggle and a respected member of Portland's Black community of several hundred, Lovejoy made a special point of personally crossing the color barrier in a state that had a history of anti-Black racism. Indeed, at a time when job opportunities for Black women were very limited, Redmond worked as a hairdresser, a servant, and a longtime janitor at Oregon's US District Court. Her emancipated parents had imbued her with the desire for full citizenship, however, and her true vocation was civic activism. She volunteered at the Oregon Colored Women's Council (later the Oregon Colored Women's Club), the Portland YWCA, and the Mt. Olivet First Baptist Church, where she organized meetings and educational lectures on suffrage. During the 1912 campaign, she was president of the Colored Women's Equal Suffrage Association, and when Lovejoy addressed one of their meetings, the *Oregonian* quoted Redmond's assurance that the audience was "enthusiastic for the cause." (During the 2012 centennial celebration of suffrage in Oregon, historians discovered her overlooked yet major contributions to the women's movement, and at Oregon State University, in Corvallis, the Women's Center became the Hattie Redmond Women and Gender Center.)

In addition to building a strong suffrage coalition, Lovejoy encouraged creative campaigning. Along with the usual buttons, banners, and flags, members of Portland's Woman's Club posted a twelve-foot-high green VOTES FOR WOMEN sign on St. Patrick's Day and sponsored a "suffrage flying squadron" that blasted small Oregon towns with signs and leaflets. Then, too, national politics also helped set a positive tone. In 1912, Theodore Roosevelt broke from the Republican Party and founded the East-centered Progressive Party—also known as the Bull Moose Party, in honor of the feisty ex-president. Unlike the more radical western Populists, who sought major economic reform, the more urbanized, white-collar Progressives accepted capitalism but wanted a more activist federal government to protect them from monopolies and corrupt political machines. The new Progressives also gained the distinction of becoming the first major party to back suffrage on a national level.

On November 5, 1912, pressure from Lovejoy's coalition and shame over lagging behind neighboring Washington and California persuaded 52 percent of Oregon's electorate to enfranchise women. Fittingly, the now frail Duniway wrote the official proclamation, signed it along with Governor Oswald West, and became the state's first registered female voter. Lest younger women take such progress for granted, she warned, "The debt that each generation owes to the past it must pay to the future."

Two other holdout states fueled the suffrage juggernaut in 1912. Forty-five years after Kansas became the first state to hold a referendum on the issue, a comprehensive campaign by its Equal Suffrage Association and support from progressive politicians finally persuaded voters to add an amendment to its constitution. In 1910, the territorial governor of Arizona had refused to include suffrage in its constitution, lest the issue jeopardize statehood. Once that goal was achieved in February 1912, however, the Arizona Equal Suffrage Association collected enough signatures to get enfranchisement on the ballot for the November election, when voters overwhelmingly approved it.

Since the territorial days of 1864 to 1889, Montana's legislature had repeatedly dismissed bills to include a suffrage referendum in a general election. In 1911, however, Jeannette Pickering Rankin and the state's third generation of talented activists disrupted that discouraging status quo with an inventive campaign. The daughter of prominent Missoula ranchers had formed her political views early. She observed that although her dynamic mother had worked side by side with her father to prove up their original homestead claim and even won a seat on the local school board, she could not vote.

After graduating from the University of Montana as a biology major in 1902, the restless, independent, fashionable young Rankin dabbled in several careers, including teaching and dressmaking, before finding her true calling in politics. Her interest in social reform and concern over the ravages wrought by industrialization drew her to New York City in 1904 to study at what became the Columbia University School of Social Work. Observing that even in progressive welfare organizations, skilled female professionals were often consigned to minor jobs, she concluded that women determined to improve society first had to wield enough political power to take on the age-old patriarchal authority structure itself. She returned to the West, transferred to the University of Washington in Seattle, and threw herself into the state's victorious 1910 suffrage campaign.

Like Eaton and Lovejoy, Rankin *was* the medium that was the suffrage message. The NAWSA quickly recognized her star quality by making her a field secretary, and for the next four years, she campaigned for the vote in the West, primarily back home in Montana. At one rally, Belle Fligelman Winestine, a young activist, wrote that "the air became electric" as soon as Rankin, dressed in a gold-colored velvet suit and radiating "friendliness and reason," began to speak. One newspaper editor agreed, reporting that she looked "like a young panther ready to spring."

Rankin's first goal was to persuade Montana's 1913 legislature to pass a bill to put enfranchisement on the ballot in 1914. She and the members of the state's Equal Suffrage Association built a powerful coalition by convincing the Republican, Democratic, Socialist, and Progressive political parties to endorse suffrage in their platforms. Then they contacted every legislative candidate, urging each to stick to his party's decision. The bill for a referendum passed with just four dissents. That same year, Rankin joined thousands of marchers in the huge Woman Suffrage Parade in Washington, DC, and also spent some time among kindred spirits in New York City, including Katherine Anthony, a writer who became her lifelong partner.

To build widespread support before the 1914 election in a huge state short on modern transportation and communication, Rankin enlisted grassroots campaigners in every county in Montana. The Missoula Teachers' Suffrage Committee distributed thirty thousand copies of their leaflet "Women Teachers of Montana Should Have the Vote." The Men's League for Woman Suffrage agreed to march at the state fair. The WCTU mobilized its 1,500 members to knock on doors in their neighborhoods. Rankin herself drove thousands of miles, speaking in churches and union halls, organizing parades, and visiting schools to urge students to persuade their fathers to vote for suffrage.

Her big hats and glamorous ensembles notwithstanding, Rankin eschewed political jargon and flowery moral arguments for a rancher's plain talk, nor was she above deploying some old political tricks to win voters. She sent anonymous activists into audiences at rallies where legislative candidates held forth; one woman would ask about a speaker's view on suffrage, then the others seemingly spontaneously applauded or booed at his response. As did many movement leaders, she shamelessly catered to anti-immigration sentiment by presenting American-born women's votes as a counterweight to those of the foreign-born while also courting the immigrants who accounted for about a quarter of the state's population.

Montana's own tumultuous politics benefited the suffragists' energetic 1914 campaign. That year, the state's powerful, pro-woman progressives persuaded the legislature to pass new democratic reforms, including the popular election of US senators. Moreover, the citizenry was up in arms over the outrages committed by the Anaconda Copper Mining Company, which crushed small competitors, backed sympathetic legislators in elections, and bought newspapers to sway public opinion. In this heated climate, suffragists argued that every vote was needed to counter the monopoly's antidemocratic hegemony. On November 3, 1914, Montanans voted to enfranchise the state's women—except those who were Natives—by a vote of 41,302 to 37,588. On the same day, the comprehensive campaign run by Nevada's Equal Franchise Society won over voters in twelve of its sixteen far-flung counties, and the state added a suffrage amendment to its constitution.

As popular maps that highlighted the West made plain, women in eleven of the region's fourteen states had now secured full enfranchisement before the women of even a single state back East. Their own victories won, some leaders stepped forward to fight on for the national amendment.

AFTERWORD

Men and women are like right and left hands.
It doesn't make sense not to use both.

—JEANNETTE RANKIN, FIRST US CONGRESSWOMAN

B Y 1914, most western women had the vote, and the *New York Times* marked the achievement with a statement from Carrie Chapman Catt, poised to resume her position as the NAWSA's president. "What is feminism?" she wrote. "A world-wide revolt against all artificial barriers which laws and customs interpose between women and human freedom." Yet despite the forty thousand marchers, many dressed in white, who gathered in New York City for the great suffrage parade in 1915, Pennsylvania, New Jersey, New York, Massachusetts, and the other eastern states still denied women the vote.

As its skewed gender ratio evened out and its society grew more conservative, even the West's women lost the advantages they had enjoyed during the experimental settlement era. Indeed, suffrage legislation still stalled in Nebraska and North Dakota, as well as Texas, officially a southern state. In New Mexico, activists faced a particularly complex problem. The state's constitution, ratified in 1912, only gave women the right to vote in school elections. Moreover, at a time when their culture was threatened by the Americanization movement, the Hispanics who made up more than half of the population used the document to protect their endangered land rights, Spanish language, and Catholic religion. By purposely making it difficult to amend the constitution without overwhelming support from legislators and voters, its drafters also made passing a state suffrage law particularly difficult. Rights activists necessarily focused on securing a national amendment instead.

The ranks of New Mexico's suffragists included well-off, well-educated Hispanic women from old landed Mexican families, such as Adelina "Nina" Otero-Warren, who were determined to win their rights as well as uphold their culture. Chic and high-spirited, she could have led the posh life of a socialite, but after a brief marriage to Rawson Warren, a White army officer, she divorced him, began to refer to herself as a widow, and devoted her energies to the public service that ran in both sides of her elite family. In addition to playing a prominent role in the state's Republican politics and education system, she was a major leader of its women's rights movement.

Despite the racist views of Hispanics shared by Anthony and some other White suffragists, Otero-Warren commanded the respect and cooperation of the eastern organizers sent by the new Congressional Union for Woman Suffrage, soon the National Woman's Party, who arrived in the state in 1915 to help rally support for the amendment. (Unlike the NAWSA, which sought state-by-state victories, the more radical, confrontational NWP, led by the charismatic reformer Alice Paul, pressed for a national law.) Recognizing a social peer, the eastern organizers heeded Otero-Warren's advice that their campaign in the state should appeal to Hispanic women's interest in policies that benefited them and their families, especially regarding education and health. At her insistence, all suffrage materials were also printed in Spanish as well as English. She was elected as the vice chairwoman of New Mexico's state branch of the NWP, then at Paul's request became its chairwoman.

Elsewhere in the West, enfranchised women looked to further political advancement. Some had been elected to school boards, and since the 1890s, even to certain state legislatures, but none had won a national office. When Montana's Jeannette Rankin ran for the US House of Representatives in 1916, she was a long shot by any measure. In addition to the handicap of her sex, she was a progressive Republican in a Democratic state, a prohibitionist, and, like her suffragist colleagues Catt and Paul, a pacifist on the eve of World War I. Nevertheless, 1916 was the first national election in which Montana's women—including the independents who accounted for 18 percent of its homesteaders—could vote. After traveling across the state to preach reform politics as the antidote to corrupt parties and monopolies, she won the seat, and with it instant national and international celebrity.

Congresswoman Rankin's triumph was short-lived. In 1917, she joined forty-nine colleagues in voting against America's entry into World War I. "I want to stand by my country," she said, "but I cannot vote for war." Back home, the Helena *Independent* called her "a dupe of the Kaiser, a member of the Hun army in the United States," and perhaps worse for a woman politician, "a crying schoolgirl." Even some suffragists who had regarded her as a hero fretted that she had set back the national amendment by years. Still, she carried on with her legislative duties, voting for prohibition and the nationalization of the Anaconda Copper Mining Company, which dominated Montana's politics and economy, and pressing for the vote.

In January 1917, Paul's "Silent Sentinels" began relentlessly picketing the White House to pressure President Woodrow Wilson to endorse a national amendment. On September 24, 1918, Rankin at least had the satisfaction of participating in the congressional debate on the Susan B. Anthony Amendment to enfranchise women, which Wilson finally endorsed on September 30. Politicians were under increasing pressure to yield, especially those who had to answer to America's four million new female constituents. The House passed the bill, but it was defeated in the Senate. That same year, however, North Dakota and Nebraska in the West, as well as Arkansas in the South, and Ohio, Indiana, Michigan, and New York in the East, finally adopted suffrage.

On May 21, 1919, the House once again passed what would become the Nineteenth Amendment, and on June 4, the Senate finally followed, albeit by a narrow margin. Before the bill became law, however, three quarters of the Union—then thirty-six states—had to ratify it, and on June 28, the Texas legislature complied. In New Mexico, Otero-Warren, newly elected as Superintendent of Public Schools in Santa Fe County and also the leader of the state's Republican women's committee, intensively lobbied wavering lawmakers until they ratified the amendment in February 1920.

On August 26 of that year, the Nineteenth Amendment was finally added to the Constitution: "The right of citizens of the United States to vote shall not be denied or abridged by the United States or by any State on account of sex." The vote did not make women equal to men, but they finally had enough power, from coast to coast, to challenge the male monopoly on politics and public life.

Once women were enfranchised nationwide, political parties in some states tried to attract these new voters by nominating female candidates for office. In 1920 in Oregon, Dr. Esther Lovejoy ran for the US Congress as the Democratic candidate for Portland's Third District but lost to the sitting Republican. In 1921, Otero-Warren became the first Hispanic woman to campaign for Congress. She made national headlines for beating her male challenger in the Republican primary, but narrowly lost the election. Unbowed, she continued her work as one of New Mexico's first female government officials. During her eleven years as superintendent of Santa Fe's schools, she battled illiteracy and championed bilingual education. Notwithstanding her own condescending assimilationist views regarding Native Americans, she oversaw the state's Indian schools for two years and defended its Navaho, Apache, and Pueblo communities, as well as Hispanics, from the forces of overzealous Americanization. (In the early 1930s, she and Mamie Meador, a close friend, homesteaded on adjacent claims outside Santa Fe; they called what became their ranch "Las Dos," the two women.)

Rankin's opposition to the war had seemingly doomed her barely launched political career, but for the next two decades, she stayed involved in public policy and in the public eye. She lobbied for women's rights, peace, and socioeconomic reforms, and by 1939, seized another chance to run for office in Montana. As Europe once again prepared for war, many Americans initially favored staying out of a second foreign conflict, and her pacifist views no longer seemed outlandish. She campaigned for a House seat as an advocate for neutrality, arguing that the nation's true enemies were poverty, unemployment, and disease.

Once again, Rankin went to Congress for Montana, and once again, her victory was short-lived. As the public cried out for vengeance after the Japanese bombed Pearl Harbor in 1941, she cast the only vote against retaliation. "As a woman I can't go to war," she said, "and I refuse to send anyone else." After hiding in a phone booth until security guards arrived to escort her to safety, she privately told friends, "I have nothing left but my integrity."

Rankin was one of the exceptions that proved the rule that once enfranchised, most women, like most men, did not vote to change the world. During the next two decades, she ranged far from her native West, spending much time in India studying Mohandas Gandhi's nonviolent politics. By 1968, her once radical ideas about women's equality and world peace had mainstream appeal, and she again returned to Washington, DC, in triumph this time, to lead thousands of marchers in the Jeannette Rankin Brigade to protest the Vietnam War.

More than a century and a half after the first western women were enfranchised, American women still struggle to become equal by acting as equals. The time is right to find inspiration in the neglected legacy of those persistent western foremothers, who also confronted an era of great social change and made it work to their advantage.

ACKNOWLEDGMENTS

Anyone interested in the history of women in the American West must be grateful to the scholars of the Western History Association and its Coalition for Western Women's History, who continue to develop new chapters of that dynamic, evolving saga. For sharing their insights with me, I thank Patricia Nelson Limerick for gamely consenting to be my first interview, followed by Katherine Benton-Cohen, Peter Boag, Cathleen Cahill, Rebecca Edwards, Richard Edwards, John Faragher, Elizabeth Jameson, Renee Laegreid, Lori Lahlum, Mary Mendoza, Paula Petrik, Cynthia Prescott, Andrea Radke-Moss, Vicki Ruiz, Honor Sachs, and Virginia Scharff.

I am especially indebted to historians Dee Garceau, Richard R. John, Renee Laegreid, Richard White, and David Wrobel, who kindly read my manuscript at various stages and offered invaluable comments and corrections. Any errors in the book are mine.

I am grateful to Amanda Boe for wonderful photographs, Lilly Cutrono for finding needles in historical haystacks, and Casey Denis, Candice Gianetti, Jane Cavolina, and the team at Penguin Press for sharing their gifts despite the challenges of 2020, a year unlike any other.

Finally, I thank Ann Godoff, my patient editor; Kristine Dahl, my stalwart agent; and Michael Segell, my sine qua non.

NOTES

INTRODUCTION: UNSETTLING WOMEN

xiv **the only acceptable career was marriage:** Barbara Welter, "The Cult of True Womanhood: 1820–1860," *American Quarterly* 18, no. 2, part 1 (Summer 1966).

xv **later termed their "moral authority":** Peggy Pascoe, *Relations of Rescue: The Search for Female Moral Authority in the American West, 1874–1939* (Oxford, UK: Oxford University Press, 1993).

xv **"It is in America":** Catharine Esther Beecher, *A Treatise on Domestic Economy: For the Use of Young Ladies at Home and at School* (New York: Harper & Brothers, 1856), 33.

xvii **woman's equality "was hers":** Frederick Douglass, *Frederick Douglass: Selected Speeches and Writings*, ed. Philip S. Foner, abridged and adapted by Yuval Taylor (Chicago: Lawrence Hill Books, 1999), 710.

xviii **the hundredth meridian:** In 1878, the American geologist and explorer John Wesley Powell drew a long invisible line called the hundredth meridian west, which was the longitude he identified as the boundary between the humid eastern United States and the arid western plains. Running south to north, the meridian cuts through eastern Mexico, Texas, Oklahoma, Kansas, Nebraska, the Dakotas, and the Canadian province of Manitoba en route to the pole.

CHAPTER 1: HOME ON THE RANGE

2 **"manifest destiny to overspread":** John L. O'Sullivan, "Annexation," *United States Magazine and Democratic Review*, July–August 1845.

2 **Of the thousands of early practitioners:** Amy Kaplan, "Manifest Domesticity," in *American Studies: An Anthology*, ed. Janice A. Radway (Chichester, UK: Wiley-Blackwell, 2009).

2 **"wild and inconsiderate step":** Sarah J. Cummins, *Autobiography and Reminiscences of Sarah J. Cummins* (La Grande, OR: La Grande Printing Co., 1914), 23.

2 **"What do you think father has done?":** Cummins, *Autobiography*, 21.

3 **under strong protest:** John Mack Faragher, *Women and Men on the Overland Trail* (New Haven, CT: Yale University Press, 2001).

3 **"the best accoutrements":** Cummins, *Autobiography*, 25.

3 **"Bible, dictionary, arithmetic":** Cummins, *Autobiography*, 27.

4 **"caused many ladies":** Cummins, *Autobiography*, 26.

5 **"profited by our experience":** Cummins, *Autobiography*, 36.

5 **"suited to the occasion":** Cummins, *Autobiography*, 18.

5 **"sermons in stones":** Cummins, *Autobiography*, 34.

5 **"the undulating movement":** Cummins, *Autobiography*, 24.

5 **her "will was not to be swayed":** Cummins, *Autobiography*, 45.

6 **"Seated on eternal snow":** Cummins, *Autobiography*, 50.

6 **"dear good" women:** Cummins, *Autobiography*, 23.

7 **"for the first time":** Cummins, *Autobiography*, 25.

7 **Ellen Smith was widowed:** Lillian Schlissel, *Women's Diaries of the Westward Journey* (New York: Schocken, 2004), 47–48.

9 **"families can come quite comfortable":** Whitman to Stephen and Clarissa Prentiss, October 9, 1844, in Narcissa Whitman, *The Letters of Narcissa Whitman, 1836–1847* (Fairfield, WA: Ye Galleon Press, 1986), 181.

9 **"wild regions, inhabited":** Cummins, *Autobiography*, 5.

10 **"the great beyond":** Cummins, *Autobiography*, 26.

10 **they had been caricatured:** As the Italian nobleman Count Francesco Arese wrote in *A Trip to the Prairies and in the Interior of North America (1837–1838): Travel Notes*: "The wife has an entirely passive role, she is almost the slave of her husband."

10 **coalition of "murtherous wretches":** Mary White Rowlandson, *A Narrative of the Captivity and Restoration of Mrs. Mary Rowlandson* (Cambridge, MA: Samuel Green, 1682), unnumbered page. In 1824, *A Narrative of the Life of Mrs. Mary Jemison*, by James E. Seaver (https://www.gutenberg.org/files/6960/6960-h/6960-h.htm), created a sensation with a very different kind of captivity experience from Rowlandson's horror story. In 1758, some Shawnee Indians in upstate New York seized twelve-year-old Jemison, later known as the "White Woman of the Genesee," after killing many of her relatives, then handed her off to some Senecas, who later adopted her. She described her new Native sisters as kind and gentle and noted that the women "had no master to oversee or drive us, so that we could work as leisurely as we pleased" (chap. 4). In short, she pronounced that "no people can live more happy than the Indians did in times of peace" (chap. 6). After two years, Mary married Sheninjee, a Delaware Indian whom she describes as admirable in every way, adding that "strange as it may seem, I loved him!" (chap. 3). She turned down a chance to return to White society after his death, and instead married an older Seneca warrior, with whom she lived for fifty years.

11 **The federal government's policy:** In 1824, the Bureau of Indian Affairs—tellingly established within the War Department—determined that Native peoples were no longer sovereign nations but merely domestic tribes. They were required by peace treaties to stop fighting the army, other Native peoples, and settlers, relinquish control over their traditional lands, and live within certain territorial borders. In 1830, President Andrew Jackson signed the unprecedented Indian Removal Act, which forced tens of thousands of people from the Cherokee and other tribes east of the Mississippi to relocate to the inhospitable new Indian Territory, in what is now Oklahoma. Speckled Snake, a chief of the

Creeks, had already anticipated the policy: "Brothers! I have listened to a great many talks from our Great Father [Jackson]. But they always began and ended in this: 'Get a little farther; you are too near me.' I have spoken."

11 **"nice, fresh venison"**: Cummins, *Autobiography*, 43.

11 **"sullen and wily"**: Cummins, *Autobiography*, 41.

12 **"Whatsoever, then, he [a man] removes"**: John Locke, "The Second Treatise on Civil Government (1689)," in *An Introduction to Political Philosophy* (Routledge Revivals) by A. R. M. Murray, 126.

12 **"little chair made of Sugar Maple wood"**: Cummins, *Autobiography*, 54.

13 **137 White men for every 100 White women:** *The Seventh Census of the United States: 1850* (Washington, DC, 1853); *Statistics of the United States in 1860: The Eighth Census* (Washington, DC, 1866).

14 **"the improvements on our claim"**: Cummins, *Autobiography*, 58.

14 **"The new claim was alluvial"**: Cummins, *Autobiography*, 58.

14 **the "marvelous manifestations"**: Cummins, *Autobiography*, 4.

14 **"one who assists" and "privilege of honoring"**: Cummins, *Autobiography*, 1, 2.

15 **the California Territory's population:** "The California Gold Rush," https://www.britannica.com/topic/California-Gold-Rush.

15 **"tearful widows of a fortnight"**: Joan Swallow Reiter, *The Women*, Old West Series (New York: Time-Life Books, 1978), 40.

15 **a man paid her $5:** Correnah Wilson Wright, "Luzena Stanley Wilson, '49er" (Oakland, CA: Eucalyptus Press of Mills College, 1937), quoted in Christiane Fischer, ed., *Let Them Speak for Themselves: Women in the American West, 1849–1900* (Hamden, CT: Archon Books, 1977), 153.

16 **"stared the white face"**: Wright, "Luzena Stanley Wilson, '49er," quoted in Fischer, *Let Them Speak*, 154.

16 **"plunged wildly into every mode"**: Wright, "Luzena Stanley Wilson, '49er," quoted in Fischer, *Let Them Speak*, 159.

16 **"The 'knights of the green table'"**: Wright, "Luzena Stanley Wilson, '49er," quoted in Fischer, *Let Them Speak*, 159.

16 **any kindly woman was "a queen"**: Wright, "Luzena Stanley Wilson, '49er," quoted in Fischer, *Let Them Speak*, 155. Over the course of two years, Harriet Behrins, who lived with her husband in a mining camp of fifty men, saw only one other White woman. Despite the isolation, she wrote, her memories of the experience were "most pleasant and sunny; situated as I was amidst beautiful scenes of nature, recipient of the simple gallantry of the men, who catered to my slightest wish." Harriet Frances Behrins, "Reminiscences of California in 1851," quoted in Fischer, *Let Them Speak*, 30.

17 **"As always occurs to"**: Wright, "Luzena Stanley Wilson, '49er," quoted in Fischer, *Let Them Speak*, 158.

17 **take her husband "into partnership"**: Wright, "Luzena Stanley Wilson, '49er," quoted in Fischer, *Let Them Speak*, 158.

18 **"every man thought"**: Wright, "Luzena Stanley Wilson, '49er," quoted in Fischer, *Let Them Speak*, 162.

18 **Her one concession:** Wright, "Luzena Stanley Wilson, '49er," quoted in Fischer, *Let Them Speak*, 159.

18 **"scareing the Hogs"**: Mary B. Ballou, "I Hear the Hogs in My Kitchen": *A Woman's View of the Gold Rush* (New Haven, CT: Yale University Press, 1962), quoted in Fischer, *Let Them Speak*, 43–44.

18 **"coffee for the French people"**: Ballou, "I Hear the Hogs," quoted in Fischer, *Let Them Speak*, 43.

18 **"Occasionly I run in"**: Ballou, "I Hear the Hogs," quoted in Fischer, *Let Them Speak*, 44.

18 **"French and Duch"**: Ballou, "I Hear the Hogs," quoted in Fischer, *Let Them Speak*, 46.

19 **"a capable, efficient woman"**: Letter from Horace Greeley, September 1, 1852, read at the 1852 National Women's Rights Convention, reproduced in full at http://www.gutenberg.org/files/28020/28020-h/28020-h.htm#CHAPTER_VI.

CHAPTER 2: THE RESPECTABLE COMMUNITY

22 **Since they could not:** In one particularly farcical instance, however, the men of Las Vegas, New Mexico, got the credit for providing the public amenity of a water fountain that had been conceived of and financed by local women temperance advocates, who hoped to discourage thirsty men from heading to a saloon.

22 **Her account of stamping:** Sarah Royce, *A Frontier Lady: Recollections of the Gold Rush and Early California* (Lincoln: University of Nebraska Press, 1977).

22 **"amenities and refinements"**: Royce, *A Frontier Lady*, 85.

22 **"roughly-reared frontier-men almost as ignorant"**: Royce, *A Frontier Lady*, 86.

22 **"appeared very generally"**: Royce, *A Frontier Lady*, 139.

23 **Respectability was Victorian society's:** Many middle- and upper-class women who had been gently reared in towns and cities had a harder time adjusting to rugged western life than farmers' daughters. Back in 1839, Caroline Kirkland, a former New York City teacher from a prominent family, had offered her explanation in *A New Home—Who'll Follow? Or, Glimpses of Western Life*. At a time when the popular works of Washington Irving and James Fenimore Cooper mythologized wilderness and lionized the men who conquered it, her arch, iconoclastic account of homesteading with her family in the then-remote Michigan Territory described frontier life as a lonely, uncivilized experience of regression. "Nobody should ever go one mile from home in thin shoes in this country," she sniffed, "but old Broadway habits are *so* hard to forget." Edgar Allan Poe and other critics relished her exposé of the settler's simple life, but Kirkland's rustic neighbors were infuriated by her descriptions of small-minded bumpkins presiding over wretched huts. Soon after she published *Forest Life*, another withering memoir, in 1842, she and her family headed back to New York City.

23 **"repeat with appropriate variations"**: *Sources of the History of Oregon*, vol. 1 (Eugene: University Press, 1899), 55.

23 **"in most of the masculine faces"**: Royce, *A Frontier Lady*, 104.

24 **Many cash-strapped men:** Arriving in the West around the same time as Royce, Elise Waerenskjold, a teacher and mother in Four-Mile Prairie, Texas,

had to wait eighteen years before her community built a school, for which she blamed a gender gap: "God only knows how our husbands could be so indifferent toward a project which is of so very great importance to our children." Theodore Christian Blegen, ed., *Land of Their Choice: The Immigrants Write Home* (Minneapolis: University of Minnesota Press, 1955), 330.

25 **"the stage for an elemental struggle":** Royce, *A Frontier Lady*, 108.

26 **"He came so near":** Royce, *A Frontier Lady*, 44.

26 **"agreed on the great foundation":** Royce, *A Frontier Lady*, 124.

27 **"weathered it in spite":** Mrs. C. A. Teeples, "The First Pioneers of the Gila Valley," *Arizona Historical Review* 1, no. 4 (January 1929), quoted in Fischer, *Let Them Speak*, 97.

27 **"each of [the four] women":** Quoted in Fischer, *Let Them Speak*, 96.

27 **"swiftly forming and dissolving":** Royce, *A Frontier Lady*, 107.

27 **"it was not always":** Royce, *A Frontier Lady*, 117.

28 **"The miners came in '49":** Quoted in Gary Kamiya, "Prostitutes from France Charmed S.F. during Gold Rush," SFGate.com, May 9, 2014.

28 **"social and beneficent societies":** Royce, *A Frontier Lady*, 139.

29 **"assistance to strangers":** Quoted in California Historical Society, "Finding Aid to the San Francisco Ladies' Protection and Relief Society Records MS 3576," 2009, http://pdf.oac.cdlib.org/pdf/chs/ms_3576.pdf.

29 **Other than the sizable enslaved population in Texas:** According to a legend set to song, Emily D. West, a free Black woman of mixed ancestry who worked as a housekeeper, played a dramatic role in securing Texas for the Anglos. Just before the decisive Battle of San Jacinto, General Antonio López de Santa Anna's troops entered the town of Morgan's Point and seized her, along with other residents. William Bollaert, an Englishman who traveled in Texas, opined in his journal that West's charms had distracted Santa Anna from the business of war: "The battle of San Jacinto was probably lost to the Mexicans, owing to the influence of a Mulatta Girl (Emily) belonging to Col. Morgan who was closeted in the tent with G'l Santana." (Quoted in https://www.tshaonline.org/handbook/entries/west-emily-d.) Her complexion might have been described then as "high yellow," but it's unlikely that a woman servant could hoodwink an experienced general in the middle of a war. In any event, West returned to the East as a free woman in 1837 (https://www.womenintexashistory.org/biographies/emily-d-west/). The tale of a beautiful woman of color who helped to free Texas, true or not, came to be associated with the popular song "The Yellow Rose of Texas." The chorus of the earliest version, published in 1853, was sung by white minstrels: "She's the sweetest girl of colour / That this darkey ever knew . . . " Quoted in Lora-Marie Bernard, *The Yellow Rose of Texas* (Charleston, SC: History Press, 2020), 27. In the 1950s, the bandleader Mitch Miller deracinated the heroine and produced a national sensation: "She's the sweetest little rosebud / That Texas ever knew . . ."

29 **the number of Black people:** Inter-university Consortium for Political and Social Research, *Historical, Demographic, Economic, and Social Data: The United States, 1790–1970* (Ann Arbor, MI: ICPSR, 1997).

30 **"strange," "mesmeric" air:** Quoted in Henry Louis Gates and Evelyn Brooks Higginbotham, eds., *African American Lives* (Oxford: Oxford University

Press, 2004), 675. When she appeared in court to testify in a lurid case concerning a forged marriage contract, the *San Francisco Call* of May 6, 1884, reported, "Mammy Pleasant, as the plaintiff calls her colored companion, shows herself in court only as a bird of passage, so to say. She bustles in, converses pleasantly with the young men attached to the defendant's counsel . . . and like a wind from the south astray in northern climes departs and leaves but chill behind."

30 **"strangely effective and influential":** W. E. B. Du Bois, *The Gift of Black Folk* (1924), quoted in Veronica Chambers, "Mary Ellen Pleasant," *New York Times*, January 31, 2019.

30 **"The ax is laid":** Quoted in Chambers, "Mary Ellen Pleasant."

31 **"still strong, vigorous, tall":** Quoted in "Clara Brown, Pioneer and Philanthropist in Early Colorado," *History of American Women*, https://www.womenhistoryblog.com/2015/03/clara-brown.html.

31 **"this new country":** Virginia Scharff, "The Hearth of Darkness: Susan Magoffin on Suspect Terrain," in *Twenty Thousand Roads: Women, Movement, and the West* (Berkeley: University of California Press, 2002), 50.

31 **She found the ladies' "ciggaritas":** Quoted in Scharff, "The Hearth of Darkness," 49.

32 **very grand "dark-eyed Senora":** Quoted in Scharff, "The Hearth of Darkness," 51.

32 **Red-haired, bejeweled Doña Gertrudis:** Deena J. González, "Gertrudis Barceló: La Tules of Image and Reality," in *Latina Legacies: Identity, Biography, and Community*, ed. Vicki L. Ruiz and Virginia Sánchez Korrol (Oxford, UK: Oxford University Press, 2005).

32 **"allure the wayward, inexperienced youth":** Quoted in Scharff, "The Hearth of Darkness," 51.

33 **"a very quick and intelligent people":** Quoted in Scharff, "The Hearth of Darkness," 49.

33 **The president was one:** Cazneau first developed her colonizing zeal in Texas, where in 1836 she applauded when recently arrived American ranchers and slaveholding planters, who styled themselves "Texians," declared their own independent Republic of Texas. After her real estate venture failed, Cazneau returned to New York and took up journalism under the mantle of Moses Beach, the *Sun*'s powerful editor.

33 **"plenipotentiary in petticoats":** Moses Sperry Beach, "A Secret Mission to Mexico," *Scribner's Monthly*, Vol. XVIII, May–October 1879, 140.

33 **"masculine stomach for war":** Thomas Hart Benton, *Thirty Years' View: or, A History of the Working of the American Government for Thirty Years, from 1820 to 1850*, Vol. II (New York: D. Appleton, 1858), 704.

33 **a "rich and delightful country":** Quoted in Tom Reilly, "Jane McManus Storms: Letters from the Mexican War, 1846–1848," *Southwestern Historical Quarterly* 85, no. 1 (July 1981): 21–44.

34 **As mining quickly became:** The underremarked history of the US–Mexican border, which extends nearly two thousand miles and is considered the world's longest, physically illustrates the hardening of racial and ethnic distinctions in the Southwest over time. The boundary was set in 1848, but a binational

commission didn't get around to marking it until the 1850s. The Rio Grande—North America's fourth longest river—took care of the Texas portion, and the overland border was merely indicated by big, widely spaced obelisks. In 1896, another survey added many more monuments, bringing the total to 257. Comings and goings across the border remained frequent and casual into the early twentieth century. Indeed, for more than six decades, there was no fence, much less a wall, to mark it.

34 **even privileged women of color:** Maria Raquel Casas, "Victoria Reid and the Politics of Identity," in Ruiz and Sánchez Korrol, *Latina Legacies*, 20–38.

36 **"That patching business":** Nancy Woloch, *Women and The American Experience: A Concise History* (New York: Alfred A. Knopf, 1984), 171.

CHAPTER 3: "WOMAN RIGHTS"

39 **"a thousand times more difficult":** Quoted in Joseph G. Gambone, ed., "The Forgotten Feminist of Kansas, 1: The Papers of Clarina I. H. Nichols, 1854–1885," *Kansas Historical Quarterly* 39, no. 1 (Spring 1973): 35, https://www.kshs .org/p/the-forgotten-feminist-of-kansas-1/13232.

40 **"The law which alienates":** Clarina Howard Nichols, "The Responsibilities of Woman," speech, Women's Rights Convention, Worcester, Massachusetts, 1851 (Rochester, NY: Steam Press of Curtis, Butts & Co., 1851), 2.

42 **"From Blue Stockings, Bloomers":** Thomas J. Dimsdale, *The Vigilantes of Montana* (1864). Quoted in Reiter, *The Women*, 199.

43 **"I am deprived":** Marilyn Blackwell, "Nichols, Clarina Howard," *American National Biography*, October 2012.

43 **"[Man's] laws concerning our interests":** Quoted in Gambone, "The Forgotten Feminist of Kansas," 20.

43 **"It is only since":** Nichols, "The Responsibilities of Woman," 2.

44 **"kind of emancipation":** Eliza Burhans Farnham, *Life in Prairie Land, 1846* (Champaign: University of Illinois Press, 1988), vi.

44 **"artificial and pernicious course":** Farnham, *Life in Prairie Land*, v.

45 **"Life is exalted":** Eliza Burhans Farnham, "Reviews and Literary Notices," *Atlantic Monthly: A Magazine of Literature, Art and Politics* 14, September 1863, 389.

45 **"to see one of our":** Mark Twain, *Life as I Find It* (Garden City, NY: Hanover House, 1961), 19.

45 **"such women lecturers":** Quoted in "Moneka Woman's Rights Association," *Kansapedia*, Kansas Historical Society, https://www.kshs.org/kansapedia/moneka -woman-s-rights-association/15158.

46 **a "male conspiracy":** Aileen Ribeiro, *Dress and Morality* (New York: Holmes and Meier, 1986), 134.

46 **"ill-health and temper":** Elizabeth Cady Stanton, quoted in Ida Husted Harper, ed., *History of Woman Suffrage* (United Kingdom: Fowler & Wells, 1881), 470.

47 **"Nearly everyone tried":** Julia Archibald Holmes, letter to Jane B. Archibald, "From the Rocky Mountains—Mrs. Holmes Ascends Pike's Peak," *Lawrence Republican*, October 7, 1858 (vol. II, no. 19), 2.

47 **Her published observations:** The Holmeses proceeded on to Taos, where Julia worked as a correspondent for the *New-York Tribune* while raising their four

children. In 1870, she divorced her husband and moved to Washington, DC, where she became a close friend of Susan B. Anthony and the secretary of the National Woman Suffrage Association. Not one to shy away from the dramatic gesture, she tried to register to vote in 1871, nearly a half century before such a thing was possible in the East; by that point, she could have cast her ballot in two western territories.

48 **"it is all the go here":** Abby Mansur, "MS Letters Written to Her Sister, 1852–1854," quoted in Fischer, *Let Them Speak*, 52.

48 **Many courts tacitly acknowledged:** Motivations for divorce varied according to the culture in various parts of the West. In Wyoming, the powerful railroads demanded that employees be temperate and married, so the likeliest causes for breakups there were binge drinking and spousal abuse. In Nebraska, where homesteads were established earlier, many divorces involved property disputes as well. In proper Victorian Helena, Montana, most involved violations of middle-class propriety committed by chronically absent or philandering husbands.

50 **Lincoln signed the Homestead Act:** Appreciating the act's importance for average people requires a little background on homesteading's history in the West. The relatively progressive Preemption Act of 1841 (http://www.minnesotalegal historyproject.org/assets/Microsoft%20Word%20-%20Preemption %20Act%20of%201841.pdf), for example, gave squatters' rights to 160 acres of surveyed public land to farmers who improved it. Yet to finalize ownership, they had to pay a minimum of $1.25 per acre—a considerable sum then; if they could not, speculators snatched up the properties at auction.

50 **As Mississippi congressman William Barry:** *Congressional Globe*, 33rd Congress, 1st Session (February 28, 1854), 503.

50 **Mary Meyer, a German immigrant:** Fred Knapp, "First Woman Homesteader Offers Glimpse of Little-Known History," NET News (Nebraska's PBS & NPR Station), http://netnebraska.org/article/news/887870/first-woman-home steader-offers-glimpse-little-known-history.

51 **285 million acres:** Robert V. Hine and John Mack Faragher, *Frontiers: A Short History of the American West* (New Haven, CT: Yale University Press, 2007), 134.

51 **included the "Exodusters":** Hine and Faragher, *Frontiers*, 152.

51 **"The scenery to me":** Quoted in Glenda Riley, "American Daughters: Black Women in the West," *Montana: The Magazine of Western History* (Spring 1988): 20.

51 **Far from freeloading:** Richard Edwards, Jacob K. Friefeld, and Rebecca S. Wingo, *Homesteading the Plains: Toward a New History* (Lincoln: University of Nebraska Press, 2017), 10.

52 **"respectfully and earnestly":** Jane Hampton Cook, "Which Lady Was Behind the Deciding Vote for Women's Suffrage 100 Years Ago?," *The Hill*, August 17, 2020.

53 **"There is a great stir":** Sojourner Truth, "Address to the First Annual Meeting of the American Equal Rights Association," May 9, 1867, https://www.lehigh .edu/~dek7/SSAWW/writTruthAddress.htm.

53 **"God is with us":** Quoted in Gambone, "The Forgotten Feminist of Kansas."

54 **"nonentity in law":** Abigail Scott Duniway, *Path Breaking* (Portland, OR: James, Kerns & Abbott, 1914), 14.

54 **"servant without wages":** Duniway, *Path Breaking*, 135.

54 **"To make thousands of pounds":** Duniway, *Path Breaking*, 9.

55 **"It's odd that men feel":** Abigail Scott Duniway, in *The New Northwest* (Portland, OR) 1871–1887, Library of Congress, quoted in Jennifer Chambers, *Abigail Scott Duniway and Susan B. Anthony in Oregon: Hesitate No Longer* (Cheltenham, UK: History Press, 2018), 58.

55 **"When women's true history":** Abigail Scott Duniway, "The Pioneer Mother," July 6, 1905, in *The Collected Speeches of Abigail Scott Duniway*, https://asduniway.org/%E2%80%9Cthe-pioneer-mother%E2%80%9D-july-6-1905/.

56 **"In looking backward":** Quoted in Reiter, *The Women*, 221.

CHAPTER 4: WYOMING MAKES HISTORY

57 **After turning a small log cabin:** A statue displayed in Cheyenne, the state capital, mildly commemorates Morris as a "proponent of the legislative act" that made Wyoming the "1st government in the world to grant women equal rights."

58 **"as good as any man":** Quoted in Tom Rea, "Right Choice, Wrong Reasons: Wyoming Women Win the Right to Vote," Wyoming State Historical Society, November 8, 2014, https://www.wyohistory.org/encyclopedia/right-choice-wrong-reasons-wyoming-women-win-right-vote.

58 **Men outnumbered women:** "Historical Decennial Census Population for Wyoming Counties, Cities, and Towns," US Bureau of the Census.

58 **"Damn it," said one:** Quoted in Rea, "Right Choice, Wrong Reasons."

60 **"a gentle white-haired housewife":** "69-Year-Old Woman Votes in General Election in Laramie," *Laramie Daily Sentinel*, September 7, 1870.

60 **According to *Frank Leslie's*:** Jessica Anderson, "Overlooked No More: She Followed a Trail to Wyoming. Then She Blazed One," *New York Times*, May 23, 2018.

60 **"a test of woman's ability":** Anderson, "Overlooked No More."

60 **In a letter to her sister:** D. Claudia Thompson, "Amalia Post, Defender of Women's Rights," Wyoming State Historical Society, November 8, 2014, https://www.wyohistory.org/encyclopedia/amalia-post-defender-womens-rights.

60 **When reporters from the eastern press:** Reiter, *The Women*, 215.

61 **While barnstorming through:** Beverly Beeton and G. Thomas Edwards, "Susan B. Anthony's Woman Suffrage Crusade in the American West," *Journal of the West* 12, no. 1 (April 1982): 5.

61 **In 1890, when Wyoming's statehood:** Reiter, *The Women*, 216.

61 **even Mark Twain could not resist:** Mark Twain, *Roughing It*, chap. 14, https://twain.lib.virginia.edu/roughingit/map/rimormon5.html.

62 **Employing trendy Industrial Age:** Michael Quinn, "Wells, Emmeline B.," *American National Biography*, December 2, 1999.

63 **Men obliged to build:** Some feisty Mormon women even defended their homesteads from malefactors. John D. Lee described the fracas that ensued when the two youngest of his nineteen wives assailed a neighbor who started to chop down trees along a creek that ran through his land. Emma and Ann Lee protested that their poultry needed the shade, but the man refused to

stop, until the women sought out their husband, who took the offender's ax away. When the culprit returned again the next morning, Lee was absent once more, and the situation escalated rapidly: "When I with several others reached the scene of action," he wrote, "I found them both on the ground & Ann with one hand in his hair & with the other pounding him in the face. In the meantime Emma returned with a New Supply of hot water & then pitched into him with Ann & they both handled him rather Ruff. His face was a gore of blood. My son Willard finally took them off him." Quoted in Leonard J. Arrington, "Blessed Damozels: Women in Mormon History," adapted from Arrington's presidential address to the Western History Association's annual convention, Omaha, Nebraska, October 10, 1969, DialogueJournal.com, https://www.dialoguejournal.com/wp-content/uploads/sbi/articles/Dialogue_V06N02_24.pdf.

63 **Christina Oleson Warnick, a homesteader:** Leonard J. Arrington, "Rural Life among Nineteenth-Century Mormons: The Woman's Experience," Symposium on the History of Rural Life in America, *Agricultural History* 58, no. 3 (July 1984): 240.

64 **"All honor and reverence":** Emmeline Wells, "Why, Ah! Why," *Woman's Exponent* 3 (October 1, 1874): 67.

64 **Describing a letter full of:** Quinn, "Wells, Emmeline B."

64 **As Stanton had put it:** Allison Lange, "The 14th and 15th Amendments," National Women's History Museum, Fall 2015, http://www.crusadeforthevote.org/14-15-amendments.

65 **The organization's weekly:** "Susan B. Anthony," Schlesinger Library, Radcliffe Institute for Advanced Study, Harvard University, https://www.radcliffe.harvard.edu/schlesinger-library/collection/susan-b-anthony.

66 **Then the justices:** Veronica Bravo and Janet Loehrke, "Women Suffragists Persisted for 70 Years to Win the Right to Vote in 1920," *USA Today*, August 14, 2020.

66 **"every sacred right":** Quoted in Karlyn Kohrs Campbell, *Women Public Speakers in the United States, 1800–1925* (Westport, CT: Greenwood, 1993), 396.

66 **"a taste of pioneering":** Duniway, *Path Breaking*, 46.

67 **"nobody but a fool":** Duniway, *The New Northwest* (1880), quoted in "Duniway, Abigail Scott (1834–1915)," Encyclopedia.com.

67 **Even her good friend Anthony:** Quoted in Margaret Riddle, "Duniway, Abigail Scott (1834–1915)," HistoryLink.org, Essay 8720, August 10, 2008, https://www.historylink.org/File/8720.

67 **"Men like to be coaxed:** Abigail Scott Duniway, "Interesting Sketch of Early Life of Abigail Scott Duniway," *The New Citizen*, January 1, 1912, 9.

67 **"as necessary as it may be":** Quoted in T. A. Larson, "The Woman Suffrage Movement in Washington," *Pacific Northwest Quarterly* 67, no. 2 (April 1976): 54.

68 **"Nowhere else upon this planet":** Quoted in Campbell, *Women Public Speakers in the United States*, 398.

CHAPTER 5: A HOME OF HER OWN

69 **of some 4 million claimants:** Edwards, Friefeld, and Wingo, *Homesteading the Plains*, 12.

70 **Most women who settled:** Anne B. Webb, "Minnesota Women Homesteaders: 1863–1889," *Journal of Social History* 23, no. 1 (Autumn 1989): 115–36.

70 **a surprising 2,400 women**: Anne B. Webb, "Forgotten Persephones: Women Farmers on the Frontier," *Minnesota History* 50, no. 4 (Winter 1986): 135.

70 **This stunning proof:** H. Elaine Lindgren, *Land in Her Own Name* (Norman: University of Oklahoma Press, 1996), 29.

73 **"the necessaries of life":** Webb, "Forgotten Persephones," 146.

73 **In addition to her wood home**: Webb, "Forgotten Persephones," 146.

73 **As cheerful as:** Pat Prince, "Researcher Finds U.S. Frontier Women," *Minneapolis Star and Tribune*, May 27, 1987.

73 **In parts of Nebraska**: Edwards, Friefeld, and Wingo, *Homesteading the Plains*, 146.

75 **"conveniences, elegancies, comforts":** Quoted in Sara Brooks Sundberg, "Picturing the Past: Farm Women on the Grasslands Frontier 1850–1900," *Great Plains Quarterly* 30, no. 3 (Summer 2010): 207.

75 **"it is best we should go now":** Sundberg, "Picturing the Past," 207.

75 **"better than I feared":** Ellayne Velde-Conyers, "Letters from the Prairie," *Marshall Independent* (Minnesota), June 4, 2018, part 1, https://www.marshall independent.com/opinion/local-columns/2018/06/letters-from-the-prairie/.

75 **"The first two years":** Velde-Conyers, "Letters from the Prairie," part 1.

75 **a hundred pounds of butter:** Sundberg, "Picturing the Past," 213.

75 **watching the "red tip":** Willa Cather, *My Ántonia* (New York: Penguin Putnam, 1999), 159.

76 **"When they can leave":** Farnham, *Life in Prairie Land 1846*, 122.

77 **"the sun, moon, or stars":** Annie Green, *Sixteen Years on the Great American Desert* (Titusville, PA: Frank W. Truesdell, 1887), 13.

77 **Carpenter enthused over:** Sundberg, "Picturing the Past," 208.

77 **Ántonia Shimerda, the luminous:** Cather, *My Ántonia*, 223.

77 **"Under the long shaggy":** Willa Cather, *O Pioneers!* (Boston and New York: Houghton Mifflin, 1913), 71.

79 **"nothing of riding":** Lily Klasner, *My Girlhood Among Outlaws*, ed. Eve Ball (Tucson: University of Arizona Press, 1972), 4.

79 **a model cowgirl:** Klasner, *My Girlhood Among Outlaws*, 4.

79 **In addition to roving outlaws:** In 1836, America was shocked by news that a party of Native Americans including some Comanches had seized Cynthia Ann Parker, then about nine years old, after slaughtering most of her family near Waco, Texas. In 1860, the papers breathlessly reported that Parker had been captured once again, this time while fleeing with her Comanche band from the Texas Rangers. After twenty-four years, the blue-eyed woman who had been called Naduah—"found one"—by the tribe that had adopted her was returned to her White relatives along with Topsana, or Prairie Flower, the youngest of her three children. The erstwhile captive was disconsolate, however, and pined for Peta Nocona, her husband and a tribal leader, and her life in the vast Comancheria. After her daughter sickened and died, she succumbed to a combination of influenza, depression, and self-imposed starvation in 1870. Quanah Parker, her Comanche son, became a legendary warrior, diplomat, and finally a wealthy, polygamous Oklahoma rancher, who died peacefully in 1911.

80 **"resources that would fit":** Margaret Fuller, *The Essential Margaret Fuller* (Garden City, NY: Dover, 2019), 82.

80 **"Your wife is elected to Legislature":** California politician James Caples, quoted in "California Woman Suffrage 1870–1911," International Museum of Women, http://exhibitions.globalfundforwomen.org/exhibitions/california-suffrage.

81 **"bawling, ranting women":** Thomas Brill, quoted in "Women's Suffrage Movement," *Colorado Encyclopedia*, adapted from Carl Abbott, Stephen J. Leonard, and Thomas J. Noel, *Colorado: A History of the Centennial State*, 5th ed. (Boulder: University Press of Colorado, 2013).

81 **Beset by lobbyists during:** Elizabeth Cady Stanton, *History of Woman Suffrage: 1876–1885* (New York: Elizabeth Cady Stanton, 1886), 786.

81 **"Hereafter no female":** Edmond Stephen Meany, *History of the State of Washington* (New York: Macmillan, 1909), 270.

CHAPTER 6: A MAN'S EDUCATION

83 **Women such as Catt:** Andrea G. Radke-Moss, *Bright Epoch: Women and Coeducation in the American West* (Lincoln: University of Nebraska Press, 2008).

84 **In 1847, while promoting:** Allison Speicher, "Catharine Beecher Educates the West," *Connecticut Explored* 15, no. 1 (Winter 2016–2017): 32.

85 **At last, the respectable single:** Quoted in Jessica Enoch, "A Woman's Place Is in the School: Rhetorics of Gendered Space in Nineteenth-Century America," *College English* 70, no. 3 (January 2008): 112.

88 **"elevated women's sphere":** Radke-Moss, *Bright Epoch*, 181.

88 **address on women's rights:** Radke-Moss, *Bright Epoch*, 283.

89 **Many such groups:** Iowa Agricultural College's women's drill team even appeared at the World's Columbian Exposition in Chicago in 1893.

90 **As the eastern writer:** Catherine Lavender, "Notes on the New Woman," College of Staten Island of the City University of New York, Prepared for Students in HST 386: Women in the City, 1998, archived from the original PDF, October 28, 2014.

91 **Many men agreed:** Willa Cather, *The Song of the Lark* (Boston and New York: Houghton Mifflin, 1915), 102.

91 **4 percent of the West's unmarried women:** Peter G. Boag, *Re-Dressing America's Frontier Past* (Berkeley: University of California Press, 2011).

91 **Then, too, "maiden ladies":** Western men who were arrested for homosexual acts appeared in the public records and newspapers, and some communities had ordinances against cross-dressing. Yet many men donned female clothing to perform on stage or so that everyone could dance at frequent all-male

gatherings, and some gay men were simply accepted by their communities. John Chaffee and Jason Chamberlain were California gold miners who lived for over fifty years on a charming farm, where they hosted many travelers. "The artistic inclination of these gentlemen is quite apparent," one guest observed, "tho which one is the 'ladies man' we could not discover, each modestly declining the honor."

92 Upon Parkhurst's death: Quoted in Tim Arango, "Overlooked No More: Charley Parkhurst, Gold Rush Legend with a Hidden Identity," *New York Times*, December 5, 2018.

93 Native societies in the West: The term "two-spirit" was created in Ojibwe and adopted in English in 1990 at the third annual Native American/First Nations gay and lesbian conference in Winnipeg, Manitoba, Canada.

93 He noted that she dressed: James Beckwourth, *The Life and Adventures of James P. Beckwourth* (New York: Harper & Brothers, 1856), quoted in "Nineteenth-Century Indigenous Women Warriors," Women's History Matters, February 6, 2014, montanawomenshistory.org, http://montanawomenshistory.org/nineteenth-century-indigenous-women-warriors/.

94 "I saw a magnificent": Eve Ball, *In the Days of Victorio: Recollections of a Warm Springs Apache,* narrated by James Kaywaykla (Tucson: University of Arizona Press, 1970), 9, 10.

94 Lozen did not marry: Ball and Kaywaykla, *In the Days of Victorio*, 15.

95 the worst violence of all: Benjamin Madley, *An American Genocide: The United States and the California Indian Catastrophe, 1846–1873* (New Haven, CT: Yale University Press, 2016).

95 In 1862, a White male settler: Benjamin Madley, "California's Yuki Indians: Defining Genocide in Native American History," *Western Historical Quarterly* 39, no. 3 (Autumn 2008): 303–32.

95 When the wife of Iron Bull: Elizabeth J. Reynolds Burt, *An Army Wife's Forty Years in the Service, 1862–1902*, unpublished manuscript, Elizabeth J. Reynolds Burt Papers, Library of Congress, Washington, DC, 158.

96 An eager collector of Native artifacts: Glenda Riley, *Women and Indians on the Frontier, 1825–1915* (Albuquerque: University of New Mexico Press, 1984), 140–41.

96 gleaming misery: Martha Summerhayes, *Vanished Arizona: Recollections of the Army Life by a New England Woman* (Salem, MA: Salem Press, 1911), quoted in Fischer, *Let Them Speak*, 137.

96 "were simply expressing the domestic instinct": Summerhayes, *Vanished Arizona*, quoted in Fischer, *Let Them Speak*, 140.

96 "know and appreciate honesty": Summerhayes, *Vanished Arizona*, quoted in Fischer, *Let Them Speak*, 146.

97 "rather solemn ceremony": Summerhayes, *Vanished Arizona*, quoted in Fischer, *Let Them Speak*, 142.

97 Vogdes boasted of her sangfroid: Riley, *Women and Indians on the Frontier*, 141.

97 At first, Caroline Winne: Sherry Smith, "Officers' Wives, Indians and the Indian Wars," *Order of the Indian Wars Journal* 1, no. 1 (Winter 1980): 42–43.

98 "confused my sense of justice": Riley, *Women and Indians on the Frontier*, 151.

CHAPTER 7: WOMEN AT WORK

100 **these allegedly dark forces:** Catharine Beecher, *The Evils Suffered by American Women and American Children: The Causes and the Remedy* (New York: Harper & Brothers, 1846), 7.

101 **Male teachers, who were fewer:** Chris Enss, *Frontier Teachers* (Helena, MT: TwoDot Press, 2008), 132.

101 **a professional missionary:** Michael C. Coleman, "McBeth, Susan Law," *American National Biography*, February 2000.

101 **the best chance of survival:** Ulysses S. Grant, *First Inaugural Address*, March 4, 1869, https://millercenter.org/the-presidency/presidential-speeches/march-4 -1869-first-inaugural-address.

102 **In his second inaugural address:** Ulysses S. Grant, *Second Inaugural Address*, March 4, 1873, https://millercenter.org/the-presidency/presidential-speeches /march-4-1873-second-inaugural-address.

103 **Catholic missionary nuns, who provided:** Anne M. Butler, "There Are Exceptions to Every Rule," *American Catholic Studies* 116, no. 3 (Fall 2005): 1–22.

104 **she was dismayed:** Reiter, *The Women*, 99.

105 **"he raised his large-brimmed hat":** Enss, *Frontier Teachers*, 11–12.

105 **"Poor wild hearts":** Quoted in Silvia Guidi, "Sr. Blandina, the Nun of the West," *L'Osservatore Romano*, weekly edition in English, September 4, 2015, 10.

106 **Many women became domestic servants:** Blue-collar women's opportunities were limited by their gender and class, then further narrowed by their race and ethnicity. Between 60 and 90 percent of Seattle's Norwegian and Swedish women were domestic servants, for example, compared to about 25 percent of women from other groups. Even free Black women were mostly restricted to domestic service.

107 *"Oh, who would":* Cather, *Song of the Lark*, 109.

CHAPTER 8: AN "AMBITIOUS ORGANIZATION OF LADIES"

110 **the Woman Lawyer's Bill:** Kristina Horton Flaherty, "A Hundred Years Later, a Trailblazer Gets Her Due," *California Bar Journal*, 2011, https://www.calbar journal.com/June2011/TopHeadlines/TH1.aspx.

111 **When she later cofounded:** "Portia Law Club. Ambitious Organization of Ladies. Its Object the Establishment of a Law College for Women. Striking Costumes," unsigned article, *San Francisco Call* 75, no. 35, January 4, 1894.

111 **"I kept my wits":** Reiter, *The Women*, 153.

111 **"I am a woman":** Barbara Allen Babcock, "Foltz, Clara Shortridge," *American National Biography*, December 2, 1999.

112 **The enterprising frontier girl:** Jean M. Ward, "Bethenia Owens-Adair," *Oregon Encyclopedia*, Oregon Historical Society, March 17, 2018, https://www .oregonencyclopedia.org/articles/bethenia_owens_adair_1840_1926/#.X39D _pNKhcB.

113 **Virtually all medical schools:** "Medical Training for Women," *Eclectic Journal of Medicine* 4 (1852): 114.

NOTES

115 **"want to be called"**: Quoted in Carson Vaughan, "The Incredible Legacy of Susan La Flesche, the First Native American to Earn a Medical Degree," *Smithsonian*, March 1, 2017, https://www.smithsonianmag.com/history/incred ible-legacy-susan-la-flesche-first-native-american-earn-medical-degree -180962332/.

116 **"I'm not accomplishing miracles"**: Jordan Pascale, "Susan La Flesche's Legacy Lives On," *Native Daughters*, University of Nebraska-Lincoln, http://cojmc .unl.edu/nativedaughters/healers/susan-la-flesches-legacy-lives-on.

118 **Whether their tie was ever:** Quoted in Carroll Smith-Rosenberg, "The Female World of Love and Ritual: Relations Between Women in Nineteenth Century America," *Signs* 1, no. 1 (Autumn 1975): 6.

118 **After de Kay married:** Quoted in Carroll Smith-Rosenberg, *Disorderly Conduct: Visions of Gender in Victorian America* (New York: Alfred A. Knopf, 1985), 58.

119 **"Desert did not seem":** Mary Hallock Foote, *Edith Bonham* (New York: Hough-ton Mifflin, 1917), 7.

119 **In 1878, *Scribner's* published:** Mary Hallock Foote, "A California Mining Camp," *Scribner's Monthly*, February 1878.

119 **one traveler who wrote of stumbling:** Quoted in Casey Bush, "Artist-Author Mary Hallock Foote and Her Angle of Repose," Oregon Cultural Heritage Commission, 2003, http://www.ochcom.org/pdf/Mary-Hallock-Foote.pdf.

120 **As the eastern protagonist:** Foote, *Edith Bonham*, 78.

122 **Propaganda aside, Cody:** "Buffalo Bill's Views: The Celebrated Indian Fighter on the Indian Problem—Never Make a Promise to the Indians Which Is Not Fulfilled to the Letter," *Times-Picayune*, October 28, 1879, http://codyarchive .org/texts/wfc.nsp00271.html.

122 **As she modestly allowed:** "The Wild West in Nottingham. The Opening Day," *Daily Express*, August 25, 1891, http://codyarchive.org/texts/wfc.nsp11464.html.

123 **She wore youthful curls:** In 1901, after injuring her back in a train wreck, Oak-ley parted ways with Cody, then endured a difficult period during which she sued newspapers that had falsely accused her of theft and drug abuse. After this unhappy interlude, she joined the Young Buffalo Show and returned to the arena in 1910 at the age of fifty, using various youthful sobriquets and still rid-ing sidesaddle in a skirt. When she finally retired, Oakley continued to set marksmanship records, gave free shooting lessons to women, and performed for charities, including the Red Cross. She and the devoted Butler died within days of each other and are buried side by side near Brock, Ohio.

124 **"Which is more cruel?":** Tom Noel, "Opinion," *Denver Post*, October 23, 2008, https://www.denverpost.com/2008/10/23/opinion-18/.

CHAPTER 9: "DO EVERYTHING"

125 **"We must choose":** Frances E. Willard, "The World Moves On and with It Woman," *Oakland Tribune*, February 19, 1887 (vol. 26, no. 41), 3.

126 **exemplar of Victorian womanhood:** Paula Petrik, "Mothers and Daughters of Eldorado: The Fisk Family of Helena, Montana," *Montana: The Magazine of Western History* 32, no. 3 (Summer 1982).

127 **These boomtowns attracted:** Between 1865 and 1870, thirty-seven of the madams and sex workers in Helena's booming prostitution industry accounted for 44 percent of women's property transactions; they sometimes lent to and borrowed from one another, using jewelry, clothing, or a good spring mattress as collateral.

127 **"how any man can be as lost":** National Park Service, The Robert and Elizabeth Fisk House, https://www.nps.gov/nr/feature/wom/2009/elizabeth_fisk_house.htm.

129 **"cleanse the Stygian pool":** Quoted in Kenneth D. Rose, *American Women and the Repeal of Prohibition* (New York: NYU Press, 1997), 36.

130 **"I cannot live wholly":** Letter of Elizabeth Chester Fisk to Azubah Chester, November 2, 1890, quoted in Petrik, "Mothers and Daughters of Eldorado," 60.

130 **"remarkably fine-looking body":** Quoted in Susan Ware, *Why They Marched* (Cambridge, MA: Harvard University Press, 2019), 38.

130 **"two heads in counsel":** Frances E. Willard, *Glimpses of Fifty Years: The Autobiography of an American Woman* (Chicago: Woman's Temperance Publication Association, 1889), 642.

131 **"stand bravely by":** Carolyn De Swarte Gifford and Amy R. Slagell, eds., *Let Something Good Be Said: Speeches and Writings of Frances E. Willard* (Urbana and Chicago: University of Illinois Press, 2007), 180.

132 **the new "settlement houses":** Hull House's famous alumni include Benny Goodman, who took music lessons there during his impoverished youth.

132 **Strict immigration laws:** The federal government attempted to keep the Chinese population limited to male laborers with stringent anti-immigration laws, including the Page Act of 1875, which specifically targeted Chinese women. Some 258,000 migrants, mostly men, had arrived before the Chinese Exclusion Act of 1882 banned even male laborers for ten years; in 1892, the law was renewed, then made indefinite in 1904, until its repeal in 1943. As a result, very few Chinese women made it to the US. California's anti-Chinese laws included bans on land ownership and interracial marriage, or "miscegenation," a term that dates to the Civil War, when pro-slavery forces used it to drum up fear among Whites.

133 **In her legalistic labor contract:** Quoted in "Chinese Immigration," Senate Report 689, 44th Congress, 2nd Session (serial 1734): 145, 146.

134 **Culbertson enjoyed a highly:** "She Gave Her Life to God," *San Francisco Call*, vol. 82, no. 62, August 1, 1897.

135 **"anti-female, anti-family":** Mary Ellen Swift, "Suffrage for Women a Handicap in Civic Work," *Woman's Protest* 3 (August 1913): 3.

136 **"We have been despoiled":** Quoted in Mildred Andrews, "Woman's Christian Temperance Union, Western Washington," HistoryLink.org, Essay 407, December 2, 1998, https://www.historylink.org/File/407#:~:text=Hansen%20proclaimed%2C%20%22We%20have%20been,win%22%20(Annual%20Report).

CHAPTER 10: WOMEN AND THE "INDIAN QUESTION"

137 **Until the Indian Citizenship Act:** In little more than three decades, Native Americans had been downgraded from the status of sovereign nations to poten-

NOTES

tial antagonists, and then in 1849 to powerless wards of the United States, which could relocate them or confine them to reservations as it saw fit. In 1871, Congress formalized this decline in status by ending nearly a century of treaty making between Native Americans and the federal government.

137 **"the privileges of protection":** Susette La Flesche Tibbles, preface, in William Harsha, aka Wolf Killer, *Ploughed Under: The Story of an Indian Chief* (New York: Fords, Howard & Hulbert, 1881), quoted in Helen Hunt Jackson, *Ramona* (Boston: Roberts Brothers, 1889), appendix D, 407.

139 **The result was:** Alice Fletcher, "Five Indian Ceremonies," Peabody Museum of American Archaeology and Ethnology, 16th Annual Report, 1884, 260–333.

139 **She also took pains:** Alice Fletcher, *A Study of Omaha Indian Music* (New York: Salem Press, 1893), 8.

139 **Fletcher's extensive muddy-boots:** Joan T. Mark, *A Stranger in Her Native Land: Alice Fletcher and the American Indians* (Lincoln: University of Nebraska Press, 1989), 354.

140 **"Allow an Indian":** La Flesche Tibbles, quoted in Jackson, *Ramona*, 407.

141 **Already enthralled by:** George Wharton James, *Through Ramona's Country* (Boston: Little, Brown, 1908), 8.

141 **Having twice failed:** Rosemary Whittaker, "Jackson, Helen Hunt," *American National Biography*, February 2000.

142 **Highlighting Ramona's dignity:** Jackson, *Ramona*, 42.

142 **She was devastated:** Whittaker, "Jackson, Helen Hunt."

143 **she rescued her father:** When her father refused to side against the army in its conflict with the starving Bannock people, they retaliated by taking him and other Paiutes hostage. Winnemucca undertook an epic ride over dangerous terrain to find the Bannocks' camp and rally her father and many others to escape.

143 **a front-page story:** "A Brave Indian Squaw," *New York Times*, June 17, 1878, 1.

143 **her "quaint anecdotes":** Gae Whitney Canfield, *Sarah Winnemucca of the Northern Paiutes* (Norman: University of Oklahoma Press, 1988), 164.

144 **Treading a fine line:** Quoted in Dory Nason, "We Hold Our Hands Up: On Indigenous Women's Love and Resistance," *Decolonization, Indigeneity, Education & Society*, February 12, 2013, https://decolonization.wordpress.com/2013/02/12/we-hold-our-hands-up-on-indigenous-womens-love-and-resistance/.

144 **Despite the shadows:** Lewis Hopkins, a former employee of the Indian Bureau who became Winnemucca's fourth husband, contracted tuberculosis, and after she paid his gambling debts from her book's proceeds, he departed, leaving her nearly destitute. She continued to promote the cause of Paiute education, but the Peabody Indian School she had managed to establish on her brother's Nevada ranch closed after four years. After reuniting with Hopkins, she contracted his disease and died in 1891.

145 **illustrated their increased confidence:** Valerie Sherer Mathes, "Nineteenth Century Women and Reform: The Women's National Indian Association," *American Indian Quarterly* 14, no. 1 (Winter 1990): 8.

145 **Working tirelessly to turn:** Quinton's speeches include "Abolition of Unnecessary Agencies" (1897), "Care of the Indian" (1891), "The Indian: First Paper" (1893), "The Woman's National Indian Association" (1893), and "Women's Work for Indians" (1893).

145 **Of course, Native American women:** Katherine Osburn, *Southern Ute Women: Autonomy and Assimilation on the Reservation, 1885–1934* (Lincoln: University of Nebraska Press, 2008).

146 **Looking back from:** *Annual Meeting and Report of the Women's National Indian Association* (Philadelphia: Women's National Indian Association, 1895), 9.

146 **Fletcher rejoiced that peoples:** "Alice Cunningham Fletcher: Ethnologist, Anthropologist and Social Scientist," *History of American Women*, women historblog.com, http://www.womenhistoryblog.com/2015/05/alice-cunningham -fletcher.html.

148 **The so-called Indian schools:** The schools were run by the Indian Service, which administered the workforce of the federal Office of Indian Affairs, now the Bureau of Indian Affairs.

148 **Proud of her unusual career:** Elaine Goodale Eastman, *Sister to the Sioux*, ed. Kay Garber (Lincoln: University of Nebraska Press, 1985). Quoted on back cover.

148 **During her six years:** Gayle Veronica Fischer, "Eastman, Elaine Goodale," *American National Biography*, February 2000.

149 **Like other well-intentioned:** Quoted in Ruth Ann Alexander, "Elaine Goodale Eastman (1863–1953)," *Only a Teacher: Schoolhouse Pioneers*, PBS, https://www .pbs.org/onlyateacher/elaine.html.

149 **Upon becoming Mrs. Eastman:** Quoted in Fischer, "Eastman, Elaine Goodale."

150 **Instead of raising her:** Quoted in Fischer, "Eastman, Elaine Goodale."

150 **"Peaceful revolutions are slow":** La Flesche Tibbles, quoted in Emma Roth-berg, "Susette La Flesche Tibbles ('Bright Eyes')," National Women's History Museum, 2020, http://www.womenshistory.org/education-resources/biographies /susette-la-flesche-tibbles-bright-eyes.

CHAPTER 11: PROGRESSIVES AND POPULISTS

153 **After her firsthand:** Luna Kellie, *A Prairie Populist: The Memoirs of Luna Kellie*, ed. Jane Taylor Nelsen (Iowa City: University of Iowa Press, 1992).

153 **"the minute you crossed":** Quoted in Deborah Fink Ames, "Gender," *Encyclopedia of the Great Plains*, http://plainshumanities.unl.edu/encyclopedia/doc /egp.gen.001.xml.

155 **"a decent mother":** Luna Kellie, quoted in Dan Holtz, "The Folk Songs of Great Plains Homesteading: Anthems, Laments, and Political Songs," *Nebraska History* 94 (2013): 42.

156 **"an instrument in the hands":** Quoted in O. Gene Clanton, "Intolerant Populist? The Disaffection of Mary Elizabeth Lease," Kansas Historical Society, https://www.kshs.org/p/kansas-historical-quarterly-the-disaffection-of-mary -elizabeth-lease/17865.

157 **"What you farmers need":** Charles W. Carey, "Lease, Mary Elizabeth Clyens," *American National Biography*, February 2000.

157 **"no government can":** Emma D. Pack, ed., "F.M.B.A," *The Farmer's Wife* (Topeka, KS), vol. 1, no. 6. (December 1, 1891), 1.

158 **Kellie and thousands of agrarian:** Charles Postel, *American Populism, 1876–1896*, "Why Did So Many Women Join the Populist Cause?," https://digital.lib .niu.edu/illinois/gildedage/populism.

159 **Despite Lease's insistence:** Quoted in "Mary Elizabeth Lease, The Populist Joan of Arc," Kansas Historical Society, 2009, https://www.kshs.org/teachers/read_kansas/pdfs/m30card01.pdf.

CHAPTER 12: SUFFRAGE CENTRAL

164 **when some male critics:** Caroline Churchill, *Active Footsteps* (New York: Arno Press, 1980), quoted in Fischer, *Let Them Speak*, 171.

164 **"The Chinaman's greatest crime":** Churchill, *Active Footsteps*, quoted in Fischer, *Let Them Speak*, 174.

165 **She even drew parallels:** Churchill, *Active Footsteps*, quoted in Fischer, *Let Them Speak*, 170.

166 **"whole precincts of voters":** Carrie Chapman Catt, "Why We Ask for the Submission of an Amendment," speech, February 14, 1900, Archives of Women's Political Communication, Iowa State University, https://awpc.cattcenter.iastate.edu/2018/03/23/why-we-ask-for-the-submission-of-an-amendment-feb-14-1900/.

166 **Favorably comparing herself:** Churchill, quoted in Fischer, *Let Them Speak*, 170.

167 **She patiently compared:** Veronica Chambers et al., *Finish the Fight!* (New York: Versify, 2020), 38.

168 **his "frontier thesis":** Frederick Jackson Turner, "The Significance of the Frontier in American History," speech, World's Columbian Exposition, 1893, https://gutenberg.org/files/22994-h/22994-h.htm.

168 **Warning of "a crisis":** Theodore Roosevelt, "The Strenuous Life," speech, April 10, 1899, *Voices of Democracy*, https://voicesofdemocracy.umd.edu/roosevelt-strenuous-life-1899-speech-text/.

171 **Nevertheless, she was presented:** "Louise Mulhall Carried Feminist Banner into the Cattle Country," *Kansas City Star*, January 11, 1941, 1. After performing in vaudeville as well as in various Wild West shows, Mulhall organized Lucille Mulhall's Roundup, her own rodeo, in 1916. Whether from social pressure or a preference for indoor work or both, most cowgirls hung up their spurs after marriage. After two brief attempts at wedded life, however, she retired to her family's huge ranch around 1922 and later died in a car crash.

172 *The Virginian*, **published in 1902:** Owen Wister, *The Virginian: A Horseman of the Plains* (New York: Gramercy Books, 1902). The book was revived as a successful TV series in 1962.

172 **strong, mostly silent hero:** Wister, *The Virginian*, 89.

172 **a parable about a hen:** Wister, *The Virginian*, 84.

173 **justice into their own hands:** The lynching of Watson and Averell prepared the ground for the infamous Johnson County War of 1892, waged by the big cattlemen's professional gunmen against homesteaders and small ranchers. This major range war inspired popular books and movies, notably *Shane*, whose eponymous hero stood with the little guys; Rooster Cogburn, the charismatic antihero of *True Grit*, fought for the dark side.

173 **Both the justice system:** On the other hand, "Cattle Queen" Ann Bassett was justly renowned for lawlessness. Her father taught her to ride, shoot, and rope on his ranch, which sprawled into Utah, Wyoming, and Colorado, then shipped her

off to be civilized at fancy boarding schools. The beautiful girl acquired the lady's mien and fine manners for which she became known, but she preferred the rough ranching life. At the age of fifteen, she began a sporadic seven-year affair with the outlaw Butch Cassidy, an unconventional suitor with whom her father had long conducted shady business. (Many observers later noted her strong resemblance to Etta Place, who accompanied Cassidy and his Wild Bunch to South America.) Later in life, Bassett was arrested for rustling and waging a range war over access to public grazing land against a neighboring rancher. She was acquitted at a trial that had to be held in an opera house to accommodate the huge crowd.

173 **In 1888, after a tuberculosis:** Richard B. Roeder, "Crossing the Gender Line: Ella L. Knowles, Montana's First Woman Lawyer," *Montana: The Magazine of Western History* 32 (Summer 1982).

174 **"the most remarkable":** Jay Burns, "Meet Ella Knowles, Class of 1884, Bates' Most Dangerous Alumna," *Bates Magazine*, March 21, 2018, https://www.bates.edu/news/2018/03/21/meet-ella-knowles-bates-most-dangerous-alumna/.

174 **If Montanans would but:** Burns, "Meet Ella Knowles."

175 **She performed so capably:** Kerry Drake, "Estelle Reel, First Woman Elected to Statewide Office in Wyoming," Wyoming Historical Society, https://www.wyohistory.org/encyclopedia/estelle-reel-first-woman-elected-statewide-office-wyoming.

176 **"not attempt to encroach":** Drake, "Estelle Reel."

176 **Moreover, despite her strong objections:** This injustice informed some tart advice Reel offered to one aspiring eastern teacher: "If you should decide to come West I think you could do better in Portland, Oregon, than any other place in the West that I know of at the present time."

176 **"The basketry as woven by Indians":** Drake, "Estelle Reel."

CHAPTER 13: NEW WOMEN SQUARED

179 **the number of independents swelled:** Edwards, Friefeld, and Wingo, *Homesteading the Plains*, 134.

180 **In 1903, twenty-one-year-old:** Lori Ann Lahlum, "Mina Westbye: Norwegian Immigrant, North Dakota Homesteader, Studio Photographer, 'New Woman,'" *Montana: The Magazine of Western History* 60, no. 4 (Winter 2010), https://www.montana.edu/empowering-women-in-ag/documents/articles-and-news/Nina%20Westbye_Norwegian%20Immigrant_North%20Dakota%20Homesteader_Studio%20Photographer_New%20Woman_.pdf.

181 **"if I had been":** Lahlum, "Mina Westbye," 10.

182 **After scandalizing a sheriff:** Quoted in "Not Just a Housewife: The Changing Roles of Women in the West," National Cowboy & Western Heritage Museum, https://nationalcowboymuseum.org/explore/just-housewife-changing-roles-women-west/.

183 **The sisters found deep emotional:** Quoted in Glenda Riley, *The Female Frontier* (Lawrence: University Press of Kansas, 1988), 137–38.

184 **The magazine ran Stewart's:** The film *Heartland* presents a dramatized version of Stewart's life.

NOTES

184 **Positioning herself as:** Quoted in Barbara Allen Bogart, "Elinore Pruitt Stewart, Writer and Homesteader," Wyoming Historical Society, November 14, 2014, https://www.wyohistory.org/encyclopedia/elinore-pruitt-stewart-writer-and-homesteader.

185 **In 1913, Hallie Morse Daggett:** Rosemary Holsinger, "A Novel Experiment: Hallie Comes to Eddy's Gulch," *Women in Forestry* 5, no. 2 (Summer 1983), http://www.webpages.uidaho.edu/WINR/Daggett.htm.

185 **The manager who interviewed:** Quoted in Holsinger, "A Novel Experiment."

186 **"for I knew":** Quoted in Holsinger, "A Novel Experiment."

186 **"My interest is kept up":** Quoted in Holsinger, "A Novel Experiment."

187 **In Tres Alamos, a settlement:** Katherine Benton-Cohen, "Common Purposes, Worlds Apart: Mexican-American, Mormon and Midwestern Women Homesteaders in Cochise County, Arizona," *Western Historical Quarterly* 36, no. 4 (Winter 2005): 440.

187 **When Rachel Bella Kahn:** Rachel Calof, *Rachel Calof's Story: Jewish Homesteader on the Northern Plains*, ed. J. Sanford Rikoon, trans. Jacob Calof and Molly Shaw (Bloomington: Indiana University Press, 1995).

188 **Following the Civil War:** Ellen Baumler, "Two Legendary African American Homesteaders," *Women's History Matters*, October 7, 2914, montanawomenshistory.org, http://montanawomenshistory.org/two-legendary-african-american-homesteaders/.

189 **Less is known:** Baumler, "Two Legendary African American Homesteaders."

189 **Between the late nineteenth:** H. Elaine Lindgren, "Ethnic Women Homesteading on the Plains of North Dakota," *Great Plains Quarterly* 9, no. 3 (Summer 1989), 157; Sheryll Patterson-Black, "Women Homesteaders on the Great Plains Frontier," *Frontiers: A Journal of Women Studies* 1 (Spring 1976): 68.

189 **Elizabeth Corey, a teacher:** Philip L. Gerber, ed., *Bachelor Bess: The Homesteading Letters of Elizabeth Corey, 1909–1919* (Iowa City: University of Iowa Press, 1990), 205. Bess took care to provide her students with some simple pleasures as well as instruction: "Wednesday evening I came home after school and made candy till half after eleven, am getting to be a gimsnuffer at making candy—can make four kinds. . . . Took a syrup pail of candy to school Thursday—it didn't take the youngsters long to make it look tired." In exchange, she enjoyed the kind of social life essential to combating homesteading's isolation. Describing "a big Hop at the hall in Hayes on Friday evening," she wrote, "The claim holders both men and women for miles around rode in and they had a fine time. People in a new country get acquainted rather quickly you know and in twenty four hours I found myself somewhat acquainted in Hayes."

190 **fabled female prospectors:** Sally Springmeyer Zanjani, *A Mine of Her Own: Woman Prospectors in the American West, 1850–1950* (Lincoln: University of Nebraska Press, 1997).

190 **Despite the challenges:** Quoted in Zanjani, *A Mine of Her Own*, 94.

190 **Impressed, the *Tonopah Bonanza*:** Quoted in Zanjani, *A Mine of Her Own*, 85.

191 **Wondering that more of them:** Quoted in Zanjani, *A Mine of Her Own*, 95.

191 **"When you're out":** Quoted in Zanjani, *A Mine of Her Own*, 282.

191 **According to her great-grandson:** Quoted in Zanjani, *A Mine of Her Own*, 83.

CHAPTER 14: THE EAST LOOKS WEST

194 As far back as the 1860s: Isabelle Saxon, *Five Years Within the Golden Gate* (London: Chapman and Hall, 1868), 57.

196 In 1919, she first envisioned: Julia Morgan, letter to Arthur Byne, in Sara Holmes Boutelle, "Morgan, Julia," *American National Biography*, February 2000.

198 Born in 1856: Cather, *The Song of the Lark*, 303.

199 In a celebrated story: In the story, Zitkala-Sa portrays her mother, who had long since been deserted by the girl's father, as experiencing the decision to let her child go to the remote institution as yet another step "farther from her native way of living," just as she had earlier "given up her wigwam of slender poles, to live, a foreigner, in a home of clumsy logs." Yet like many Native parents faced with two poor choices, she also believed that schooling's practical benefits would outweigh its emotional costs: "This tearing away, so young, from her mother is necessary, if I would have her an educated woman. The palefaces, who owe us a large debt for stolen lands, have begun to pay a tardy justice in offering some education to our children. But I know my daughter must suffer keenly in this experiment."

200 "neither a wild Indian": Jacqueline Fear-Segal, "'Use the Club of White Man's Wisdom in Defence of Our Customs': White Schools and Native Agendas," *American Studies International* 40, no. 3 (2002): 15.

200 "a marriage in high life": "Gertrude Simmons Bonnin (Zitkala Sha [*sic*]—Red Bird) Army Spouse," Arlington Cemetery, November 20, 2005, http://www. arlingtoncemetery.net/gsbonnin.htm.

201 "out of clear sky": Quoted in John Clayton, *The Cowboy Girl* (Lincoln: University of Nebraska Press, 2007), 34.

202 No conventional "tawny skinned": Caroline Lockhart, *Me-Smith* (Grosset & Dunlap, 1911). Quoted in Clayton, *The Cowboy Girl*, 34.

203 They admired the western argot: Caroline Lockhart, *The Fighting Shepherdess* (Boston: Small, Maynard, 1919), 220.

203 At the age of fifty-four: Quoted in Annie Hanshew, "Writing a Rough-and-Tumble World: Caroline Lockhart and B. M. Bower," *Women's History Matters*, June 10, 2014, montanawomenshistory.com, http://montanawomenshistory.org/writing-a-rough-and-tumble-world-caroline-lockhart-and-b-m-bower/.

203 Late in life: Quoted in "Caroline Lockhart," National Park Service, July 19, 2015, https://www.nps.gov/bica/learn/historyculture/caroline-lockhart.htm. In 1952, nearly twenty years after the publication of *The Old West and the New*, appropriately enough her last book, eighty-one-year-old Lockhart moved back to Cody. She owned one of the town's few televisions and invited local children to watch episodes of *Hopalong Cassidy*, in hopes they would grasp something about the past she had long tried to preserve.

204 The natural athlete was: "Tillie Baldwin Weeps over Death of Will Rogers," *The Day* (New London, CT), August 17, 1935, 18.

207 Ackley's pride in her family's rise: In 1857, Ackley married someone identified in her diary simply as "a man from Sacramento." In contrast, she recorded every detail of her bridal gown and tulle veil crowned with orange blossoms, as well as her "traveling costume." This hapless husband, she wrote, ignored her shrewd advice to invest in local real estate, moved their family to Nevada, then died shortly after they returned, impoverished, to California.

207 especially important to women of color: Cathleen D. Cahill, *Recasting the Vote: How Women of Color Transformed the Suffrage Movement* (Chapel Hill: University of North Carolina Press, 2020).

208 "We're Colorado's colored women": "Elizabeth Piper Ensley and the 100th Anniversary of the 19th Amendment," February 18, 2020, HistoryColorado, https://www.historycolorado.org/story/womens-history/2020/02/18/elizabeth-piper-ensley-and-100th-anniversary-19th-amendment.

209 "confusion and chaos": Cahill, *Recasting the Vote*, 137.

209 "a race whose lands": Cahill, *Recasting the Vote*, 138.

209 "Did you ever know": Marie Bottineau Baldwin, quoted in "Indian Women the First Suffragists and Used Recall, Chippewa Avers," *Washington Times*, August 3, 1914.

211 "Now the time is at hand": Zitkala-Sa, "America's Indian Problem," in *American Indian Stories, Legends, and Other Writings* (Washington, DC: Hayworth Publishing House, 1921), 183.

211 As the first president: Jennifer Medina, "Overlooked No More: Jovita Idár, Who Promoted Rights of Mexican-Americans and Women," *New York Times*, August 7, 2020.

211 She urged women: Marlena Fitzpatrick, "Jovita Idar: Journalism Pioneer," *Latino Rebels*, March 4, 2016, https://www.latinorebels.com/2016/03/04/latinahistorymonth-jovita-idar-journalism-pioneer/.

211 "Women are no longer": Alexis Chapman, "Women in HerStory: Jovita Idár, 1885–1946," Museum of Motherhood, June 25, 2010, https://museumofmotherhood.wordpress.com/2010/06/25/women-in-herstory-jovita-idar-1885-1946/.

212 During the Mexican Revolution: The US-Mexico border aroused little controversy until 1911, when the cattle industry in the northern Great Plains reeled from an epidemic of tick-borne disease, and government authorities hoping to prevent the spread of such illnesses by wandering cattle erected the first fence along the international boundary. This physical barrier and the distinction between American and Mexican cattle, which had to be deloused at the fence, began to reinforce ideas about Mexicans themselves as inferior, dirty, and perhaps diseased. Crossing the border was no longer a casual, everyday affair, and by the 1940s, the first fences designed for people kept Mexican women from joining their male relatives enrolled in the Bracero guest-worker program. By the twenty-first century, the border would become a symbol of America's power to exclude people according to color.

212 "Educate a woman": Kerri Lee Alexander, "Jovita Idár, 1885–1946," National Women's History Museum, https://www.womenshistory.org/education-resources/biographies/jovita-idar.

212 They pointed out that: Quoted in Susan Schulten, "The Crooked Path to Women's Suffrage: The Senate Ratified the 19th Amendment a Century Ago. What Took So Long?," *New York Times*, June 4, 2019, https://www.nytimes.com/2019/06/04/opinion/the-crooked-path-to-womens-suffrage.html.

213 **a trendy slogan:** Laura de Force Gordon, "Woman's Relation to the State," *Sacramento Bee*, February 2, 1895 (vol. 77): 2.

214 **As *Votes for Women*:** John C. Putman, "A Test of Chiffon Politics," *Pacific Historical Review* 69, no. 4 (November 2000): 595.

CHAPTER 15: THE ENFRANCHISED WEST

216 **To reduce friction:** Matt Overfelt, Gianna Sherman, and Zach Wright, "Biographical Sketch of Mary E. O'Neill," Biographical Database of NAWSA Suffragists, 1890–1920, Alexander Street, https://documents.alexanderstreet.com/d/1009860206.

218 **"crude, raw, half-formed commonwealths":** Quoted in Schulten, "The Crooked Path to Women's Suffrage."

220 **When the state's women:** "Tye Leung Schulze," National Park Service, https://www.nps.gov/people/tye-leung-schulze.htm.

221 **Dr. Esther Clayson Pohl Lovejoy:** Kimberly Jensen, "'Neither Head nor Tail to the Campaign': Esther Pohl Lovejoy and the Oregon Woman Suffrage Victory of 1912," *Oregon Historical Quarterly* 108, no. 3 (Fall 2007): 350–83; Kimberly Jensen, "Esther Pohl Lovejoy, M.D., the First World War, and a Feminist Critique of Wartime Violence," in *The Women's Movement in Wartime: International Perspectives 1914–19*, ed. Alison Fell and Ingrid Sharp (London: Palgrave Macmillan, 2007), 175–93.

221 **"none of the boys threw eggs":** Esther C. P. Lovejoy, "My Medical School, 1890–1894," *Oregon Historical Quarterly* 75, no. 1 (March 1974): 19.

223 **Lovejoy's democratizing message:** Sara Piasecki, "Valentine's Bonus: Romance a la Lovejoy," Historical Notes, Ohio State University Historical Collections and Archives, February 15, 2008, http://ohsu-hca.blogspot.com/2008_02_10_archive.html.

223 **During the 1912 campaign:** Janet Dilg, "Harriet 'Hattie' Redmond," *Oregon Encyclopedia*, Oregon Historical Society, July 6, 2020, https://www.oregonencyclopedia.org/articles/redmond_harriet_hattie/#.X2-J-5NKhcA.

224 **Lest younger women:** "Abigail Scott Duniway, 1834–1915," Secretary of State, State Archives, *On Her Own Wings*, https://sos.oregon.gov/archives/exhibits/suffrage/Pages/bio/duniway.aspx.

226 **At one rally:** Mary Pickett, "Jeannette Rankin and the Path to Women's Suffrage in Montana," *Billings Gazette*, November 2, 2014, https://billingsgazette.com/news/state-and-regional/govt-and-politics/jeannette-rankin-and-the-path-to-womens-suffrage-in-montana/article_83307d2b-2888-558d-9e1d-907d6518101f.html.

AFTERWORD

231 **"I want to":** Nancy C. Unger, "Rankin, Jeannette Pickering," *American National Biography*, February 2000.

233 **"I can't go to war":** Unger, "Rankin, Jeannette Pickering."

SUGGESTED READINGS

Armitage, Susan, and Elizabeth Jameson. *The Women's West*. Norman: University of Oklahoma Press, 1987.

Benton-Cohen, Katherine. *Inventing the Immigration Problem: The Dillingham Commission and Its Legacy*. Cambridge, MA: Harvard University Press, 2018.

Boag, Peter G. *Re-Dressing America's Frontier Past*. Berkeley: University of California Press, 2011.

Cahill, Cathleen D. *Recasting the Vote: How Women of Color Transformed the Suffrage Movement*. Chapel Hill: University of North Carolina Press, 2020.

Clayton, John. *The Cowboy Girl: The Life of Caroline Lockhart*. Lincoln: University of Nebraska Press, 2007.

Cummins, Sarah J., *Autobiography and Reminiscences of Sarah J. Cummins*. La Grande, OR: La Grande Printing Co., 1914.

Edwards, Rebecca. *Angels in the Machinery: Gender in American Party Politics from the Civil War to the Progressive Era*. Oxford, UK: Oxford University Press, 1997.

Edwards, Richard, Joseph K. Friefeld, and Rebecca S. Wingo. *Homesteading the Plains: Toward a New History*. Lincoln: University of Nebraska Press, 2017.

Enss, Chris. *Frontier Teachers: Stories of Heroic Women of the Old West*. Helena, MT: TwoDot Press, 2008.

Faragher, John Mack. *Women and Men on the Overland Trail*. New Haven, CT: Yale University Press, 2001.

Fischer, Christiane. *Let Them Speak for Themselves: Women in the American West, 1849–1900*. Hamden, CT: Archon Books, 1977.

Garceau, Dee. *The Important Things of Life: Women, Work, and Family in Sweetwater County, Wyoming, 1880–1929*. Lincoln: University of Nebraska Press, 1997.

Haywood, C. Robert. *Victorian West: Class and Culture in Kansas Cattle Towns*. Lawrence: University Press of Kansas, 1991.

Hine, Robert V., and John Mack Faragher. *Frontiers: A Short History of the American West*. New Haven, CT: Yale University Press, 2007.

Jameson, Elizabeth. *Writing the Range: Race, Class and Culture in the Women's West*. Norman: University of Oklahoma Press, 1997.

Jeffrey, Julie Roy. *Frontier Women: "Civilizing" the West? 1840–1880*. New York: Hill and Wang, 1998.

Klasner, Lily. *My Girlhood Among Outlaws.* Edited by Eve Ball. Tucson: University of Arizona Press, 1972.

Laegreid, Renee, and Sandra Mathews, eds., *Women on the North American Plains.* Lubbock: Texas Tech University Press, 2011.

Lahlum, Lori Ann, and Molly P. Rozum, eds. *Equality at the Ballot Box: Votes for Women on the Northern Great Plains.* Pierre: South Dakota Historical Society Press, 2019.

Limerick, Patricia Nelson. *The Legacy of Conquest: The Unbroken Past of the American West.* New York: W. W. Norton, 1987.

———. *Something in the Soil: Legacies and Reckonings in the New West.* New York: W. W. Norton, 2001.

Mead, Rebecca. *How the Vote Was Won: Woman Suffrage in the Western United States, 1868–1914.* New York: New York University Press, 2004.

Osburn, Katherine. *Southern Ute Women: Autonomy and Assimilation on the Reservation, 1885–1934.* Lincoln: University of Nebraska Press, 2008.

Pascoe, Peggy. *Relations of Rescue: The Search for Female Moral Authority in the American West, 1874–1939.* Oxford, UK: Oxford University Press, 1993.

Petrik, Paula. *No Step Backward.* Helena: Montana Historical Society, 1987.

Prescott, Cynthia Culver. *Gender and Generation on the Far Western Frontier.* Tucson: University of Arizona Press, 2007.

Radke-Moss, Andrea G. *Bright Epoch: Women & Coeducation in the American West.* Lincoln: University of Nebraska Press, 2008.

Riley, Glenda. *The Female Frontier: A Comparative View of Women on the Prairie and the Plains.* Lawrence: University Press of Kansas, 1988.

———. *Women and Indians on the Frontier, 1825–1915.* Albuquerque: University of New Mexico Press, 1984.

Rohrbough, Malcolm J. *Days of Gold: The California Gold Rush and the American Nation.* Berkeley: University of California Press, 1997.

Royce, Sarah. *A Frontier Lady: Recollections of the Gold Rush and Early California.* Lincoln: University of Nebraska Press, 1977.

Ruiz, Vicki L. *From Out of the Shadows: Mexican Women in Twentieth-Century America.* Oxford, UK: Oxford University Press, 1998.

Sachs, Honor. *Home Rule: Households, Manhood, and National Expansion on the Eighteenth-Century Kentucky Frontier.* New Haven, CT: Yale University Press, 2015.

Scharff, Virginia. *Twenty Thousand Roads: Women, Movement, and the West.* Berkeley: University of California Press, 2002.

Schlissel, Lillian. *Women's Diaries of the Westward Journey.* New York: Schocken, 2004.

Wagner, Sally Roesch. *The Women's Suffrage Movement.* New York: Penguin, 2019.

Ware, Susan. *Why They Marched.* Cambridge, MA: Harvard University Press, 2019.

White, Richard. *The Republic for Which It Stands—The United States During Reconstruction and the Gilded Age, 1865–1896.* Oxford, UK: Oxford University Press, 2017.

Wrobel, David M. *America's West: A History, 1890–1950*. Cambridge, UK: Cambridge University Press, 2017.

Yung, Judy. *Unbound Feet: A Social History of Chinese Women in San Francisco*. Berkeley: University of California Press, 1995.

Zanjani, Sally. *A Mine of Her Own: Women Prospectors in the American West, 1850–1950*. Lincoln: University of Nebraska Press, 1997.

ILLUSTRATION CREDITS

p. 1: University of Washington Libraries, Special Collections, UW9168.

p. 2: top right: The Church of Jesus Christ of Latter-Day Saints; middle left: Collection of the Grace Hudson Museum & Sun House, City of Ukiah, California, 2003-9-4; bottom right: Courtesy of the California History Room, California State Library, Sacramento, California.

p. 3: Courtesy of the Sisters of Charity Archives, rights retained.

p. 4: top: Courtesy of Hampton University's Archival and Museum Collection, Hampton University, Hampton, Virginia; bottom: Foote, Mary Hallock, *A Pretty Girl in the West*, United States, 1889. Courtesy of Library of Congress, Prints and Photographs Division, Washington, DC, https://www.loc.gov/item/2010715869/.

p. 5: top: Buffalo Bill Center of the West, Buffalo Bill Museum, MS006-William F. Cody Collection, P.69.0071; bottom: Frances Willard Memorial Library and WCTU Archives, Evanston IL.

p. 6: Polly Bemis with Horses in 1910, 62-44-7, Idaho State Archives.

p. 7: National Portrait Gallery, Smithsonian Institution.

p. 8: top right: The Scranton Tribune, Scranton, Pennsylvania, June 5, 1900; middle left: The Denver Public Library, Western History Collections, C MSS WH113; bottom right: kansasmemory.org, Kansas State Historical Society.

p. 9: University of Wyoming, American Heritage Center, Caroline Lockhart Papers, Accession Number 00177, Box 7.

p. 10: top: Courtesy of California State University, Chico, Meriam Library Special Collections; bottom: via http://www.elinorestewart.com.

p. 11: Courtesy of Chris Durban.

p. 12: General Photograph Collection/UTSA Libraries Special Collections.

p. 13: Courtesy of Pictorial Review.

p. 14: top: Courtesy of OHSU Historical Collections & Archives; bottom: Courtesy of Oregon Historical Society.

p. 15: Rep. Jeanette Rankin of Montana, United States, Washington DC, ca. 1917–18. Courtesy of Library of Congress, Records of the National Woman's Party, http://hdl.loc.gov/loc.mss/mnwp.276027.

p. 16: Public domain, via Wikimedia Commons.

INDEX

marriage (*cont.*)
  rarely discussed, 6–7
  remarriage after divorce, 48
  and reproductive lives of women, 114
  and women's ineligibility for homesteads, 70
  and women's lack of rights/legal protections, xiv, 39–41, 43, 54
Married Women's Property Act, xvi, 81
Massachusetts, xiii
Maxwell, Martha, 123–24
mayors, female, 136, 213
McBeth, Kate, 102
McBeth, Susan "Sue," 101–3
McKinley, William, 169, 176
Meador, Mamie, 233
measles, 13
Mejia, Rafaela, 187
men
  achievements of, reliant on women's support, 19
  alcohol consumption of, 41, 126
  attributed with women's achievements, 22
  fraternal lodges of, 218
  nostalgia/anxiety for lost virility, 168
  women passing as, 92
Mesa Verde National Park, 205
Mescalero Apaches, 79
mestizo (mixed-race) culture, 32
Mexican-American War, 15
Mexican Revolution, 212
Mexico
  and Cazneau's championing of western expansion, 33–34
  egalitarianism of civil law in, 32–33, 42, 187
  and Magoffin's life in Santa Fe, 31–33
  and mestizo (mixed-race) culture, 31–33
  social mobility in, 32
  US–Mexican border, 242n, 259n
Meyer, Mary, 50–51
Michigan, 232
migration to West
  of Blacks, 29–31
  Carpenter's experience on, 75
  Cummins's reports on, 1–2, 3
  demands made of women on, 4
  and fitness of women, 7
  and gender roles, 4–5
  Holmes's demonstration of equality on, 46
  and Native Americans, 8–11
  to Oregon Territory, 1–3
  in post-war years, 53
  Royce's spiritual experience during, 26
  value of women's work on, 5–6
  and women's enlarged sense of place, 7
  See also domestic role of women; homesteaders
military
  conquest of Native Americans, 94–95

  Smith's service as infantryman in, 92
  washer-women working for, 96–97
  and wives of officers, 94, 95–96
Miller, Ida Mary Ammons, 182–83
millinery shops, 54–55, 112, 114
miners and prospectors, 15–17, 190–92
mining industry, 163–64
Minnesota, 70–73
Minor, Virginia, 66
missionaries, 101–4, 116, 132–34
Mission Indians of California, 34, 141–42
Modocs, 95
Mojaves, 95
Moneka Woman's Rights Association, 45–46, 47
Montana
  Black homesteaders in, 188–89
  divorce in, 244n
  homesteaders in, 51
  Knowles's activism in, 173–75
  Lockhart's travels to, 201
  temperance movement in, 126–27, 130
  voting rights in, 225–27
  women employed in, 99
Montana Woman's Suffrage Association, 174
Montez, Lola (aka Eliza Rosanna Gilbert), 27
Moore, Lucy Morrison, 203
moral authority of women
  Beecher on, xv
  in benighted causes, 115
  and calls for full enfranchisement, xvii
  and community building efforts, 21
  Duniway's objections to argument, 68
  as educators, 105
  and Farnham's advocacy for equal rights, 45
  and Lease's progressive leadership, 156
  and Nichols's advocacy for equal rights, 43, 55
  and rallying of "citizen mothers" to suffrage, 129
  and temperance movement, 125, 129
Morgan, Agnes "Annie," 188–89
Morgan, Julia, 193–96
Morgan-Case Homestead, 188–89
Mormons
  and "civilizing" effects of White women, xviii
  mainstream attitudes toward, 26–27
  and polygamy, 26, 61–64, 135, 245n
  pride in enfranchisement, 64
  in Utah Territory, xxi, 26
  and women's groups, 206
Morrill Land-Grant Act, xx, 51–52, 69, 83
Morris, Esther Hobart, 57–58, 61, 245n
Mott, Lucretia, xv–xvi
Mulhall, Lucille, 171–72, 255n
municipal elections, 135, 176